Praise for **Breakup**

"Leo Averbach relates the process of experiencing the hurt, anger, and pain of betrayal and loss in full and uncut."
—Deborah L. Baker. Reader's Choice.

"...a sensitive, insightful, detailed and inspiring book."
—Jay P. Granat, Ph.D. Psychotherapist and a Licensed Marriage and Family Therapist.

"Leo Averbach has been there...inside the hell of divorce."
—David Knox, Ph.D. Professor of Sociology at East Carolina University, Marriage and Family Therapist.

"Gritty and powerful, **Breakup** is an emotion-filled, heartrending read."
—Cherie Mangum. Apex Reviews.

"Very well written and documented. It was revealing to have such an intimate male perspective with its perceptive exposure of male attitudes and vulnerabilities."
—Norman Silver. Amazon Reviews.

"This book will give you perspective to see you are not the only one struggling to make this life-changing decision—to end your marriage."
—Kristi Leeper-Hensley. Divorce to Happiness.

BREAKUP

ENDURING DIVORCE

LEO AVERBACH

Lexicon Books

© 2011 Leo Averbach

All rights reserved. No part of this publication may be reproduced or transmitted in any form or by any means electronic or mechanical, including photocopy, recording, or any information storage and retrieval system, without permission in writing from both the copyright owner and the publisher.

Requests for permission to make copies of any part of this work should be sent to Lexicon Books using email: lexiconht@gmail.com

ISBN: 978-0-9831820-0-9

British Library Cataloguing in Publication Data. A catalogue record for this book is available from the British Library.

Printed in the United Kingdom by Lexicon Books

For those who stood by me. There were some.

If you are going through hell, keep going.
—Winston Churchill

AUTHOR'S NOTE

In order to protect the privacy of individuals who appear in this memoir, certain names and other identifying details have been changed.

Leo Averbach
August 2009

Contents

Prologue   i
Foreword   xiii
Introduction   xv

1. Betrayed   1
2. Man of Sorrows   26
3. She's Left, Kind of   46
4. My Prerogative   71
5. The Family is in Ruins   86
6. The Dust has Settled   99
7. Take the Next Step   115
8. I Don't Want Her   138
9. We Need Healing   165
10. Do I Want Her?   182
11. An Unexpected Turn of Events   198
12. End this Limbo   214
13. I am Still Standing   235
14. There is No Civilized Divorce   241
15. Clear the Decks!   253

Epilogue   265

Prologue

I

Towards the end of the nineteenth century, all four of my grandparents landed on the shores of South Africa from Lithuania. Both my parents were born in Cape Town and I was too, in 1944. The city was beautiful and, like the rest of the country, a relatively tranquil backwater.

I don't remember much from my early childhood. I struggle to think what the atmosphere was like in our house when I was a young child. My feeling is that my mother loved me and that my father could barely tolerate me. I believe she gave me a good start: a few precious years. What the relationship was between them I have no idea though, after she died, my father professed to have loved my mother very much.

When I was about six, my mother became ill and underwent two abdominal operations. She seemed to be fading away as a presence, but at the time I did not know that she had cancer and I certainly did not understand that her condition was terminal. I was aware of a pall hanging over the house. She remained a shadow in our lives and died on July 29, 1955, without saying goodbye or revealing her feelings. She was only thirty-five. I was ten and my sister was six. I was left with almost no sense at all of my mother except what she looked like, kept young through photographs. She bore a certain resemblance to Demi Moore. People say she was creative and artistic.

The other significant figure in my life, my father, was psychologically and physically brutal to me until I left school. He demeaned me, saying I was hopeless and worthless. He routinely threatened to send me to boarding school, to thrash me, and to beat me black and blue. He would often beat me with a belt and shake me violently, adding for good measure, "I'll knock the living daylights out of you." Despite being a talented sportsman, he never found the time to play with me, yet he seldom failed to cast a stern eye over my homework, usually accompanied by a disparaging remark or two. Throughout my childhood I suffered his autocratic violence.

I have never really understood the reason for his brutality. Was it his own feelings of inadequacy and rage, or the fact that I did not meet his expectations of me? Was he simply jealous of my mother's affection for me? He was under emotional and financial strain from my mother's illness and death, having known all along that her cancer was terminal. It does not excuse his behavior, which he later regretted.

My life at home up till the age of sixteen, determined largely by the combination of my mother's death and my father's rage, was miserable. It also became increasingly empty. My mother's input faded as her condition deteriorated, and left a hole when she died. There was good food on the table, I had decent clothes to wear and we had a servant who cleaned and cooked, but there was no warmth and no nurturing, no encouragement of my talents or interests, no gentle pat on my shoulder.

Outside the harsh circumstances of my home life, growing up during the fifties in the southern suburbs of Cape Town was a privilege not only in the sense that I was white-skinned, although that helped. When we moved into the neighborhood of Newlands the street was not yet tarred, there were woods and open fields close by, and the Liesbeek River was at the bottom of the road. There were lots of kids my age around and no television to keep us indoors. The weather was good, so we played outdoors: cricket in the street, marbles on the sandy sidewalk, all sorts of games in the woods. On the river we built dams, ate watermelon, and hopped along the rocks up to Kirstenbosch Botanical Gardens. It was a kind of children's paradise.

Instead of family, I had friends. During my early teens, five of us often got together to play touch rugby, just to ride our bikes, or to listen to records. Tom Lehrer's witty lyrics were much loved, but we also liked Harry Belafonte's gentle rhythm and the emotion in *Porgy and Bess*. I always preferred to go to my friends' houses, as they had moms who made us crumpets. Girls featured in our fantasies but hardly in reality.

I started school early, at the age of about four, and from then on was always a year young for my class as well as being small for my age. I eventually finished high school in 1960, at the age of sixteen. School was overall an agreeable social experience but very limited educationally. Good teachers were few, and the system did not encourage critical thinking or originality. Moreover, we were subjected to the political agenda of the apartheid regime and its reading of history. On leaving school, I was offered a place at Cape Town University to read either Medicine or Mechanical Engineering. I made a fateful decision: it was to be neither.

Being an ardent member of a Jewish youth movement, I decided to go on a youth leadership course in Israel instead. I was dead keen and, surprisingly, my father agreed. The year I spent in Israel (1961) as an impressionable teenager was extraordinary. I was gripped by the experience of being a free agent in a vibrant, new country and by the exposure to all it had to offer. In particular, our visit to the trial in Jerusalem of the Nazi war criminal Adolf Eichmann, seeing the evil man in his glass enclosure, left an indelible impression on me. The trial was intended to impress upon Israelis and upon the rest of the world a clear message: "never again." Israel was the only guarantee against a Holocaust recurring.

I was lucky to be part of a really nice bunch of people. A few of us were so caught up in the energy of the country and of the kibbutzim in particular that we decided to form a group with the aim of settling together on a kibbutz.

Now fully committed to eventually settling on a kibbutz, I returned to South Africa. In line with my belief that a technical training was the best preparation for kibbutz life, I started an apprenticeship in Fitting & Turning at the Bus Company in Cape Town. I spent three years in the workshop, on pitifully low wages, making replacement parts for buses.

Social life for me revolved around my youth movement activities, to which I was passionately devoted. My involvement with girls during this period was curtailed, conveniently perhaps, by my fanciful "commitment" to Daniella, whom I had met and exchanged a few words with at the tail end of the course in Israel. She was Italian and had beautiful dark-green eyes. We had a brief correspondence but it came to nothing. Later, and much closer to home, I was infatuated with Gabriel, a lovely young woman who had been my next-door neighbor for many years. We went on hikes together, went to see *The Condemned of Altona*, and sat in the car afterwards talking about the movie. However, it never turned into a relationship.

Like many in the sixties generation, in the movement we loved Joan Baez and Bob Dylan. We spent hours together singing protest songs and Negro spirituals and, at some level, we believed it was possible to change the world. Unlike the crowds who later gathered at festivals such as Woodstock, we sought to channel our youthful idealism and utopian inclinations in a very specific direction—Israel. This conviction gained impetus from the fact that many of us saw no future for ourselves in a racially-riven South Africa.

II

The group I was part of, consisting of thirty-six youngsters, arrived on kibbutz Etgar in early February 1965. I can still recall the day of our arrival, with its mixture of pungent farm smells, mud underfoot, and the excited buzz of lots of people around to welcome us.

Perhaps I was running away from home, looking for a new family and a community—a sense of belonging. But at the time I was ideologically committed to the idea of kibbutz as a framework that would ultimately lead to a better world. I saw myself as part of a pioneering experiment in social engineering—the kibbutz, within the wider framework of national renewal, the nascent state. We were participating in a utopian project!

Above all, the years I spent on kibbutz proved to be a memorable and formative personal experience: the first of two five-year crucibles in my life. It was an exciting time, a time of warm and intimate friendships, of togetherness, of numerous infatuations and brief romances, of laughter, of hardship endured alone and together. We studied together, worked together, showered communally, and ate salad together in the dining hall. Evenings were often taken up by intense discussions about serious and trivial subjects alike.

Initially, I went to work in the metal workshop, which was the natural place for somone with a technical training. The work day was long and hard, but we also had fun. Later, when I was asked to leave the metal workshop and start working with the sheep, I was a bit resentful but accepted that that was what was needed. I learned to milk, to take the 360-plus sheep out grazing in the valley or on the hillside, and to tend to the lambs.

Like all Israelis, we were due for army service. In the summer of 1966, about twenty of us from the kibbutz began our national service. We were conscripted into a branch of the army that combined regular army service with work on kibbutzim. We spent the first five months at a basic-training camp, where we were knocked into shape through a combination of fairly strenuous physical exercise, forced marches, arms training, and army discipline. Somehow we battled through, and I even excelled in a few areas. At school I had been a mediocre athlete, but here I was one of the best in the whole camp, completing the obstacle course in record time.

From basic training I went straight on to advanced training, which made everything we had done before feel like a romp in the park. This really was tough. Very long, hard marches, exhausting training exercises, weeks out in the field in the bitter cold, and very little sleep, combined to make this six-month stint extremely exacting. The week of parachute training in the middle was a breeze by comparison. Only a small percentage of those who began the training actually finished it. I was one of those who did make it to the end, proud of my parachutist's wings and red beret. Our combat skills were never tested during this period. It was all a bit unreal.

By the time I returned to the kibbutz in early May 1967 I was, together with a few others, a bit of a celebrity. After all, we had recently come from South Africa and here we were—fully-fledged Israeli paratroopers.

Naively perhaps, when I was first conscripted and even during the rigorous training I underwent, I had no thoughts or expectations of actually fighting in a war. It wasn't in my script. Yet, in June 1967, when the Six Day War broke out, I found myself in northern Sinai, confronting well-entrenched Egyptian troops. At the end of that first day, as the sun was setting, I stood in the battlefield with the acrid smell of burning flesh and materiel in my nose, shrapnel in my left hand, witnessing corpses being loaded onto a truck. The rest of the war turned out to be fairly uneventful for me.

After the war, I got back safely to the kibbutz and started working in the factory. By this time, I was beginning to have reservations about the extent to which the kibbutz could realize the ideals of social justice and equality I had, perhaps unrealistically, ascribed to it. But quiet kibbutz life suited me, and occasionally it was spiced up by the odd sexual liaison. One of these was to change the course of my life.

In the summer of 1969, an attractive South African woman by the name of Paula came to visit a cousin of hers who lived on the kibbutz. She was on her way to London to start a doctorate in microbiology and wanted to spend the summer in Israel. One night, at a small party, we danced together to the hypnotic sound of Bob Dylan singing *Mr. Tambourine Man*. A tender love blossomed between us and, by the time she finally left for London a few weeks later, feelings were so strong that we promised faithfully to keep in touch. I planned to visit her in London soon.

III

I was upset that Paula was not at Heathrow to meet me when I arrived at the end of January 1970 but tried not to think about it too much. Friends took me to their apartment in Wimbledon, where I was able to stay for several months. I felt like a country bumpkin coming to the big city—London. Almost everything was unfamiliar and a little intimidating: the sheer scale of it all, the masses of people, the underground, the strange houses. I was unused to the freezing cold weather, the unremitting grayness, and the narrow streets. The contrast to the rural lifestyle and blue skies I had become accustomed to on kibbutz, and to the expansiveness of Cape Town, was enormous.

My exchange of letters with Paula had given me every reason to think we would carry on our relationship more or less from where we had left it a few months earlier on the kibbutz. Much to my surprise and disappointment, this was not the case. Soon after we met, she told me she was involved with Robin. Her love letters were a sham. Why did she keep up the pretence when she could easily have written to say that things were off? Our meetings were tense, and I could sense she was not very interested in me. I did not know what to do. My instinct said "hang in there," and being a bit lost and somewhat dependent I clung to what I thought would give me hope, security, and perhaps love—my prospective relationship with her. I was keen on her and was desperate for it to work out. At some point soon afterwards, standing outside Dillons bookshop, I got quite bold and said she needed to choose between Robin and me. Her reply was that Robin was going off to India. We began to spend time together, in the student milieu of Mecklenburgh Square, going to movies, cheap restaurants and concerts in the park, all wearing duffle coats. I, too, joined the student ranks at London University when I started a degree in Middle Eastern History and Arabic. Later, following an interest in language development in young children, I completed a post-graduate teaching diploma.

Slowly, Paula and I were becoming a couple. But it wasn't an easy, flowing relationship; there was underlying tension. On the whole, the days continued to be better than the nights. Nevertheless, via a separation and reunion, it was not a long hop from there to living together in a rented garden apartment in Hampstead and eventually to marriage. Our marriage took place outside, on the common behind the apartment in September 1972, in the presence of my father and sister, Paula's mother, other family members, and friends. The setting was delightful, a small troupe played baroque music, and the rabbi said it was an auspicious beginning to the Jewish New Year.

We built up a cosy circle of friends from among the cosmopolitan student community and various other contacts, whom we met with regularly for walks, talks, and parties. I also kept in close touch with my friends in Israel, who visited us now and again. Paula and I enjoyed doing things together, whether it was our frequent walks around Hampstead, visiting museums and galleries, camping in Wales, or traveling overseas.

We both wanted to have children, although we never took a conscious decision to "get pregnant." All the same, our first child duly arrived in January 1975, by Cesarean section. Unspoilt by the travails of a normal birth, she was the most beautiful creature I had ever seen. I held her close. Our lives now revolved around Jessy, the new baby. All our love was showered on her. Nothing was held back. We adored her, we hugged her, we dwelt on her every move, and marveled at her development. Both of us were utterly besotted with her. Paula had maternity leave and my work commitments, as a special needs teacher, left me plenty of time to be with my daughter. And I wanted to be the kind of father I never had: warm, loving, caring, involved.

We carried Jessy everywhere with us. At first we wrapped her up well and went walking on the Heath with Zippa, our dog. She was going to be an outdoor girl, just like her mom and dad. When she was a year-and-a-half, I walked down to the bottom of the Grand Canyon and up again with her on my back. By the time I took her down the Samariá Gorge in Crete a year later, Paula was pregnant again, and the "Jessy only" period was coming to an end.

In February 1978, Jake came into this world via a normal birth. Naturally, I was there to hold Paula's hand and wipe her brow. We were both thrilled to bits with the beautiful boy, a gentle, smiling soul virtually from the first minute. Now, possessed of some experience, things were much easier for us as parents, and Jake no doubt reaped the benefit of our growing confidence. It was all more casual and carefree, though our fascination with their development never ceased—from crawling to walking to talking. Unbelievable.

Both Paula and I had permanent jobs and we'd purchased the apartment we had been renting. We were just beginning to settle down as a snug little family —the standard package of two kids, a dog and a mortgage—when I started to get restless. Despite my new-found interest in pottery and having the great little pottery studio I had built in the garden, I was looking for more excitement, more intensity. Dreary London was getting me down and the prospect of being a teacher, albeit in a very special environment, did not thrill me. Paula also liked the idea of "doing something different" and together we planned to go and live in the south of France. Paula and I joined a beginners' class in French.

After considering a few different possible arrangements for the initial period, we eventually agreed to stay in a house belonging to acquaintances of ours located in Nizas, a small village in the Languedoc, near Pezenas. The arrangement we came to was that we could stay in the house rent free, in return for which we would supervise the renovation work that had been planned and also make some general improvements. We rented our apartment, and after we bought an old left-hand-drive Taunus, we were all set to go. It was the end of February 1981. Jessy was six, Jake was three.

What struck us first about Nizas was the calm, the contrast with bustling London. We soon came to appreciate the fresh air and the simple, rustic beauty of the village—houses with red-tiled roofs surrounded by vineyards, a little square with a fountain in the centre. It did not take us long to settle into country living: shopping at the markets, exploring the surrounding area, swimming in the rivers, the lakes, and the sea, doing a bit of "learning" with the kids, picnicking, playing games, going on walks, riding bikes, flying Jake's kite at Lac du Salagou. Our favorite spot was undoubtedly the Gorges d'Héric, whose crystal-clear pools gave us endless joy. Gradually, our broken French notwithstanding, we befriended some of the locals, and there were usually a number of foreign visitors around to chat to. We all seemed to be in our element. For the most part, these were wonderful times, a sort of idyll. I hoped it would last.

The plan was to make our life somewhere in the vicinity, but it did not work out that way. By the end of the summer, when Paula's mother arrived and we all helped with the grape harvest (the *vendage*), we knew we would have to move on. By then, Paula was pregnant again and we decided to return to London.

Rachel was born in March 1982, a gorgeous bundle of joy from the word go, full of smiles and forever the communicator. She just blended into the family, and the new dynamic of "two adults, three children" worked extremely well. Apart from the fact that the children related well to one another, the burden of their parents was now shared among three rather than two. The old pattern of one-on-one was broken. Rachel's arrival had opened things up.

While the family setup felt good, I felt lousy. I didn't want to be in London, and I was constantly hatching schemes to move to somewhere warm, sunny, and peaceful. Not wanting to get back into teaching, I resorted to my technical skills and started making furniture for clients. Soon afterwards, I met Rob and we joined forces to make furniture in a tiny workshop in West Hampstead. Our product range grew, and before we knew it we had orders for children's furniture from the John Lewis partnership, a large chain.

This period saw a sea change in our family dynamic following Paula's professional reorientation: she shifted from research in microbial genetics to human genetics. She found suitable work in the field at a decent academic salary and started to take seriously what she was doing, with ever more enthusiasm. Her job required her to travel a lot, both in the UK and internationally. By contrast, I was struggling to build up Rob & Leo Designs as a profitable concern. Both Rob and I put our heart and soul into the task, as well as money. Despite acclaim for excellent designs and sales in the UK, Europe, and the US, the business never took off. Only at odd intervals were we able to draw salaries from it. I found myself caught in the trap of, on the one hand, being determined to make a go of the business, and on the other, needing to earn a living.

When, in the mid-eighties, we moved from our apartment in "desirable" Hampstead to a family house in the slightly "less desirable" but far friendlier West Hampstead, we all had more space and we also had a room or two to let to students. The rent we made from the many language students from all over the world who came to stay in our genial home in Solent Road certainly helped to pay the bills. Often, there were seven or more people seated for dinner around our extended dining room table. Still, we regularly received letters from our bank manager politely informing us that we had exceeded our overdraft limit. It was painful, and because I was not earning anything, I bore responsibility for the shortfall. However, the decision to continue with the business in the hope that it would eventually prosper was always taken jointly by Paula and me, though she was undoubtedly influenced by my commitment to it and my lack of any clear alternative.

In effect, Paula became the family's sole breadwinner, which of itself was not a problem for either of us. But as time wore on and the financial pressure persisted, the imbalance began to put a strain on our relationship. In addition, her professional star was rising; mine was wavering. Naturally, this affected the way we each felt about ourselves and our lives. After much deliberation, I reluctantly returned to teaching children with learning/behavioral difficulties in various state schools.

Paula and I functioned well as parents. We agreed on virtually all matters related to our children, whose welfare was our prime concern. We both happily invested a lot of energy in the family, striking a good working balance between over-protectiveness and laxity. Perhaps we were avoiding having to examine our own relationship, but the net result was that we neglected it and the relationship suffered. In addition, between us there had never been a lot of passion, and what there was seemed to drain away with the passage of time. I knew I wanted more from the relationship but was not able to negotiate for what I wanted and, ultimately, was unsure whether the greater intimacy I sought was available. The two key areas—love and work—were both unsatisfactory for me.

Clearly, Paula was feeling something similar, at least in the realm of love, because about a year later, in the early nineties, the whole edifice came tumbling down.

FOREWORD

Several weeks ago, Leo Averbach asked me if I would be willing to write a foreword for his new book. Apparently, he had read some of my writings about marriage, family and divorce and thought I would be a good person to read and critique his manuscript.

I was quite flattered, but I did not know this man and I knew nothing about his writing ability, his story or his life. When I received the book, I was intrigued, captivated and impressed from the start. Leo is a fascinating fellow with an interesting history.

He has written a sensitive, insightful, detailed and inspiring book about the pain and the growth which a person can experience as they go through the end of a relationship, the divorce process and the healing process.

Breakup: Enduring Divorce is a personalized and detailed chronological account of the author's sadness, depression, conflicts, insights, and last but not least, his growth and his discovery of peace and contentment.

The author does an excellent job of depicting the range of feelings and experiences which a person is apt to have as they mourn the loss of their partner and their relationship. In addition, Averbach shows us how earlier losses in one's life can make the loss of a spouse particularly painful.

The author tells how his work with two therapists furnished him with much insight and expedited the healing process for him. People who are curious or uninformed about the therapeutic process and its role in helping people recover from a divorce will learn a lot from the author's accounts of sessions with his two skilled and compassionate therapists.

This is a well-written and stimulating book about loss, love, marriage, growth and a sensitive and wise person's search for tranquility.

In America, almost one out of every two marriages ends in a divorce. Consequently, I believe this book can have real value for millions of men and women who are struggling with this significant psychological challenge.

Breakup: Enduring Divorce is not just another self-help book. It is beautifully written in the form of a personal journal and filled with the author's thoughts, feelings and engaging candor. It is a sincere, honest and intelligent work which demonstrates the emotional benefits of journaling one's life.

This fine book is also a must read for lawyers who represent people in matrimonial matters. Likewise, therapists, psychiatrists, psychologists and social workers who counsel divorcing individuals or people who are involved in or getting out of dysfunctional relationships can learn a lot about how these struggles can impact patients in these transitional states.

This book can be a powerful healer for a person who has been wounded by the termination of a relationship or by the divorce experience.

Jay P. Granat, Ph.D.
December 2009.

Jay P. Granat, Ph.D. is a Psychotherapist and a Licensed Marriage and Family Therapist in River Edge, New Jersey. Dr. Granat has appeared in major media outlets including The New York Times, Good Morning America, The BBC, The CBC and New York Magazine. He writes a weekly self-help column for four New Jersey newspapers and has developed a number of self-help programs. He has been a guest columnist for www.divorce360.com. Dr. Granat's dissertation was on marital disintegration and he has counseled hundreds of people struggling with relationship issues. He now spends much of this time counseling athletes and their families and he is the Founder of www.StayInTheZone.com and www.DrJayGranat.com.

INTRODUCTION

On July 4, 2005, I slipped and broke my ankle. While waiting for my fibula to knit, I decided to resurrect the journal I had kept when my marriage broke up in London in the nineties, and had neglected since then. The result is this memoir, an abbreviated version of the journal, which chronicles the painful dissolution of my marriage and my slow process of recovery from divorce.

At the time, my journal became my confidant, my figurative "shoulder to cry on": receptacle for all my pent-up emotions. I avidly poured my innermost thoughts, all my feelings and experiences into it. The simple act of writing was cathartic; putting things down on paper added a certain clarity that had not been there before. In addition, the journal served as a record of my therapy sessions, both individual and group, which continued throughout the period of the breakup.

I wrote in longhand on sheets of paper that gradually piled up, each one dated. I also kept a little diary with me at all times to record my thoughts as they arose. On some days, the intensity of my feelings led me to write ten pages or more, and altogether I wrote close on two thousand pages. For the purposes of this book, the journal had to be shortened, but the text that appears here is taken word-for-word from my journal, with no additions, only minimal cosmetic alterations and division into chapters.

Due to its having been written in the midst of my marital-cum-personal crisis, *Breakup* may often seem uncomfortably raw to the reader, especially as the narrative holds nothing back. The journal's intimate nature takes you right into the cauldron of marital disintegration, revealing the anguish and disorientation I experienced, virtually day by day. The account lays bare my obsessive machinations and my radical mood swings as I struggled to cope with the whole gamut of emotions—loss, abandonment, rejection, grief, regression, powerlessness, jealousy, anger and rage—stirred by my wife's betrayal.

This frenzy gains a measure of sanity from the reports of the therapy sessions that took place as my world was crumbling around me. They provided me with a link between my intense, often outrageous feelings, and my established emotional patterns, particularly with regard to my mother Julia. The therapy subtly aided my gradual process of self-acceptance and healing and helped me lay my demons to rest. Individual sessions tended to deal with specific incidents, and were often interspersed with snippets of wisdom from the therapists. But taken as a whole, the therapy profoundly affected the way I negotiated the crisis, until it was finally resolved and I moved on to a new life with a new partner.

With the advantage of hindsight, I can see that the breakup of my marriage inadvertently turned out to be a transformative experience for me. The upheaval, coming like a bolt from the blue and feeling like hell, jolted me back to life and forced me to begin afresh. Akin to a wake-up call, it shook me out of the fog I had been living in for years and liberated me in the process.

By presenting this account, I am expressing my belief that my story transcends my own experience. Although I am aware that the experience of crises varies enormously from person to person, I feel that this story offers ample food for thought and could impact on the lives of many people.

1: BETRAYED

16 Feb 1990
London.
I am feeling sorry for myself and a bit lost in the world. I have only ever managed to do things for brief spells, like living on a kibbutz, studying, teaching, designing furniture, and so on. Now I live in the shadow of the failure of Rob & Leo Designs. I thought I could run a business when I don't have a clue and cannot now redeem the situation. It's lost forever. What I have learnt is not to go into business again. Anyway, it's no use berating myself. I have to look on the plus side. I am healthy, have a nice family and lovely home. So, why do I find my situation so uninspiring?

I returned from a short holiday in Israel in the summer determined to do something about my "situation." Therapy of some sort was the obvious answer for me, so I started looking for a therapist. One day I noticed an ad in Time Out *for a therapist by the name of Clive, who described himself as a "biodynamic therapist." Taken by the ad and curious about biodynamic therapy, I phoned him. After we had exchanged a few words he suggested that rather than chat over the phone I should come to see him. The following Friday evening I went over to him in Putney, taking with me a small tray of dates as a gift. After we had chatted for a few minutes Clive said, "This is love. We are going to work together." I readily agreed.*

13 Nov 1990
Two things were on my mind before my first session with Clive: my relationship with my wife Paula and work. We started off by talking about Letting Go: in the present, of the past, of what I think I am, ought to be, etc. He remarked that I am up tight about little things, so I cannot get on with life and have stood still for years.
　　According to him, "There is a general emptiness and depression in you, no joy. It is better to throw it all away." We spoke about the figure I cut against the world; the phases of my life. It seems I have built up a legend of being a king in Israel—the im-

age of myself I cling to. He asked what feelings I have in relation to my mother and her death. I am unsure. My father was throttling. That I see clearly.

Clive was surprised I cope with my situation without either drugs or alcohol.

After the session I felt calm and a bit empty. I was not very coherent and was not clear what Clive said about Mozart's *Magic Flute*, particularly the significance of the *Maiden of the Night*. I'm thinking about the ways my style worked in the past but I realize I am out of touch with reality now.

20 Nov 1990
The second session with Clive.
"Why are you feeling tense and disgruntled?" he asked. I said, "I am frustrated at school/work and dissatisfied at home." Clive thinks I am cut off from the world. I distance myself; I am fastidious. His impression is that my father did not speak because he was depressed and I never mourned for my mother. That is the focus of being cut off from feelings. I am reliving the dynamic that existed between my parents: father's anger with mother—unfinished business. And I am doing the same thing with Paula.

Clive says the facts are that I am here now and that my mother died of cancer. To some extent I am in a foreign country. What is unresolved is bridging the void between how I am now and how I need to be.

27 Nov 1990
The third session with Clive.
I related a very vivid dream. I am working in some engineering business. It has a shady feel about it. I have to dig a hole because water is coming up. While digging I come across a car, a 1962-model Porche. It's blue and in pristine condition. I raise it to the surface and put it in the garage. My job is to look after it but suddenly I can't find it so I go looking. I run down the road, exhilarated. I feel young, fit and strong. Eventually I find the boss, who wants to sell cars and create the right image.

Clives's interpretation: 1962 is where I am stuck, an eighteen-year-old teenager—young, immature, fragile. Nice guy. A great

BREAKUP

idealist and believer with enormous determination and integrity, looking for and needing something outside myself.
I told him that things are cold between Paula and me. Clive says sex should be pure recreation, not a coin of the realm. He suggests that Paula wants me away so she can fulfill her role as mother and father (like her own mother). We talk of potency and impotency—my images in relation to Paula. He asks, "What is the worst that can happen in case of breakup?" I say, "I will miss the kids."

04 Dec 1990
After the fourth session.

Clive intuits a story of my continuing my mother's unfinished business. I am living out my mother without admitting her femininity. She didn't die, she contracted cancer. She exists in the ideal world therefore I am searching for the ideal world. I died in her place. I did not allow her to die. I died for her. I internalized her death. I am this dead woman!

It has taken me all this time to reach this point. Still, it is only in my head; not yet integrated. I have created this ideal world in order to avoid having to face the real world—why my mother died. There was a strong element of my mother protecting me from my father. When she died my protection went, adding fear to loss. How brutal was my father? Did I really suffer? I think I did.

I mentioned my ambivalence regarding Paula, saying that when we are together there is tension and anger. An impossible situation has developed. I want affection, feel terrible and can't generate it. Catch 22. We are not even kissing. Clive asks, "What if you were to know of an affair. Allow yourself, what then?"

According to Clive being adult means accepting my situation and making the best of it: London, relationships, work, kids, friends. This is it. Relax. There is nothing better.

11 Dec 1990
After the fifth session.

I am upset and angry. Paula won't kiss me and I wonder what it means. Clive asks if we can forget the rough period and move ahead. I have grave doubts. Am I scared to declare my love in case it means death—refusal? There is so much anger that I cannot sort out what is what.

Clive's aphorism: Marriage is fucking; otherwise it is friendship. As he sees it, in order to achieve manhood I have to extricate myself from this web.

04 Jan 1991
We are into the same old pattern. Paula is strutting around like an excited bird. At night there is no affection. We are like two cold fish. She is sexually dead; I feel bored and empty. All I want is to walk a long way, to escape to a retreat in France or Italy. I feel like going out in the rain with just what I am wearing. Why should I be enslaved to this situation?

08 Jan 1991
After the session with Clive.
We spoke about being a "Man Without Qualities" (Robert Musil), whereas I want to be nice guy, achiever, etc. I am bored with myself and my life. I need to lose control. Seems like I am hiding my dark side and I need to get in touch with it. This is the really heroic journey.

There is no situation, only meaning, i.e., how I perceive it. No objective reality. There is no problem out there, in the world. It is just my perception of it that is at fault. I have to give myself a break. Enough suffering. I have to change in relation to all the things in my life: work, wife, London. I don't have to change them. I have to find answers within myself. There is nothing outside.

24 Jan 1991
The session with Clive.
We discussed the story of the Eagle and the Elephant, of pretending to be something other than you really are. The lesson being that "you have to be who you are." Clive keeps reminding me that I think the situation lies outside myself. It doesn't.

He makes the point that I am a perfectionist. I look for perfection in everything, including my wife and job. I am constantly

BREAKUP

looking for more satisfaction, more everything, and therefore I am dissatisfied. I cannot accept mediocrity. DROP PERFECTIONISM.

Paula has a lump in her breast. It could be breast cancer! Shock & confusion. Thoughts of sickness and death flood me again, and about recreating my father's situation. What will happen to us?

05 Feb 1991
The session with Clive.
My mother died at a brilliant moment. She cut me off just as I was about to enter manhood. This way it preserved her image as a perfect woman/mother. I have continued to preserve this image, by remaining a child. And if I cease to remain a child, that image is no longer preserved. I have to say goodbye to her. I have not yet buried her properly.

Letting go means being able to detach myself from my past, from my mother and father. I am still caught in the triptych. It is an ossified process. I have to de-ossify but I don't want to. Why? Because I am afraid there is nothing else.

20 Feb 1991
The session with Clive.
We talked about male/female—both elements are there in an integrated individual. My female is heavily idealized. A more realistic picture is that there are three faces of Eve: creator, nurturer, destroyer. I am stuck in Phase 1.

26 Feb 1991
The session with Clive.
I am the supplicant and the consummator. I am waiting for my mother to give me permission to grow up and do adult things. Grant it myself—I am the mother and the son; I am the asker and the giver.

I want joy and fulfilment, I am yearning for it. I can provide it too. I don't need Clive or anybody else. I can do it by myself. In fact, only I can do it. Nobody else can. So be it. I can grant myself happiness, joy, light even in the midst of misery—London, teaching. I have been waiting for other people, places to bestow joy on me. It can only come from within me. I am the prince; I am also the pauper.

06 Mar 1991
Yesterday Clive introduced me to the Corals. Somehow he knew it would touch me.

Where Corals Lie by Richard Garnett, first set to music in Edward Elgar's Sea Pictures (1899). (The version I heard is sung by Dame Janet Baker.)

The deeps have music soft and low
When winds awake the airy spry,
It lures me, lures me on to go
And see the land where corals lie.
The land where corals lie.

By mount and mead, by lawn and rill
When night is deep, and moon is high
That music seeks and finds me still,
And tells me where the corals lie.
And tells me where the corals lie.

Yes, press my eyelids close, 'tis well,
Yes, press my eyelids close, 'tis well,
But far the rapid fancies fly
The rolling worlds of wave and shell,
And all the land where corals lie.

Thy lips are like a sunset glow,
Thy smile is like a morning sky,
Yet leave me, leave me, let me go
And see the land where corals lie,
The land, the land where corals lie.

Nothing has been so evocative of my mother. There was something about the tone and cadence that gave me a very strong

BREAKUP

sense of my mother: the image of the corals lying on the seabed—my mother lying preserved, intact. Clive suggested that I have kept her preserved; she has kept me as I was. I have to live my life; she has to die. She has to rot, ferment, disintegrate. I often try to imagine what my mother would be like now. I don't think what she is actually like—bones.

Clive asked about my relationship with Paula. "How did it all start? What were you attracted to in her?" I replied, "The way she carried herself in the world: her spontaneity, ease, intelligence—life force." He pointed out the contrast with me feeling dead.

16 Mar 1991
After yesterday's session.
Clive: "We are running out of ice."
I am stuck at the age of ten. For thirty-five years I have remained ten because I think that I have to keep my mother alive in order for the concept of mother to live on. But she is dead, ex, deceased. I have to provide the warmth, love and affection I need.
I see Julia as a skeleton in a smart men's suit, which is hiding my dead mother. She is just bones, some sublime form floating gently on the bottom of the sea, and I have no mechanism for saying goodbye to her. I am unable to get words out.

Clive says I am possessed by my mother. He saw it from the first minute. It does not matter who Julia was. I have projected the image of truth, love, beauty and affection onto her. I tend to be tolerant and accepting, not assertive. I should be looking for the male side—assertiveness, more fire and power.

I mentioned my inability to cry. He observed that my body armour is too tightly locked. I could not remember the last time I cried. Then it struck me. It was not long after my mother died, when I saw the film *A Kid for Two Farthings*. Clive was brought to tears by the image of the old Jewish man in the film. I remember coming out of the film and being comforted by Ada K.

To mourn Julia means to mourn lost time—thirty-five years. The lost me.

16 Apr 1991
Session
We talk about opposites: Wimp/man; Apollo/Dionysus.

We all have both sides so we have to recognize it and accept.
At the same time we have choices:
a. Can create the world internally, in the imagination
b. Can create part internal, part external
c. Can have all external

Freedom is having control of one's imagination, having one's own gods. Call them up when needed. I still need land and community. Once I have created my gods in my imagination I can walk around Golders Green.

The child in me suspects that Paula has given up on me. The child in me is never wrong.

18 Apr 1991
I imagine a conversation with Paula.

I think you have given up on me, or did I push you? Something in me says you are involved with somebody else. I suspect it is Shawn. He needs it; you need it. Your anger and mine are genuine. I more or less declared my love for you and you did not respond. You were silent. What does that mean? I guess we can live like this. You have found your independence, as you call it. I will find mine. We can live together with minimal emotional investment from either side. Keep the ship running. Maybe your "freedom" does not have to interfere with our relationship in the least. It could even enhance it, because you will be a happier person, more fulfilled.

It is all a bit reminiscent of '70–'71, when I got to London. I came to be with you and you were with Robin.

20 Apr 1991
After an extraordinary night.

I confronted Paula and she told me what was happening. As I suspected, since February she has been involved with Shawn, a guy she has been working with for a few years. I was relieved I was right and kind of accepted. It is better knowing, for the moment.

Leo, the ultimate nice guy. *Mensch.* Where is my anger? Can I just take this with equanimity? Why do I feel so calm? Am I scared to explode the whole thing? Am I trying to win her back?

BREAKUP

She says she loves me for it. How ironic. And yet, it feels okay. I can handle it. It is weird being in a situation I cannot talk about with friends. This is the central theme in my life and I won't be talking about it.

How long will it last? She may want to stop but he needs her desperately. I have grown up a bit; I can call up my gods. I don't feel like rushing off to find someone to caress.

Paula says I have saved the marriage by my action. Well, do we really want to save it? She says, yes. Let's try and keep it going for a while. She needs lots of space. I think I can give it to her. We have been more affectionate lately than almost ever before. There was some release of tension, especially last night.

I feel hurt, very. The love I wanted from you, you have lavished elsewhere. That is painful. But, I can recognize the pain and bear it. Somehow, I see the world clearer today. *The colours are sharper and I am more certain of myself.*

Again I ask: Am I just burying my anger and rage, like I did when I was a child, or am I just aware of the pain, anger and rage and therefore able to tolerate it? What I felt in the past, the deathly sickness in my guts, is not there now. That was powerlessness, insecurity, rage and fear.

I went for a walk on the Heath and tried to find the warm, all-loving mother within me. It's not easy, but I am more accepting of myself. I am not Tom Jones or Sigmund Freud, yet able to be "average." Almost.

It seems crazy to me that I might not need love from another person, that I can supply all the love I need. This is a turning point in my life. Now I have to move towards real independence and integrity, although I am still not able to regress. Where is the four-year-old me?

21 Apr 1991

Can I sit and watch her in a love relationship? They say the worst pain is at the beginning; it gets easier as time goes on. At what point do I throw in the towel, cut my losses? Don't expect me to wait around. What has this changed, anyway? Our relationship is not worse, perhaps better. If I can bear it it's a better situation. But what about me? I am her slave.

She says she is basically monogamous but is torn. She is torn between love, passion and care on the one hand and family, mediocrity, boredom on the other. What choice?? *You are caught between nice guy Leo who you can't really get it together with and nice guy Shawn who is problematic to live with.*
I see my wife has found a love situation and I am looking on it from the outside. I envy her situation. I am not really jealous of Shawn because I don't think Paula and I could find that love.
Did I push her into it? What were my unconscious motives? Did I want an excuse for my own longings? Did I want the titillation that comes from extreme emotion, i.e., self-flagellation? And what am I going to do about it? Just take it as it comes. There is more passion there than I first thought. That is not surprising. At the same time, there is more passion between us than there has been in a long, long time. We are intimate. I am thinking warmly about her. I want her to love me.
I find myself trying to gain her love, but maybe I should just push off. I am not going to find love here, only aggravation and pain. She says, "Wait a while, I'll be back." Will she? Do I want her?

22 Apr 1991

I am sad, I am angry, I am in tears. I feel alive. I feel the loss, I feel the pain, but I still go on.
What was I like as a little boy? I had some sense of it in the shower. Nine, ten years old. Helpless, scared, uncertain and yet something in me said, "You'll be okay, Leo. You'll be fine." And I smiled. That was the voice of my internal mother. I was crying because I felt such an utter failure, so helpless, so pathetic. I was angry with Paula, so angry I could have throttled her.
Surely it is plain as daylight—she doesn't love me. She thinks I am a nice guy. A *mensch*. Something in her says, and has always said, "He is the one to marry and live with. I can trust him, he will love and care for me. But he has never really excited me, made me want to do cartwheels, made the world sharp and my skin tingle."
I alternate between wanting to please her and wanting to throttle her. I have said how much I love her and that she does not have to choose. I have said that I love her so much that I can

even tolerate her loving someone else. But at the same time I AM ANGRY. I AM MAD. I AM FURIOUS.

Ultimately, I can take care of myself. It would be nice to have someone to comfort and love me, but I can manage. I feel the strength inside me. That is what counts. At some level I feel she should not let go of what she has. Life is short. If you find a love relationship then you have to go with it. Also, for us it can never be the same again. She will always be comparing, although their delight and passion will not last. We should not settle for the mediocre. It hurts, really hurts, but it's plain truth.

Why do I feel this way? Why am I prepared to give her up? Because I think it is better for both of us. What we have is reasonable but it is not really the right stuff. There is a lot of history, attachment, fondness and dependency. It is not actually love. Only it's so hard to give it up. I need to use one of the formulae: find someone outside, or find someone inside. It may be possible to conduct life this way. Is it good for me? Is it good for us? I don't know.

What about the light-hearted view. So she plays around a bit, she loves another guy. So what? Maybe I will do the same. In fact, I do not see how it will balance out unless I either leave or do the same. If I reject her she can go to him. She has choice, she can't lose. This is a painful time. I want it to pass and it cannot pass quickly enough.

I can call up my gods but I feel sad at the loss, the deep loss of myself over all this time. The voice said, "You'll be okay, Leo." That is my greatest strength, the real me.

There will be still more pain, especially regarding our family. That will be tough for me. We just have to handle it in the right way. We have to. I feel it in my bones that it is going to happen. That is scary. That is what I fear, the collapse of our family. It is not my relationship with her that I mourn; it's the passing of our family. So, keep it together, keep up the pretence. It is possible. I see now there are two levels: our relationship and the family. It's the family I really care about.

Who is going to hold me in the world? I cry. I am very emotional. I can hold myself, just about. I spoke of a five-year plan to Paula. "Let's live together for five years and then go our own way. See what happens."

23 Apr 1991
I woke at about five and started thinking about Gleneagles (in Scotland), where they got together, and got that sick, panicky feeling. Then Paula held me and we loved passionately. Afterwards I lay in bed by myself and felt this calm descend on me. I have never felt so calm.
    It's not anger I feel, it's grief. It is sorrow and sadness. It's the Corals. I cried like I have never cried before.

I phoned James (an old friend in Israel) and spoke from my heart. I told him I felt okay, that I had sensed my inner resources. I said I had reached the lowest depths and the top of the hill, and it was all downhill from here. Not true. Yesterday I was nine-ish; I still have to get to screaming and shouting at four-ish. What could get me there?
    Perhaps at the back of my mind I still think she will come back to me. She says she has never left! Am I still trying to please, to curry favour? How do I use my imagination, my fantasy? Is it really controlling things if I fantasize about being intimate with someone? She is helping me through this, partly out of genuine feeling, partly because she needs and wants it all to stay together.
    The real pain has still to come. I am not right at the very bottom yet. That will come if I get fully rejected, if I want her and she does not want me.

Hill Garden, Golders Green.
I am crying for me, nobody else. The lost me, the little boy. Fuck her.

24 Apr 1991
What we covered in yesterday's session.
I am the Christ child, prepared to suffer for the good of my mother. I'm on the cross. I have been forsaken in favor of a new child, and all this is reminiscent of my childhood pattern. What did I feel then and what do I feel now? Helplessness. I also ask, "What have I done wrong?"
    Clive insists that there is no male figure in my life. No male firmness in me. I am being mother to her as well as child. I need to be father too. I am trying to please, as ever, whereas I need to break patterns.

What I want to say to her: *You were prepared to risk your husband and family for a relationship with a man you cannot live with. Not all flings are legitimate. You are playing with fire.* When push comes to shove the family and your relationship with me can go down the tubes. The fact is, till Friday night you thought it was going that way. Then I saved you, so you feel relieved. *Why don't you look at other ways of resolving your problems with me? There might be a resolution; there might not be.*

Later
Do nothing. Sit and watch yourself from 1 mm up; the higher, the better the view. Everything is to the good. It will work out. Things will come to me if I find my centre. First I have to plumb the depths. I have to experience nothingness, then there will be a re-birth. Now that all is open and possible we are going back to what we know, what is familiar—the family. We think we have seen the void so we run back to the familiar, to the family.

25 Apr 1991
I feel it in my bones that we are parting, if not physically then emotionally. I feel very weepy, brought on by thoughts about the past—what was, the good side. The loss.
Paula says, "Things are moving fast." I realize now what this means. This is the supreme pain. *What you have must be fantastically strong. It is impossible for me to be clear about my feelings for you. It's too emotional. You are just placating me, keeping me quiet.*

Just breathe deep and call up my gods. Call up my mother. That is what I need, to fall into her arms and be taken into her womb again. Mother, I have been rejected. I am nobody. But, I smile because I can almost see my new self. All I have to do is survive, for a while.

I feel the anticipated pain of the children. They will be knocked sideways. I care more for my children than I do for myself. Sad. I feel ashamed because I may appear a wimp. Okay, I am not what I seem to be. I am imperfect, vulnerable and insecure. I think I can now accept this in myself. She is head over heels. I am nothing. I see and fear a life of sterile spirituality, when I want joy and sparkle.

I like the idea of going to France by myself. Somehow spiritual sterility feels better there. I don't want to teach or do psychotherapy. I want to do pottery and make tables, look after property, breathe fresh air.
An emptiness pervades. I am looking for her.

Yesterday's session.
I learned two things: 1. Let it be. It will be okay, probably better. There will be pain, a lot of pain, but after the pain there will be calm and re-birth; 2. I need to seek the perfect forms of mother and father. My real parents were gods with feet of clay. I can now conjure up the perfect, all-loving, caring mother and the father. These are the two forms I need for my own protection and safety and I can give them to those I love. I need to look a little harder for father but I see him now. I feel something growing inside me, a ray of hope.

I am beginning to realize what it means to "deeply resign," and I weep. I have to deeply resign my previous life and then I will be able to start a new life.

It has been a morning of turmoil, brought on by hearing the tape she shares with Shawn when I went downstairs. Music is magic. I realized what it means to her and I resent those tapes being in my house. I do not want them here.

This morning Rachel (my younger daughter) and I hugged each other and listened to Corals. She said she cried and I told her I had cried yesterday. She wanted to know why it was so sad for me. I told her it reminded me of my mother.

I am so weepy. Every ten minutes something makes me cry. I am thinking of contacting all my friends, whoever I have in the world. I need them a little now and might need them a lot more later.

I fluctuate between anger and resentment and trying to please; between wishing it would all end and hoping we will recreate family bliss. Also, I am a bit embarrassed in the eyes of the world. Not a man, not who you thought I was.

The family. I pain over what I expect to happen. Don't split the family. We have to find another way. Looked at differently, I can't *want* the family to stay together. Either it will or it won't. Is this so? Will my actions not affect things? I don't understand this dynamic.

My manhood is diminished. My pride is hurt. My core is shaken. Fuck her, in a big way. I am worried. I am anxious, fearful, shaking. Think of all the people involved.

I fear the emptiness, the void. But I am assured it is the beginning of life.

Between the ages of six and ten I was waiting for death—of my mother. I probably wanted it to end but was not allowed to have those thoughts. That situation is recreated every now and again, like now.

26 Apr 1991

Passion is in the groin. It's there for her with him. That is my greatest worry, desire. What is desire? I can just about bear it. How much harder can it get?

Console yourself. It won't kill you and you will be better, stronger for it. *But it hurts, mother. I am diminished. I am demeaned.* Don't tell that to anyone, boy. That is your dignity and it's all you have left. Reminds me of Viktor Frankl.

For the last twenty years you have been trying to make the earth move for her and it has drained you totally. Now you feel relief because the load is off, though you feel a failure. Don't; it was an impossible task. Do you see that? You set yourself a Herculean task and you are not Hercules.

I have spent the last twenty years trying and he did it in two days. Magic. Maybe I should tell him to piss off. I want to see him face to face. I feel like blowing the whole thing open. What will happen then?

And what did the Corals say today? There was a ray of hope, of looking forward. They said: go forth, my boy. Deeply resign, go into the world, don't be scared. And I smiled. There is awareness of loss. Loss. Loss. But there is hope for the future, for growth and joy, tinged with sorrow and regret. That is what is in me now.

27 Apr 1991

What a night. Now I feel it is all over. I just feel that they are right for each other, whatever that means. At this stage of her life it is he that she needs. It might blow over and it might not. A breakup is inevitable. She is torn; I am cut to shreds. Thinking about the way it happened for them: the right atmosphere, a few drinks, electricity. How will it happen for me? Passion is chemistry. You cannot teach it. That is a hard, bitter lesson. The emotional house is crumbling. I have to step outside before it falls. Jay said the flames of passion die. Possibly. But Paula will be unfulfilled without this. I want her to be fulfilled. I dread the prospect of an unhappy woman as my partner. Can she be happy with me? Can I be happy with her?

Am I engaged in another heroic struggle, this time to save our family? I always seem to find a cause, one that does not do me any good. Is it pissing against the wind?

Letter from Paula, written before she left for Denmark:
Leo,
Take care—please don't be too sad—I'm coming back to you. I'll be thinking of you—trying to work things out for myself—it's not easy—I'll phone.
P.S. Rachel's rolls are in top shelf of freezer—ready made. Jake's bagels are one shelf down in carrier bag—there aren't enough for whole week—there is salami but you'll have to buy a few more bagels.
I love you.
P

28 Apr 1991

It's a time for breaking away. Holding on is like alcohol dependency: I want it, I need it—it's killing me. What about training as a hypnotherapist, getting a job in a community, doing pottery seriously, dog breeding? I see the next stage now. Gradually move away and create my own world. She has work and love—fulfilment. I envy her. I envy anybody like that.

There is a little voice inside that says all the time: I want it to work with Paula. This is the voice of dependency and attachment, the cry of habit, the hope of avoiding pain. It's a false hope. What seems like the easy solution now is not the correct one. I am sure of that.

I look at your short love note. It is all true: you are coming back to me and you will be thinking of me. You love me and I

BREAKUP

am reasonably certain you will continue to love me, partly because you know how much I love you and a side of you says, "I want a pure, faithful man." That stage has passed. Accept it. Now you want passion and you seem to have it.

For me, at a certain stage, you were the person to be with. There was deep affection and attachment. We brought up a wonderful family. Now I have to move off, to cut my own path and find work I can get absorbed in. And maybe love will come too.

Leo, let me speak to you as a father:
My boy, things are hard for you at the moment. Stay calm and confident. You will be okay. You have great resources and strength. Let them come to the fore.

At an earlier stage in your life you chose the heroic path in thinking you could create paradise on earth, first on the kibbutz and then with Paula. Those things worked for you, more or less. But, as you can see, the attempt to create paradise with Paula nearly killed you. Put down the load now. You managed to create a wonderful family. You will always have the positive side of that and you can continue to be a good father to your kids.

Now is a time for moving away gently, to create your own life, in a small way. You need to find work and possibly real love. However, love will not come easily to you. As to work, you need to see what is right for you; you have a lot of skills and talents. You can find a new self. It will mean deeply resigning what you have had up till now—almost everything. I think you are ready for it.

I have faith in you. You will be okay.

I spoke to James. He said, "The kids have had a brilliant innings. It will be hard for them, not terrible. You have my total and full support."

Later I spoke to Harry (another old friend). He wanted to know where my anger was. Did I get into rages? He has been rejected by two women. He feels they took all the good with them and left nothing. He wanted to know what will happen when the passion goes *fut*. He said I could phone him anytime, day or night. He felt my pain. I must develop a clear sense of me, which takes a long time.

Paula phoned from Copenhagen. I said the wrong things, like I missed her. She laughed and got short, wanting to speak to her kids. I panicked, like a four-year-old.

Jan (a family friend) feels it is real, deep love between them that could really flourish and grow. I think so too. She thinks Paula is asking phenomenal maturity and understanding from me. It is fine to give it. She would not have got to where she has got without the fathering I have given her. It's an earthquake. Nothing will be the same again. Paula is so high; there is no speaking to her. With a love of this sort you just want to be together all the time. Maybe she can love two people.

Jan's advice to me: "Go back to pottery. You are a very good potter."

29 Apr 1991
6:00 a.m.
Sick, sick, sick in my tummy.

It's not just hard, it's terrible. It is far worse than I thought it could be.

Things between them are too wonderful for me to believe and it goes through me like a knife. How can she have so much and me nothing? I am just an empty vessel shouting for help and salvation. Where will it come from?

And I cried, but not for long. I tried to be in my ideal mother's arms. My ideal father spoke a little. He says it will be okay, even if it doesn't look like it now.

La Bohème is my music. Sad, sad joy. I can hear it inside me. I feel quite contented, seeing that look on her face after we were in bed together on Saturday morning. Someone helped to push her to the top. What a relief. Now I can do my thing.

I am absolutely powerless, like a child, like I was as a child. What power does a child have over a parent? None. Here she has all the power. She has the ability to say: *I don't love you.* It's not true—she can't deny it. She loves me.

I want to say something to you right now. I want to give you space. At the same time I want your love too. I need it. Don't reject me. I

BREAKUP

need your help to find my way. I think we have enough between us for you to give it. Our love for each other is greater than it has been for twenty years so there is no reason to part. Not true, but there is reason to stay together.

It's panic stations, I know. I need to find a quiet spot and look into myself. I am worried about being dependent on her. Her every move will affect me. She's going to Chicago. Will she come back?

I feel a big part of me is lost, is absent. I feel it in the solar plexus. Maybe that is where I have felt something is missing. I want to look at some photos of me as a baby. Corals. *Mother, I weep for you. I am powerless.*

I want her to phone and say: "Hi Leo, I am missing you. I do care for you and I look forward to seeing you." That would be a relief because I am uncertain of her feelings. The child is uncertain of his mother's love. The pain of rejection is what I must have felt when my mother died. I am feeling it only now.

30 Apr 1991

I sense the modest beginnings of power.

I get the feeling that everything that has gone before was nothing. This is a new phase in which I can look at the past and reject it. I can continue to be a good father and the kids will be okay. I am thinking of Robinson (in *Friday and Robinson* by Michel Tournier) in the cave. He expects darkness and finds light. Friday guides him towards a new life.

I hear a different sound from Corals now. It used to be sad and mournful—the sound of my mother; thoughts of my mother lying at the bottom of the sea, preserved perfectly. Now it is the sound of growth, movement and change. The last verse now puts a spring in my step. I AM WALKING.

Give her up, deeply. Find the corals elsewhere. I need some coral. What about Eilat?

I dread the endless cycle of on and off with Paula. I cannot let it go on. I am doing mental gymnastics: sometimes I just pretend it has ended in order to ensure the opposite. *I hate you for what you have done. I hate you so much I feel like destroying your rela-*

tionship, getting revenge, feeling a bit of power over you. How? What is the worst thing I can do to her?

Who says things have to work out all rosy? Where is it written? Not all relationships work. She might have left me in all but name but I don't think she has. I have not accepted that she has. The thought of her moving out chills me, makes me panic. It may only be a matter of time. I have to disinvest emotionally. How?

I feel absolutely powerless and helpless. No money, no status. Just a little, little me inside. I hope it's going to come out. Generally though, I feel better.

After the session with Clive yesterday.
I am thinking about the stigma and the degradation. I am not a real man. And now everyone can see I am frail and fallible. That's me. On the other hand I now have the luxury of being ordinary. I do not have to be anybody, not even Adonis.

To remind myself, it is like trying to come off heroin. I see it is eating me up and I have to drop the habit. Everybody wants to kick ass and my ass is being kicked.

The pain in this phase (which might last years) is going to be tolerating their relationship. Contrast this with a death, where the loss is greater and more obvious but it ends there. Here it continues.

James says I stumbled with the stretcher; a reference to our army days. "Who can keep going without falling? In twenty years' time you will be laughing at what is going on now." I don't think so. Guts and determination were there but you just didn't have everything it needed. Try a lighter load next time. You may have an easier journey and even reach the summit.

Echoes of Nietzsche: What does not kill you makes you stronger.

I am still waiting for her to call from Copenhagen.

01 May 1991
I had a horrible dream. I dreamt that somebody I know, an ugly child, was stealing things from our house. I kicked him out.

She is drunk with Shawn, besotted. That's the rub. *You have deserted us. Go, go, flourish with him. And let me go to the land where the corals lie.*

BREAKUP

Is it going to be a question of who is first out of the door after Jessy's exams? Paula wants out. She also wants her kids and me. It's a tough choice. She'll probably prefer not to choose. I need to know where I stand. I deserve that, otherwise we split soon.
But a little voice inside me says: how boring to go back to Paula.
Tendency to merge; tendency to part.

03 May 1991
I feel like her eunuch, on the cross and in a flaming rage. Helpless. I am like a ship in a storm, being blown about by the wind. Don't do anything rash. Calm will return and you will be able to decide. Watch yourself.
My underlying feeling is that I want her to scream out for me. Yet, a side of me does not want her, does not feel right with her. This is not just reaction to rejection. I want my mythical woman, call her Marta, not Paula. There are other fish in the sea. Explore.

06 May 1991
Paula—"I'll be back to sleep."
Pain, yes. Fear, no.
Clive—"Cut the Gordian knot."
I don't actually like Paula. She is not my affair. Just see through the pain, it will cleanse. Come out the other side. Whether it lasts or not is not my concern. I have to decide what I want. I do not have a problem—just float.

22 May 1991
I really think we should split but I can't face it. I cannot face loss, being alone. Can't face seeing her so full. I would like to feel generous, magnanimous and loving. I can't. I am your husband. I feel rejected, dejected and empty. Float in the world. No decisions. Empty now but will fill again; life will return. Let go. What's gone is gone. Know when to quit.

25 May 1991
I took off my wedding ring. She can live downstairs (on the middle floor of three). Maybe we will have to live like this for a while.

I am not moving out. I don't know what I want but know what I don't want—more of what we had. In fact, I prefer the idea of a new love. It will take time but it will come. In the meantime there is pain, but not too bad. I don't really want her so why should I care if she loves Shawn. It's hard to be rejected but I know it's right. There is almost nothing between us. We are bored with each other; we have grown apart. She may be an attractive woman but not the one for me. So, I'll find a new life. I believe things will go well for me. I have power and tremendous resources. She is not my concern.

They may be at it right now. That hurts a bit. He can have her; she can have him. I'm okay; I'm smiling.

29 May 1991
After the session with Clive yesterday.
Clive: "There is nothing, man. Just do down into nothing and you will realize you are still alive. When you are still you begin to pull things in. There is no hope. Just wake up every morning and feel some pain—know that you are alive. Don't be a bleeding heart. You are too feminine (Yin) and need to find the masculine (Yang). Be genuine, authentic. The only thing that counts is authenticity. That is your power and strength. You need to put a boundary around chaos."

I am giving up my power in every direction. I am only powerless if I think I am. All I can do at the moment is hang in, eat well and sleep well. Time will pass. Decisions are not mine. They will be taken by others. He doesn't give Paula and Shawn more than a few months. The whoosh will drop out, not him but what he is providing. She is charged up and can spread it around. We are all charged up. Something is hidden in the situation but I don't know what.

My task now is to let go, to separate. Just explore my emotions. Take each day as it comes. Each second. Get in touch with the void. Discover the child in me. Stay in between fullness and emptiness, that's the trick. It's in me. Use this incident to transform myself. Live the moment. Smell freedom. Work can loosen the bonds. HOLDDD. DON'T SPLINTER.

Love: two people trying to stay afloat on the sea. They look at each other and say "Doing okay?"
And in my desperation I turned to a tarot lady. It's all good news:

BREAKUP

I have the Winner's card: celebration, hopefulness, expansion, growth, good luck, good karma. I am the Fool: the world is my oyster. The slate is clean: new incarnation. No expectations. Go and do it. It was her choice to make disruption. She will have to eat it. Be more of a real person. Express rage. I have to stoke the fire of spiritualism. Get involved in a cause. Writing—get out that pen. Listen to the child within. The little boy has a story.

30 May 1991
I just feel so empty. My mind is constantly mulling possible scenarios. I went to see a man about the legal situation. It looks bleak. One can't force the other to leave. We are forced to live under the same roof.

Thinking I might need to opt out, leave her with the house and kids then agree to sell the house in about a year's time. Why should I stay in this situation? Perhaps I need to make a clean break. It will be hard at first but I will manage. I will have freedom but still have responsibility to the kids. I am their father and always will be. Only, I cannot stand the thought of Shawn moving into my/our house. That's a hard one.

Stay empty; it will fill again.
I don't want harmony, I want separation. Non-belligerence. I don't want to go out with you or be in your company. We talk of your moving out of the bedroom, to "cool off." Good idea. What I want is revenge. I hope it comes soon. Betrayed, that is the word. She has betrayed me and will ask for forgiveness.

03 Jun 1991
Reflecting on a weekend workshop with Clive...
I am beginning to recognize my program. I take on suffering, remove myself from reality, hold in and on.

People there said, "The lion (Leo) is a noble, graceful creature, kills and lives. Fight, man, don't die. Scream and shout against the injustice done to you."

We are all in the shit; one big toilet. Get in touch, not by reaching out but by letting go. Let go of everything—love, kids, wife, marriage. Every fucking thing. When I have reached the bottom I can start coming up again. Leave them alone. They are not my affair. Thank heavens I am out of it.

Something profound happened. I realized I preferred being in hell with my mother to being out of hell without her. Julia is dead. Dead, dead, dead. Gone, finished. I need to suffer. Why? I won't let go. Why?

Most of all I got in touch with the lost child, the vulnerable child clinging to mother and looking around for signs of love and affection. I need to have a sense that there is something inside me—wild horses—then I can gradually get in touch with it.

04 Jun 1991
I am beginning to feel the wild horses are in me. I don't have to reach out for them. I am them. All I have to do is let go, stoke the fire. This is the time when I can harness them. I am ready to fight, to fight for my side. All the way. I also have a sense of the brutal, restless caveman. I visualize him/me lashing out with a rock in his hand. He is powerful, he is motivated, driven. That's me, too. I realize I am capable of anything: brutality and tenderness.

I can use the present situation to turn myself around—to know deeply that it is all in me. It's funny how it comes slowly, almost imperceptibly.

Fight, fight, fight. I'll nail them if it's the last thing I do. I am the power. She just touched my button. This is not the time for harmony; it's the time for confrontation. Take up the cudgels. September will be too late. Let the battle commence. Make plans. I'll do what I want to, use every possible means. *You'll see what you took on when you got into bed with Shawn at Gleneagles.*

No reason, no compassion. Just rage.

05 Jun 1991
Clive and I talked yesterday.
About walking out, about leaving, about going.
If we have reached this point there is a choice:
   a.   Reconciliation
   b.   Break

As neither of us wants reconciliation there should be a break. I have to move out on my own. This is the only way for me to find my way. Worst case scenario: I move out, Shawn moves in; the kids forget about me. Well, what is wrong with that? It's

BREAKUP

where I started from. It's all just a bad investment. Cut my losses. Twenty-odd years ago I did not know Paula and now I can forget about her. It was just an episode. Thank heavens it was only twenty-odd years. She is not blood. The kids do not belong to me. All they need is a mother or father figure. I have to sort out my own internal family.

Charles: "Forget her, man. She is nothing to you but bad news. You will find a better mind, better body and better fuck elsewhere. Don't you realize that, man? She is just habit. You need to go into nothingness for a while, go and live in a community or by the sea."

Yesterday I had an enormous sense of rage and fury. I was the primitive man with a rock in my hand. Today I feel like the helpless child. No power. I just wince when I see her smile. I puke when I smell her perfume. What can I do? Nothing. I am scared to leave. I fear the loneliness. I fear the void. I don't want to lose my comforts. I don't want to see her flourish without me.

The point is she is not my affair. Whether she is just going through an incredible fantasy or whether this is true love is not for me to think about. I have to extricate myself from the situation now. It is bad news for me.

Should I go or should I stay? Do I love her or do I not? Confusion: don't burn bridges vs. cut everything; the pain of staying vs. the pain of leaving. Give it time. Can we separate while under one roof? I want her to want me back vs. I don't want her.

What do I do?

2: MAN OF SORROWS

06 Jun 1991
Corthauld Institute, Somerset House.
I have just glimpsed an aspect of the void, the divorce courts, and I can take it. Now at the gallery looking at van Dyck's *Man of Sorrows*. I identify with the figure in the painting. I am somewhere between a rock and a hard place. I feel empty and anxious. The point is that today not only can I see us living apart but I am at one with it. I even welcome it. *You were just an episode.*

07 Jun 1991
Paula was relaxed this morning and held my hand at the table. She says she feels warmly towards me. I just find it difficult to see her smiling and feel uncomfortable about the twitch of feeling in me towards her. I want her to get into bed with me. I'm smitten by her largesse and reduced size.
　　Let her go, let her go her way. I can do better. Yet, I want her, I desire her. And it's hard, man. Abandonment, rejection.

10 Jun 1991
I think our relationship has ended. She wants it that way, I want it. It's just a question of facing it. For me it will lead to better things. Maybe, as per Gill Edwards, we need to end with unconditional love, forgiveness and grace. Love frees, hate binds. I can cut the cord more easily than I can cut the cord with my mother. Or can I? Which reminds me, Paula is due to have her breast lump removed soon.
　　As to the house and kids, I feel we should settle as soon as possible, share the equity and each go our own way. She can have the kids. I want my freedom. I want to reach for my dreams. I want to jump off the cliff and see if I can fly.

11 Jun 1991
I just lay in bed this morning trying to understand what is in my heart. Do I love her and want her or not? Obviously I still feel for her, I still desire her and I don't want the pain of separation. But, I

BREAKUP

don't think I want to be tied to her. I think I want to be alone, separate and free. There is a gap between head and heart still. In my head I know we should part; in my heart I still feel like merging.

I feel I want to reach for the sky, be pulled by my dreams. I see staying on here at no. 25 and continuing our life together as boring, confining and restricting. I feel trapped and this is the chance for me to get out. I have wanted to separate for a long time and couldn't. I need a bigger canvas to paint my life on. I need to do something wild, crazy, outrageous. I sense the tiger inside me. I am slowly, slowly becoming aware of my true self.

12 Jun 1991

Can I avoid the void? I am restraining myself from going mad, holding on to sanity. It's painful but I realize there is only one way it can go. I don't want her. I want a life away from Paula.

Clive and I talked yesterday.
About cold anger and power. Don't give it up. If I feel I am powerless, I am. I don't feel I am. I am deciding what I want and intend to get it. I am searching for the masculine in me and have held back masculinity for forty-six years. There must be a good reason. Am I scared of it?

Clive has the feeling that if I want Paula back I need to start acting. I don't think I do. I want to plough a new field. I got some comfort when he said she is not in love with Shawn but with what he represents. With an exact look-alike it would be the same. She will wake up as soon as she realizes he is flesh and blood. This is the nature of human relationships (and will be true for me too).

I told him I want to up and go—explore, visit, experience. Clive replied, "It's all here; you don't have to go anywhere." And I left with a sense of unexploited power and freedom that comes with control of my own destiny. It's all in me. If I want to have it in the real world I first have to have it inside, especially self-love. All else will flow.

13 Jun 1991

Letter to Paula (not sent).
I know what I want. I want the house to be sold and for us to share the equity. You take the kids. That's it.

I will use any and every possible means to achieve this and I won't let up.
Leo

I am faced with a *fait accompli*. It's happening. We are splitting. She is moving out. I feel sick. Why? Do I want her back? Am I scared of the future? Am I just sad at the loss? Should I be responsible and stay on or should I do as my heart dictates and run away? The pain is hard to take. It seems it will not end. I just need to HOLDDD, walk, breathe. I need to call up my guardian angels, be my own parent. Don't splinter. Don't be a victim or resent.

What would the real father say?
Son, I see things are hard for you. Stand firm, you'll be okay. These things happen and you need to adapt and fight for what you want. There is no certainty of outcome but if you handle it correctly things will work out for you. You cannot avoid the pain but it will pass and you will be cleansed. Express your rage and anger. Be real. Be true.

Mother:
My darling boy. Let me hug you and hold you. I love you absolutely and unconditionally. You have been wronged and I feel terribly sad for you. Never mind that. You need to find your own path. You will. You will find life and love because you have it in you. Remember, I am with you all the way. You are empty now but it will fill again. That is the way of the world. Then you can put this episode behind you and find new life.

Child:
I am frightened. I am scared. I don't want you to abandon me. I will be lost and vulnerable. I need your protection and love. I am nothing without you. You have everything and I have nothing. Please, please don't go. Come back and be with me forever, Mommy.

BREAKUP

Leo:
My head tells me I will grow through the change and pain, that I had outgrown our relationship and can look forward to a new and better one. I want it and I need to have the guts to go and get it. Holding on is just force of habit and the weight of history and common experience.

My heart says cuddle and hold, relax and reconstruct so that we do not have to go through the pain of parting and living apart. Is the pain of separating greater or less than the pain of staying together? Wanting to blend; wanting to part. I feel the choice is not mine. She will decide. The outcome is uncertain but there is one certainty—it will be okay. I will be okay.

I need to look after the kids. I'll be there for them.

14 Jun 1991
Last night Rachel (now nine) tried to run away. Anything could have happened to her. Paula and I were both shocked, to the point of thinking we should try to live under one roof. We were scared something terrible might happen. Perhaps we should stay together for the kids.

Impossible.

15 Jun 1991
It is a fantastically hard time.

We have told the kids, separately. I am sad, yet strong and determined. Paula is using every possible means to convince herself that she is doing the right thing. She doesn't realize it is just the first flush of love. However, it could work for them.

Paula was away last night and came back later than intended. Jessy got upset so I hinted to her about the situation. I said I knew the truth but Paula had to tell her. Anyway, she did and then we both spoke to her together. Jessy was angry. She feels we have always argued and recently we gave her a hard time over her exams. We did. I feel terrible about it. She is sad and I want to communicate with her. It's hard.

Then we sat down with Rachel. She was amazing. She listened, she said a little, she cried a little and seemed to be relieved. Then she went off to play the piano. We assured her of how much we care for her.

Later we spoke to Jake. He was very distressed, as I knew he would be. He wanted to run upstairs but I restrained him. And I talked to him from my heart. I said, "Maybe Paula and I were brought together to have three amazing children." I cried. After a while he was able to hug me and then he hugged Paula and we hugged together.

Paula told me that she had met people who convinced her that it can work for her and Shawn. I said it reminded me of GBS and the Webbs, who went to Russia after the revolution and naively proclaimed, "We have seen the future, and it works." Did it?

Later.
I am constantly thinking about the future and wondering whose predicted scenario from all the people I have spoken to and consulted is going to prove correct. Secretly thinking that Sharon, who thinks it will mend, will be right, but I don't think so. Whose pattern will we follow? We can be creative and imaginative—friends, companions and occasional lovers. Go away for a week every year. Will we be able to stand each other?

I cried while listening to *La Bohème*. There is sadness; there is joy. There is strength and power. Let them out. Paula feels I am kicking her out of the house until we sell but I am firm about staying here. I'll manage. We will streamline and the kids will pull their weight. I'll get the games out.

17 Jun 1991

Myriad feelings but most of the time I just feel a dull pain. At the moment I feel sick—the abandoned child. Rachel asked me what she should tell people. I didn't know what to say. She is troubled. Jake is putting on a brave face, for the meantime. It is also a time of tenderness with Paula and pleasant sex. She says she doesn't love me any less. Only now she has something extra. She is torn, very torn.

18 Jun 1991

We had a fight last night. I was angry because Paula called Shawn when we were about to get into bed together. I had been feeling very warm and loving towards her and I felt rebuffed. I suppose I acted like a thwarted child. I lost control, possibly helped by the Herault wine I had got for dinner. I lost my sanity for a while, I splintered and then calmed down. We both felt shit afterwards.

To quote Clive, "Your home is a bomb site. You are emotionally attached to a parental/family home but need to leave."

19 Jun 1991
5:00 a.m.
I woke up early, as usual. Paula says she wants to be my friend. Shawn is her lover. That goes through me like an electric charge. The pain, the agony. What can I say: *ah-so!* She has made him her love object, which she never chose to make me.

Who I am seems tied up with being husband, father, owner and occupier of this house. It's hard to imagine any other state of being. Wait. These things are peripheral. I am me internally. I have to feel me from the inside, not in relation to outside people or objects. I think I can let go—of everything: kids, family, P, house, London. I want to be free, maybe take a year off.

Now, one hour later, I feel my kids need me at a time like this. I have to be responsible. I can't stand the thought of being here but it might be crucial for the kids.

20 Jun 1991
I chatted to my friends, the Kings, last night and am more realistic about our situation as a result: you can't stop love; between us it was never very good; this is a ticket to ride for me. Do my bit—explore, meet people, screw around. Talked of people they can introduce me to and I got a little excited at the prospect. Typical me. Lyn thinks I am an attractive man, the sort women are looking for.

I woke up early this morning with a sick feeling. I cajoled Paula to lie down with me for a short while and I talked a little about my feelings. She says her feelings for me "have not changed."

Later I took her to the Royal Free Hospital and sat around, blank, watching cricket on the TV while she underwent the small op to remove what proved to be a benign lump from her breast. I then went to her room, where she lay still slightly drugged. I felt I care for her. We talked of remaining friends, partly for the sake of the kids, and I left feeling it was like a final parting. Maybe it has something to do with hospitals. Paula was almost totally cut off from me at the Free and I remember feeling that about my mother after I had gone on my own, at the age of about eight, to visit her at Groote Schuur Hospital and taken her a card.

21 Jun 1991
I woke up in a low state thinking that not only does she not love me now but she never did. She never loved me as a man and I did not love her as a woman. Anyway I more or less dealt with the pain by letting it go through me. Then I moved on to some smiles and joy by managing to call up my ideal mother, father and lover. I have never done all of them so successfully. On the way to school I started telling myself I need to experience Leo the man, the adult, the sensitive, likeable, handsome, friendly man, who also has a dark side—full of deviousness, anger, jealousy and irresponsibility.

I sense the tidal wave. I have to step aside and let it pass without getting caught in the deluge. Hanging on to the house, a bomb site, and the family, a wreck, is just a neurotic emotional response, like hanging on to the family of my childhood.

My life with Paula falls into perspective when I think we did not love each other. It makes sense all of a sudden. Who withdrew first? Does it matter? Blame! I was trying to hurt her; she withheld sex and affection from me—an interesting dynamic. No wonder I was in such bad shape and she was so angry and unhappy. We never sorted out our problems and never tried to deal with them seriously. Could we have loved? We will never know. Yet, not all relationships have to work. Ours didn't.

In the Michel Tournier version of the *Friday and Robinson* story Friday kills his goat-rival. Something in me says I should challenge Shawn. No. Accept. The animal instinct is not appropriate and I would not feel any better. Unless I forced him away and won Paula back. Impossible, ridiculous, undesirable. Let it be. *Ah-so!* Go on to better things, man. You can. In a way I need to do what Friday did: jump off the precipice and see if I can fly. He did and got a bit grazed but came out smiling. In fact, he didn't intend to jump but got carried away. I can do the same. I have to. Question is: What is my equivalent of jumping off a cliff? Moving into a bed-sit and starting psychotherapy?

I am floating, like a piece of wood bobbing on the ocean. I have no hates, no loves, I am not fat, not thin, not nice, not clever, not stupid, not handsome, not ugly, not a psychotherapist, not a teacher, potter, designer, father, lover, friend or foe, not a writer or a person of talent. I just am.

22 Jun 1991
What is the real pain? The loss: the loss of the last twenty-plus years. We never loved each other! Is that possible? True, the love could have been greater but there was a bonding, an affection and closeness. It hurts me to think that she wants a second chance at life, a second bite of the cherry. It implies that the first bite was worthless. I also want a great love, a more liberating love, instead of the oppression and confinement of the last few years.

Still, I am caught between wanting to run away and knowing I have a responsibility to the kids. Some people make me think that there will be a "they all lived happily ever after" ending and I sort of hope there will be but it doesn't look like it.

Last night I danced the Lambada with Frankie at Ben's farewell party. I let go a little and it felt good.

24 Jun 1991
Paula and I are kind of talking a little. She is harping on this "care" bit. She says I never cared for her. I said there is no point in expending energy on what was—did I care for her, did she care for me? I cannot tell if she is really torn or putting on a show, or if she is trying to ease her conscience, or even having second thoughts. I have not come to terms with the parting yet.

I met Yael last night. She is interesting and attractive and I felt quite relaxed with her. We chatted, she told me her story and I told her mine. I liked her vibes. It felt good walking her to her car, comfortable at my side. Fantasies arose of going away for a weekend with her, perhaps even to France. It's early days with her but it makes me feel different and throws my relationship with Paula into perspective—or does it? I just feel a bit more human. Almost wanted, desired, believed in and accepted.

25 Jun 1991
Paula is going crazy. She hates me, is mad at me, supposedly for telling everybody and getting people to gang up against her. She says she has no support, feels isolated and insecure. She attacked me while I was lying in bed this morning and hurt my finger. She says she is "not going."
Paula: "Why should I? You have to pack your bags and go."
I said she can't force me. She said she will change the locks when the kids and I come back from France. Pure anger, hatred and frustration. I think she spoke to her sister last night, who got her thinking that she is mad to give up the kids and support us. Has she decided to stay? In any case, I am staying too.

She wants to mull over the past and how pathetic I was. She says I have acted like a baby now. I have not. For a week I was upset but since then I have been open and honest. At no time have I tried to run her down or take a moral stand against what she has done. I have just said: I am hurt but things were not right between us and we have decided to part. People are naturally sympathetic towards me as I am the injured party. They know me, like me and feel sorry for me. But, I don't need pity and sorrow.

It could all turn nasty.

And she asks, "Who are all these people you are seeing and talking to?" The fur flies!

Part of me wants to think that this behaviour of Paula's shows a change of heart. It doesn't. I know it won't be all rosy again. She is more determined than ever.

I am better able to cope with the pain. I don't have that sick and scared feeling of the abandoned child. That is growth. I just feel sad and mad at having to expend so much energy on this crap. Can't we just get on with our lives? It would be so much easier if I left. Perhaps I should become a hermit and go and live in the desert. I have the smell of freedom in my nose. Free from responsibility, free from people, free from material possessions. Just me and the air, the wind, the water and the earth.

Just float, boyo. Do nothing and it will happen.

26 Jun 1991
After the row yesterday morning Paula phoned to apologize. I accepted.

BREAKUP

The session with Clive:
I am not fully in touch with my feelings. If I were it would be unbearable. Paula is my conduit to earth. Without her I have a tendency to fly, as I want to now. Free of Paula as wife I relate to her as mother and I am venting all the hatred and anger I have for my mother on her. Cf. going to the hospital now and when my mother was in hospital.

I had a dream about dogs and a gorilla. I am the Alsatian, seemingly wild but actually held in control by Paula, while the old, wise gorilla (Shawn) looks on. I need to become the gorilla. Our relationship was a negative bind: I was unhappy playing the child; she was not happy playing the mother. There is something to be said for understanding the relationship so that we do not perpetuate the same patterns. To me it seems so late in life to wake up.

I was in the depths of despair when Paula left last night to spend the night with Shawn. I was lying on my bed taking the pain when the phone rang. It was Yael. She said she was prepared to come straight over, which made me so happy. She did come over. We chatted and held hands. She saved me. I want to see her again and she seems keen.

Take your ticket and ride, boy. That is the right and only choice. It has been made for you but it is right for you. It's hard, very hard, but you have to bite the bullet. There is no other way.

28 Jun 1991
I feel low, I feel sad, I feel depressed. I want Paula back. I see her around; I see her shape and want her. She is going out tonight, tomorrow night and Sunday. Maybe I shouldn't wait for her to leave but just leave. It is agony like this. She is with us/me but not with us/me. Trouble is that I think parting is bad news. It won't be. I will flower.

My feelings: a sense of abandonment—like a child; wanting her—like a man.

30 Jun 1991
I feel strangely calm and centred. She is now going up and down like a yo-yo. She says she cannot be away from the kids. She was

with Shawn's boys today but actually wanted to be with her own kids. The rub.

Now she is saying she wants to be here and "sleep a few nights a week with Shawn." Well, I don't like the idea but I didn't say anything. Last week she said she could not live with me at all. She is just playing games with me. She wants Shawn *and* her kids.

01 Jul 1991
I am constantly looking for images to help me understand the situation. What about looking on marriage as a car rather than a relationship? Keep it neutral and unemotional. The car has broken down. Do I/we want to repair it? Either we have to trudge along in this one or abandon it. We have chosen to trudge along in it as neither of us wants to abandon it. With time attitudes might change. If one abandons completely the other is forced to abandon too, but may try to hold on.

03 Jul 1991
Strange things happened in the night. Saul (a family friend) came over to talk to me and we went into the lounge. Paula was pissed off. Afterwards she came to me while I was in the bath and went crazy. She threw everything she could in my face: I am a cry baby, I am crying on people's shoulders.

What is she on about? Is she just plain mad with me and feels I am kicking her out of the house, or does she have feelings of ambivalence and is expressing them as anger? James says Paula is showing signs of worry and is beginning to realize the implications of what is going on.

04 Jul 1991
All I have to do is survive and separate from Paula.

In the meantime I am trying to learn more about the whole scene, to know more about other people's experience. I am reading Susan Jeffers' *Opening our Hearts to Men*. She refers to her friend Bobbie who wrote an account of her breakup from her husband of twenty-eight years. She describes it as a moving book about her odyssey from excruciating pain to a sense of inner peace. She struggled to let go of her rage and her victim role. They got back together again.

BREAKUP

Message from a tarot lady:
I am onto a good thing. The second half of my life will be the better half. Let down my hair, go for it. Things will work out. The road is open for me. My life with Paula is not over, even though she is in love with Shawn. Their relationship will not last, perhaps till the end of the year. Be patient. She will be back. It pains now but it's nothing to get upset about. So, she has fallen in love with somebody else. Re-birth, new life and renaissance lie ahead.

06 Jul 1991
Saturdays are hard. She comes back from Shawn's, is tense but looks sated. She is thin (for her) at the moment. Today she wants to be friendly. Their making it together in the future threatens me.

I just sensed something of my inner emptiness. I am afraid that I will run out of things to say to people, that I will dry up. It's the child in me, lost for words. Unappreciated, put down.

I am still waking at five-ish but I have got my appetite back after hardly wanting to eat for the past few months. It is hard to imagine I will go down again but I probably will. Now, at least I know that if I go down I will come up again. That is enlightenment; that is growth. I am now sitting at my desk, alone, with the sun in my face. I have never felt better.

08 Jul 1991
I want revenge. Will I get it?

It's the grim prospect of future life that bothers me. Imagine what it will be like if she has the kids and lives with Shawn and I have to have access to the kids. Images of fights and tension fill my head: me kicking him out of this house, having to force my way back in, etc. Ugly.

Don't be trapped in the future, boyo. There is nothing to be done, just float. Pain yes; fear no. The pain will pass.

09 Jul 1991
We have reached the state of acrimony and I want to go for it. I went to speak to her when she came home at seven o'clock in the morning. I told her how I felt, that I want an "I do what I want" approach, not the friendship I had spoken of before. On matters relating to the kids she wants co-operation, e.g., for Rachel's re-

port meeting today. I don't want to go with her. Finally she made an appointment. In general, she is competing for the kids. Suddenly she wants to do something with Jake on Sunday (Shawn is away). I am agitated and don't know whether to cool it or heat it up. Again this morning she said I should think about leaving. I was adamant that I would not. I had thought of locking her out but decided not to.

I am meeting lots of women but am worried that I won't meet the "right" one.

The *Friday and Robinson* story comes up again in my mind. In the end Friday leaves and Robinson is about to die. He is prepared to die. Then he hears a noise—the young boy; optimism and hope in the form of Sunday. A new life, new beginnings. Is this the paradigm of my story? It feels like death then life returns.

10 Jul 1991

I woke up early feeling like death. It felt like there was a whole building collapsing on me. There was a heavy scene yesterday as we somehow got into massive verbal abuse. She also attacked me physically a few times. I kept quite calm and just shouted at her.

It started in the morning on the way back from Rachel's report meeting, which we both went to in the end. She informed me that Shawn will be with her when she takes the kids on Sunday. She presented me with a fact after we had agreed that this would not happen yet. Then she went on about what sort of father I am. I saw red and shouted at her. The shouting continued at home. She was wild, "Leo Averbach has nothing going for him. He stinks. You are weak and have behaved terribly." She is feeling so terrible about herself as a mother that she tries to accuse me of being a lousy father.

I went off to see Alexa. Man! Is she lovely. I came back and Paula said she was prepared to talk—i.e., to tell me what she wants.

Just survive the day, the hour, this minute. Let go of expectations, of models, of patterns. Of what other people will or won't do.

What I covered with Clive yesterday.
Stand still. That is all I ever have to do.

BREAKUP

Coming to terms with my mother's death means realizing that as she nose-dived into the ground, I shot up in the opposite direction, producing the Golden Boy. Israel perpetuates the Golden Boy image and I want to remain the Golden Boy. There are two worlds, the imaginary and the real. I can have it all in the imagination but don't have to act it out. I will have my revenge. Paula will be back but I should not touch her with a barge pole.

11 Jul 1991

I am only holding on to my sanity because I don't want to appear defeated by Paula. I am scared I am going to konk out or go barmy. Hang in there. Breathe. Feel the pain; it will pass. I am thinking of phoning Clive. I won't. I can manage. I feel I need to be held. Who will hold me? I have to hold myself. Yes. That's growth.

I'm having these small tiffs with Paula. She made snide, bitchy remarks when I told her I was meeting Justine in Primrose Hill. Jealousy? She is so edgy. All I need to do is get her out of my head, which is not easy to do in the present situation. But, when I go away, when we go away, I'll be free.

12 Jul 1991

We are both talking about sleeping out at night. She is angry with me because she feels she has to leave with nothing and says I will be unreasonable. I will be. I'm angry. She says she will try to change. In other words, change her tactics. I still want it to end with Shawn—or do I?

I feel angry, just plain, irrational, brute anger. Paula betrayed me. She let me down; she gave me up and she carried on without telling me. I want revenge and I want to get my own back. I will. I'll have my day. Why should I be nice, reasonable, etc.?

I am agonizing about what to do. If I leave, if she leaves. What about the kids? Do I relinquish everything? Do we try to patch things up? Surely not. We would just revert to the same crap. Slow death. Cut the Gordian knot. And if I go away, would that be "reaching for my dreams"? Will I fly?

Women: Julia is very attractive. How far will it go? She is young and wants to see much more of me. I like her shape. She is more my type and likes the outdoors, etc.

13 Jul 1991
Paula is sleeping out and comes back beaming. The pain just goes through me. What can I ask for besides revenge? Just breathe, boy. It will clear. I want to cry but don't want to show her my feelings.
    The mornings are difficult. I wake up early and start thinking about things. I am a bit tense. I know it is over but it is hard to accept fully. I can call up my gods, mother and father, but can't call up Lover easily. I start thinking about Paula and it gets obfuscated.
    The full whack. I asked her what she really wants. She wants to be in the house with Shawn and the kids. She thinks any place they will be able to afford will be grotty and she resents having to live in a lousy place while having to contribute to keeping up this house.
    Paula says, "I will surely want a divorce."
    Okay, it is clear where she stands. What is my response? She is clear and I am not.
    I spoke to Shawn's wife yesterday. She says Shawn needs a mother. Will Paula be prepared to mother him? I am still looking for things to fail there, though it will probably work.

14 Jul 1991
It is just past midnight.
I have never felt better. That's all. I feel like thanking Shawn for giving me an extra lease on life. He has freed both Paula and me. Weird.
    I am thinking a lot about Paula, especially about sex. I think she is having "good" sex as in the movie I saw with Yael tonight—*Thelma and Louise*. I think that they are in the real world and I am in this make-believe world of the tarot. When am I going to come down to earth?
    What does it mean to accept the situation and start living? Does it mean stay still or does it mean "let my hair down"? Does it mean moving into a bed-sit and starting psychotherapy? Does it mean pissing off for a while? Why is it all so difficult? How can I be subjected to so much pain?
    Maybe I should say something to Paula. What? *You bastard. You are causing me so much pain. I can never forgive you. I am going to make you suffer if it's the last thing I do.*

I am toying with phoning her now to say the arrangement for tomorrow is off. She can't take Jake and Rachel to meet Shawn. I am not worried about the arrangement but it is another step in the relentless process and she promised me she would not rush things. There is nothing I can do. I am powerless. Recognize it.

15 Jul 1991
It is a goddam terrible morning. I woke up early feeling grim about her sleeping out and coming back in the morning. What is it? Jealousy, loss of power, helplessness, anger. And I can't do anything about it. I would rather she stayed away altogether. We cannot stand each other's company. She does not want me around and I don't want her. Feel I want to explode the whole thing. Just blow it up. Will my day come? What do I have to do?

Paula is not my problem. As long as I am full nothing else matters. What is happening for me is growth, change and a new life. That is what I have to see. It's not easy. I phoned her from Westmoor School (one of the three schools I teach in) and we had a long conversation. She is upset and wants to be friends. Says she intends to live the rest of her life with Shawn. She has made a commitment. What does that mean? Shit. I do believe it's over. Pain. Just breathe. Try to let go. I know it's better but still it's a shock. I have nothing external going: no love, no work prospects.

Separate and survive. This is the new feeling.

16 Jul 1991
I woke up feeling a strong desire for Paula and went down to see if she was there. She was not. I was prepared for it so didn't feel so bad. I lay in bed and sort of managed to call up my perfect lover.

I spoke to Paula again yesterday. All she wants to talk about is future arrangements. She thinks the kids should be here with me as a main base. She is going to be out of the country for work in September and October anyway. She constantly wants to know what I am doing and who I am seeing. I don't ask her what she is doing. I don't want to know.

I hope it is not going to get worse than this. It's hard but bearable. I am convinced that when I don't see her at all I will be fine. Let go deeply. It's the only way. I do ache when I imagine their intimacy. Somehow the thoughts come up at odd moments, induced by words, sights, flashes of thought. There is nothing I can do about it. Just feel the pain. At other times I feel she is just another person. The truth is that I can have better. And I will have. It is ALL in me. There is NOTHING outside.

Midnight.
I have been up since four thirty this morning and I feel okay.

I met Neera tonight. She is a lovely lady, relaxed, warm and friendly with a spiritual touch. Attractive, lively and open. We have a common language and I hope to see her again. In a very small way it makes me think how little I need/want Paula. It is much more exciting with somebody new. Feeling close to other people makes it easier to let go of what I had. I got a nice perspective from Neera: I thought I had no shoes till I saw a man with no feet.

17 Jul 1991
Just sitting on the deck, calm and peaceful, also excited. What is lost is the trust. Don't expect it again. I realize I am in love with aspects of the relationship we had, not with Paula. In my heart of hearts I want to make it with somebody other than her. I can do better. I feel I want more kids.

What I covered with Clive yesterday.
I started by telling him how good I felt on Sunday. He remarked that it does not last. True. We spoke about passion. It fades. You cannot be excited about somebody you have breakfast with every day. I must not blame myself. I was in a terrible situation vis-à-vis Paula—her control of things, particularly sex. She is not powerful: controlling, rather. Somebody who is powerful and strong does not need to control. The opposite. Now I am still being controlled by her and I have to get away from that.

I can hear Clive saying clearly, "Loosen the hold of the demon that it is not happening for you." I was not valued as a child so I think the "other" is better.

18 Jul 1991
There must be something good in it if I am feeling better than I have for ages. I could not kid my body. I am more aware of what

BREAKUP

is going on outside, too—I have started to listen to the radio: Three, Four and Gold.

I was thinking that I had an idea something was up when Paula came back from Gleneagles in February. What if I had managed to stop it then? I probably would have if I could have. I think I would regret that now. In other words I am "happy" that it has happened. The noose was around my neck. I was going down the tubes.

I am now closer to realizing that we will separate for all time. It has taken three months to get to this point.

L − P = 1½L (Leo − Paula = 1½Leo)

19 Jul 1991

There is a lot of tension around the house. Paula came back last night after being away for about two days. We are supposed to spend time together to talk and it just descends into bickering and nastiness. We are competing for the kids and she is purposely saying nasty and untrue things about me in front of them. She tried to force me out of the kitchen and wanted me to leave the house. The phone is a source of tension. She says I don't tell her if there are calls for her and neither of us has real privacy when we are taking calls. She is paranoid about incoming calls and lifts up the receiver on another phone to hear whom I am talking to.

20 Jul 1991

I am painfully aware of their love-making. She has given her love to him, not me. If I can endure this I can endure anything. I have been rejected. She is with Shawn, perhaps for the rest of her days. She left here last night to sleep with him and is back in the morning. It pains me.

Is this the bottom? Not yet. I feel I have been through torture. Now I have to get rid of the demon—that it is not happening for me, that out there is better/right/good. It's not. Only my own reality counts.

I got up early. It's a lovely day and I feel I want to share it with somebody. I went for a walk with Rachel and Lassie, a collie dog who has joined us. It all seems to be going Paula's way and that is hard to swallow. At the same time I feel good physically. Maybe the parting is good for us. She is a good woman but not when living with me. I have strength and drive but not when living with her. The conclusion is obvious. There is no hope of pulling it off together.

21 Jul 1991
At Archway pool under the waterfall I let go of Paula, as sex fantasy, as receptacle for emotions, as partner and support. I see the issue now as being one of whether I should try to act as the responsible adult or like the carefree child. My heart says: be the child, go, enjoy, taste freedom. This is your ticket to ride.

22 Jul 1991
I am angry, I am jealous, I am outraged. Most of all, I am relieved.

Paula is to all intents and purposes living with Shawn in Hampstead. "I'll see you Monday or Tuesday," she said as she left. I am mad at her. She should either leave or stay. Now she is doing both. I can't win.

I spoke to Elaine, our close mutual friend, last night. She observed that we go on living old patterns. For me, another major rejection; for Paula getting rid of her husband and going off with someone else, like in search of her father. Can we stop the process of perpetuating what we went through?

23 Jul 1991
The session with Clive today—the last one before the summer break.
Be compassionate towards myself. Just sit and watch what is happening. My life is in tatters. Thank God for that. I need it, I wanted it, I set it up. I must not be attached to person, place or thing. Don't give myself a hard time. Go easy on myself.

Shawn now possesses Paula, a bit like my father possessing my mother, and I want to get in the way and take over. What they are doing appears neurotic because romantic love is like a drug. But it will probably work and I am powerless to stop what they do. Just get in touch with that powerlessness. Get in touch with the fact that my life is cracking up.

I don't need to choose between being the child (leaving) and being the adult (staying). I can do both. We are all living our myths. There is no right/wrong or good/bad. There just is.

BREAKUP

I woke up at four thirty in the morning, feeling good, relaxed and at ease. I didn't even need to call up my gods. Later I called up my lover. Nice. I don't want to see Paula and I don't want to communicate with her. It's easier not to. There is so much anger, acrimony and recrimination that we cannot function. It just drains me.

At the back of my mind I am still thinking that Paula and Shawn will break up next year, as some people have predicted. I am not sure I really want it to happen and, in any case, I cannot "want" it to happen. Either it will or it won't.

24 Jul 1991

I had breakfast with Jake and Rachel. It was quite cheerful. I am not sure how they are doing but they seem okay. I have so much anger in me and I am restraining it. Why?

Yet overall I do not feel so bad. I feel better than I did six months ago. I have energy. I want to live.

I find myself "wanting" romantic love, even with Paula, possibly because I am caught in this strange, unsatisfactory situation where I do not see and cannot imagine other attractive women. Paula is probably the most attractive person I see. It's not objective but I know her. I desire her. I want her to want me. Yet it's not real for her to be my lover/wife. How do I let go of her? Vague thoughts of a three-way relationship crop up.

25 Jul 1991

I had an amazing night with Neera. After a movie and a Chinese meal in the West End we came back here to my home. It was such easy contact with sensual hands and a bit of Joan Baez and candles to soothe the way—the whole way. How weird. I felt confident but strange. I felt she really wanted me. However, my mind was not fully focused. I had creeping thoughts about Paula!

3: She's Left, Kind of

26 Jul 1991
I feel serene. Paula has "left," kind of. I took her up to Hampstead, where she is staying in an apartment with Shawn. I tried to patch things up with her as I thought it would be better and easier if we parted on good terms. But she is too angry. Four times I approached her and opened myself up. Four times she rejected me. I am not going to make any more approaches for the foreseeable future. We are not talking. She can talk to me in '92 if she wants to. I don't want to see her either. I don't want anything to do with her. I said I am prepared to forgive. I realize I am not. Accept, yes; forgive, no.

I am in the house with the kids. No hassle, no pressure. It's a bit empty but fine. I want to stay on here, at least till January.

28 Jul 1991
I feel I want life more now than I have ever wanted it before. I feel calm and yet I have a sense of energy and vitality. I am also a bit tired because I have not slept a lot over these past months and there has been so much going on. Today I finished cleaning the house in preparation for the tenants who will stay while we are away. I rode my bike up to Hampstead. I feel free and young.

I met Neera and we went to have dinner in Highgate Woods. It was very pleasant. She is emotional. We walked and sat and talked. She is a lovely woman. I have vague thoughts of going to India with her in December. When my life is in shape in five years time I'll look back on this time and say it was a turning point.

30 Jul 1991
I am sort of getting used to the idea that the family is split and that I am "on my own."

I got a wee bit drunk last night at a barbeque. I felt light-headed and nice. Valery, an old friend, is around. We spoke about how we relate to what happens to us. Is the future there for the reading? Do I have to have faith for things to happen, or will they happen anyway?

BREAKUP

31 Jul 1991
On the ferry to Calais with Jake and Rachel.
Earlier today I met Paula and the kids in Hampstead. In Gap I held her and she responded. I wanted to kiss her. I told her to open her mouth. She resisted, but did, a little. I said I would miss her and she said she would miss me.

There was tension in the car on the way to Victoria. She got onto the track of, "You'll have to decide how you'll be feeling when you get back," and she mentioned a note Tony left Gail saying she looked good. Paula said we would not be where we are if I had done things like that. I found that maddening. I just said, "We are both responsible for what happened. It is better for us to be apart but we have to behave decently." I realize that Paula will be the same in separation as she was in marriage—difficult and angry.

It's a strange feeling being with the kids alone. I can give myself to them, but feel a bit lonely. This is my new feeling in the world. I look at couples, thinking they have things sorted out. I know it's all in me. I suppose I want to know what Paula really feels about me. Is she having second thoughts? Don't think so.

02 Aug 1991
Bardou, Languedoc, France
I woke up feeling relaxed and calm. This is a beautiful place. It is simple and primitive but comfortable. It's so romantic and I would love to be here with someone I really feel for. Maybe I'll return. The kids are great.

We are with the Lewis's (old friends) and have spoken about the situation. The message is: keep contact and communication to the absolute minimum. It is not yet time for friendship. It's too soon. The split is inevitable and I just have to handle it as best I can. She feels for me, I feel for her, but contact will just lead to hurt.

They say Paula is angry with me for not protecting her from change, from having to go through this, from worries about the kids, the house, etc., so she will vent her anger, and I will vent mine.

03 Aug 1991
Bardou.
It was a lovely day yesterday. We went to the Gorge l'Eric. *Magnifique*. The water, the waterfall. I just let it flow over me.
    I feel relaxed and easy. I think I am letting go. This is the new life; more or less living the moment. There is a slight emptiness but I feel very good. I got a bit drunk on wine at dinner, which is unusual for me. Nice. My confidence is growing and I have a greater sense of self. I want something/somebody new.

09 Aug 1991
Bardou.
My thoughts over the last twelve hours have been dominated by the effects of a phone call to Paula in London. I hate the feeling that she can still manipulate me, that she is having a good time with Shawn, that she is competing with me, e.g., by going to a nudist beach and seeing *Don Giovanni*.
    I am still operating as if things are better outside me, i.e., that what other people do is worth more, especially Paula. This is bullshit. It's ALL in me; the rest is fiction.

11 Aug 1991
Bardou.
I have had intense feelings of love/hate towards Paula. I shout inwardly about the injustice done to me. It's outrageous, unacceptable, and a betrayal—the betrayal of us, of our past, of our Judaism, of our youth movement connection, of a lot of what we had together—our culture, our civilization.
    I am traumatized by them together, and yet able to get over it easily. The great thing is the relief. After all is said and done, I am relieved. I might go on to better things. That is the bottom line. Yet I cannot bear the thought of returning to London life: the financial pressure, the burdens, the contact with Paula and her mother, who will be visiting.
    I'm scared of my feelings for Paula. On the one hand there is the violent anger and hatred; on the other there is the tenderness of love. Don't know if it is love or just habit, dependence, etc. In my case I cannot allow it to develop because it will be thwarted.

BREAKUP

14 Aug 1991
Béziers, Languedoc, France.
No more Bardou. Will I ever see the place again? We all had a fantastic day at Cap d'Agde yesterday. Just peace, calm, sea and sun, spoilt a bit by a phone call to Paula at the end. She never did really love me, never really felt for me; nor me for her either. She is not my soul-mate. I think I can safely say we will never be together again. I need to know that in my being, totally, and without hoping that by denying, it will happen.
    And...to another life. Slowly. Let it happen. And who is the woman of my dreams? Soft and adoring, gentle and spiritual, with some joy and oomph.
    As I sit here I have no idea which way things are going to go, what I will be doing, where and with whom. Should we try to sell the house? I think so. Holding on to the house is holding on to the past and also allows us to think we might be there as a family again.

A bit later.
I am fantasizing about sleeping with Paula. We still have a soft spot for each other. Dangerous. I am opening myself up to being hurt. Don't initiate it, she'll refuse. On the other hand, if I don't suggest it then nothing will happen. It is nice to think about it, of playing with her parts. I can live in my imagination and do not have to act it out. Maybe she is scared to have sex with me because she might be torn. Not likely, but who knows.
    I really do feel fine. Fuck the future. Right now I'm okay. Loosen the hold of the demon that it is not happening for me, that it is happening for Paula and Shawn, Tom Dick and Harry, whoever. It's happening for me. I am the wild horse. The life force is in me. I feel it welling up inside me.
    Why can't I come to France? Why can't I be like this for a year or two or three? Just sit in the café drinking a beer, reading, writing and chatting. What about fixing up places in the area? I need company. I could put an advert in *Time Out*: Wanted: female partner/lover to make a life together in the south of France.
    It's a time of calm, a moment to savor. No decisions now. See what turns up.

15 Aug 1991
On the ferry to Dover.
I realize that Paula undermines me. Now, more than ever, I feel under attack from her. I feel undervalued and belittled. She does not like my way of carrying myself, my habits, my looks. Therefore to be around her is demeaning and undermining. It was bad enough when we were together, how much more so now that she has a model she is in love with. It make me anxious and on edge and I should not have to suffer it. I need to minimize contact. Wash her out of my hair.

Don't be the nice guy. Don't try to please. Cut the Gordian knot, boy.

London, 25 Solent Road.
Back home again. Firstly, I feel fine. I just had a shower and it is a cool night after a hot day. I am sitting here in the nude, relaxed.

Paula was all smiles when she came to fetch us. I was most surprised. She tried to be warm and friendly, really wanting to make arrangements that suit her—to come here one or two evenings a week to be with the kids. Jessy will not go to her.

I want to keep contact to a minimum and this is an infringement of my privacy. I feel put out. We argued. She accused me of stealing back the earrings I had given her! I was very insulted. It shows how neurotically suspicious she is. She says she is crying and is upset about her contact with the kids. I do not want to deprive her of contact. I just want each of us to go our own way.

I have decided to go to Israel for two weeks from 20 August. Anything to be away from here.

16 Aug 1991
I have just been to the Hill Garden on my bike. It is lovely to be in the saddle again—free spirit. On the way there, meandering through the trees, I thought that I should be tough, not give in, and not let her come to the house at all.

On the bench I thought: what does it matter, what am I really trying to achieve? Don't know. I cannot decide what I really want so I let her have it her way. We'll take it a month at a time. I'm almost at the point where I can say I want it to work for them and mean it, because I want an alternative to work for me.

Earlier, when talking about the arrangement/agreement, Paula said, "What if I want to come back?" with tears welling up in her eyes. I went over to her and said, "I'll have you back." Later I said both of us had said things at a weak moment. We'll negotiate if the time comes. I don't anticipate it will.

17 Aug 1991

In my heart of hearts I want to make it with somebody other than Paula. I can do better. It is not just a dream. There is a general trend of softening on her part. She now says we should not sell the house for six months to "see what happens." I regret I softened to her yesterday when she cried and said, "What if I want to come back?" I should have stayed away. Not sure. I felt for her. I think her feelings were genuine, though only a temporary lapse, not the real thing. I am trying to keep any talk with meaning or feeling out of our conversation.

19 Aug 1991

I am very aware of the imminence of the separation and wondering where my redemption is going to come from, if it comes at all. Who says it will?
Tomorrow: Israel.

Every time we talk about the agreement she says she wants to put in a clause about divorce and the reality hits home and it hurts. I know it will happen, should happen, and yet I find it hard. Why? Loss, change. What can I do about it? Breathe. Just breathe.

20 Aug 1991
Gatwick airport.

At Kilburn she got out of the car to say goodbye. I just said, "See you," and walked off. Given the choice, I'll act tough. I have to try that from now on. I can't expose myself to hurt and feeling. I know (almost) that it is over. Know that it should be over. *I am angry with you. I am mad. I don't want to see you and I am sorry that you have to come to the house at all. I'd rather not have* anything *to do with you.* I suppose it has to do with realizing that it is over between us. I am one step closer to integrating the idea. Takes time.

Later.
I feel a lot better. Be my own everything: father, mother, lover, astrologer. Look after the child. My own star forecast: things seem bleak now, but take heart. If you can let go of relationships, etc., that are no longer valid things will blossom for you in a spectacular way. Life will bloom beyond expectation because you have life and love.

21 Aug 1991
Herzlia, with Paula's sister.
I got up early and took it easy. We went to the beach and then had lunch. What a good feeling it is being on holiday in Israel, yet strange because I am thinking a lot about Paula and London. I suppose it is inevitable because people here want to know what is happening. I feel slightly empty but know it will fill again. The present is okay and that is all that counts.

Separation is staring at you in the face, man. Accept it fully. I'm accepting and also clinging to hope. But I know the truth.

24 Aug 1991
Herzlia.
It's a hard time. I feel an intense anger and don't want to see Paula again. *Get fucked in a big way. I don't want to know you or your troubles.* I take heart from Haya, who says this is a second chance for me too.

Mother, I am angry with you. Paula, I am angry with you. The three faces of Eve. I see it clearly now: destroyer.

05 Sep 1991
London, 25 Solent Road.
Man. I came home yesterday from Israel. No Paula. She has left. Totally and completely: taken all her things. Gone. She left a note and a friendly birthday/farewell card. She ended it "much love."

What the fuck. I hate her. I feel very, very angry. I don't want to see her but I have to deal with her. I am angry about her rejecting me, about her leaving me, about the way she has behaved like a total bastard for the last six months. I can't forgive that. She is my enemy. *You bastard, you wanted to destroy me, to ruin me. Okay.*

BREAKUP

I'm here; I'm fine; I'm breathing and walking. I won't give you ice in winter and I don't know whether to hope the road is open or closed for you. It doesn't make any difference what I hope anyway. On the one hand I want you to fall flat on your face; on the other, I want you to provide a home for the kids so I can do my thing.
Once more you trod on my fingers when I was down. We'll see. Maybe I'll get my revenge. Maybe. There are tears in my eyes at the moment but I feel okay. I am my own boss and there is no tension or pressure. I can handle the house and the kids. They are pretty well, getting on with their own thing. Jessy is sad and Paula is making a big thing of this.

Hill Garden
I was shocked when Paula said, "We want to buy a place." Why? My deep feelings arise: rather hell with mother than out of it without her. Crazy.

06 Sep 1991
What am I going to do? It's hard. I am weeping. I am sad. I feel the loss. I think I still love her. At the same time I know it is sentimental bullshit. It was hell together so why hold on. It did not work. That's it. But right now it feels like death. I know that life will return but it hurts. It is hard to be alone, to be fully and totally responsible for myself and everything I do. I am not used to being single, alone.
It has a sweet side, too. I am looking to new things, looking to build. I have considered evening classes, perhaps trying yoga. I have had thoughts about starting group analysis and have decided to have an "At Home" on Sunday afternoons.
Today Jessy and Jake are upset. Rachel is pretty fine. It's going to be hard: I am mother and father to them—cleaning, cooking and doing the laundry. Paula is giving Jessy pocket money; a reversal of roles. I don't like it. I need to be more the man, the father. How?

07 Sep 1991
Dare I admit it? I feel like dying. I feel defeated, rejected, humiliated, outdone, helpless, pathetic and lost. And I don't know if I'll

ever be any different. My life is in tatters. Clive says, "Thank God for that." Maybe, but it doesn't feel I have anything to be thankful about.

I am rid of Paula but I cling to her like I clung to my mother. "Don't leave me, Mummy. I need you, I am nothing without you. I am lost without you."

08 Sep 1991
I feel absolutely marvelous. I had a very pleasant evening at the Roth's for Rosh Hashana and then came home to the kids, who feel close and warm.

I have found someone on whom to vent all my anger, anger at my mother for dying on me, anger at my father for being so cruel, anger at the world. I am going to be angry with her. At last I can get something out of her; at last she will do something for me. Although I do not need reason or justification I have it. I have reason aplenty to feel angry and enraged. I do. It feels good and I hope it lasts. She turned the knife when it was inside me, not for the first time. But for the last. From now on I do the turning.

09 Sep 1991
It's a good date and I have a sense of urgency. I want to go, move, travel. Sell the house as soon as possible and divorce. I need to set things in motion; there is no point in hanging around. My logic is that I just have to try something else. I have taken drastic steps in the past, like going to live on kibbutz and trying to live in France/Nizas, and they have not worked out as I intended or hoped.

11 Sep 1991
I am calm and sane, with a slight boost to my confidence, having spent a romantic few hours with Alexa. Just nice and relaxed. I realize the importance of hands, how they look, how they feel. But for me the eyes and the kiss are all important. We talked of traveling together, maybe to Prague or cycling across France. She says women will be queuing up for me. It's hard to believe. But she is a woman who loves to make love and that is what I need.

I still find it hard to imagine that Paula is deeply involved with Shawn. It requires a real leap of the imagination. Yet it is there for all to see. Nevertheless it is hard to accept. But she probably never loved me or was never able to show me love, except for short periods here and there. We were brother and sister and not man and woman. She was angry with me most of the time.

There is a slight glimmer of hope that a new dawn is about to break, that good things will come up. Yet the uncertainty is debilitating. I have approached three women who advertised in *Time Out* and wonder if any will reply.

14 Sep 1991
It's great to be free and single. I do what I want and see who I want. I have just come home from a bike ride with Joe and Jessy had made delicious brownies. Jake and Rachel are out. I just lay on my bed in the nude listening to *La Bohème*. I feel relaxed. The world is my oyster. I am going out with Alexa tonight—restaurant and bed. No worries. I have spoken to Toby and he will help me with money, which is a relief, for a while at least. Down and up in the space of a few hours.

15 Sep 1991
This is the most relaxed feeling I can ever remember. It reminds me of the feeling of Saturdays on the kibbutz twenty-five years ago. It comes after a long night of love with Alexa. She left and I remained in the bed by myself. She says she feels for me like she has not felt for anybody else. I am not really excited about her but she has a nice body and is adventurous. I switched on Radio 3—Vivaldi—and read a little from *A Year in Provence*.

I am slowly accepting that Paula has gone forever. If she were to say today that she wants to return I would refuse. No doubt. Almost no doubt. (No need to worry, it won't happen.)

16 Sep 1991
Westmoor School.
I don't want to give Paula the satisfaction of knowing that what she did has led to better things, or worse, and don't want to acknowledge that she has power over me. I want her to suffer, to regret, to feel guilt, to agonize. I want to grind her down and make her squeal.

The ideal father says:
Son,
I can see that things are very hard for you at the moment. You have been through difficult times and they are not over yet. But I can tell you without a shadow of doubt that it will be okay.
Just stay calm, breathe and watch what is going on. Get in touch with your sadness, your grief, your loss and your powerlessness. It pains now but the pain will pass. It's all very fresh but you can expect to start feeling better and stronger after about six months. Your confidence will return.
You lived with Paula for twenty years. That is a long time and you have a lot of common history and three kids. However, it was not working. She was unhappy and angry; she tortured you and you did not give her what she wanted. Not all relationships work. The time has come for a change. She took the initiative but it was, in fact, mutual. You wanted out. You wanted more, better, different.
It's right now. You will have better: better mind, better body, better fuck. You have had it already. You need someone who accepts you, who loves you for what you are, someone who adores you and will give you what you need. You are attractive and desirable and women will be drawn to you.
This is a blessing in disguise. It's the time of your life. Let down your hair; get drunk. Go for it. Your fifteen best years are ahead of you. Go out and live. Put the past behind you and let go of Paula and your old life. Get in touch with that inner fire. It's there and it has been repressed for a long time. Maybe you are already beginning to feel the surge of power and energy that you have in you, that life force that you have been out of touch with is there and available.
What is important is to be healthy and to separate from Paula. The rest will follow.
Your dad.

17 Sep 1991
I went to Clive yesterday for the first time since July.
He laid it straight, "It's over with Paula. Twenty years, three kids. You can patch it up but it won't be any good. She is looking for a

big daddy to be tough with her. Pity Shawn. You were fine for marriage and as a father to the kids but no more." As for me, I am a lover so I will find women. I need it. She is just habit; I am not in love with her but what she represents. I let her throw her shit at me. No more. Just feel the pain, the terror. And it passes.

As to the question of facing issues as opposed to running away, I cannot act out the child. I will not find my mother and father anywhere. It's all inside. It is easy and convenient for me to pile my anger onto Paula but it is better to let go and to face it. A bit of my anger is intended to get her to come back but it is too late.

Sometimes I despair of ever making inroads into my shit, yet I go back to Clive to try. He says that if I don't face things now I will face them in twenty years time and it will be terrible then.

When I got back home Alexa phoned. It was so nice to hear her voice. She talks of marriage and kids. Slowly. That is a change. Paula could not open up to me and accept me. I was always on trial. She was giving orders, dictating. Alexa loves me and appreciates me. I turn her on. She wants me. I feel wanted, desired. Nice.

19 Sep 1991

Nothing is going to change. I feel I should start divorce proceedings. Get it out of the way as it is no use hanging on. Also, it may be dealing her a bit of a blow. On the other hand it may be giving her what she wants. Either way it does not make any difference.

We had a long chat on the phone today about practical arrangements. She was emotional over small issues and feels bad that she cannot come into the house. I felt a bit sorry for her. She said she has been thinking about our anniversary. What? She is probably just feeling sad, like me.

20 Sep 1991

The *rite de passage* is to a new life, not to a renewal of life with Paula. Take it, boy. Take it with all your body, heart and soul. Grab it and hold it tight. I see that the new life will be better. That is the leap of faith, reaching for my dreams. Jump into the new life. Leave the safety of the known; off the cliff.

I am so fed up. I won't stand for her shit. I won't even talk to her. I will cut her down. I will rub her nose in the ground. There is nothing to lose, nothing to redeem. It's all lost and gone. So I might as well take out my anger on her. Don't give her an inch. Read her the rule book. I will even lord it over her. I'll exert my power.

I like being in bed by myself, even waking up by myself. I am king of the castle.

21 Sep 1991
A year ago I felt like dying. Now I feel alive and have a zest for living. I have Alexa to lie with (and who knows who else!). She is great for now. She is understanding and insightful, uncannily so, and sexy and most of all she wants me very much. She may be the one to give me my ticket to ride. She has faith that I will flower. I think she genuinely wants what is good for me, even if it means "losing" me. And I feel the same about her. She has good ideas and she is down to earth. Oh, just to lie next to her. The acceptance, the desire, the climax. She suggested I write to Jessy.

My dearest Jessy,
These are hard times for you and I know you are feeling low and very sad. To see your parents split and on bad terms must be terrible for you. You probably cannot understand how all this happened and perhaps you are wishing that things will go back to what they were. You may even be blaming yourself for what has happened. You may be feeling angry with me now. I can accept that but I hope that the time will come when you feel you can approach me. I will always be there for you.
Let me assure you of a few things.
Firstly, that I love you very, very much and that nothing in the world will ever change that.
Secondly, that I will do everything I possibly can to assist you, to make things easier for you and to help you on your way in the world.
Thirdly, that you are in no sense to blame for what has happened between Paula and me. I only regret that you have had to suffer for something for which you are not responsible.

BREAKUP

Fourthly, although things look and feel grim now they will improve. With the passage of time you will feel better and we will all get used to a new way of living.

Lastly, that you have the inner strength, resources and beauty to carry you through thick and thin. You can do it, my girl.

With much love,
Dad

I gave Jessy the letter.

25 Sep 1991
I spent the afternoon with Alexa at Liberty's. Then a movie and meal at Café Flo in Camden Town, after which there was silence on the way home because I had taken a French fry from her plate with my fingers. I said maybe we should cool it for a while. We kissed and parted.

The session with Clive yesterday.
I am like Alice (from *Alice in Wonderland*), trying to make myself small in order to go back to my childhood. I got in touch with utter powerlessness—what it was like to be a child, crouching in the corner. I have to be father to that child.

26 Sep 1991
I spoke to Shania, my homeopath, yesterday. She said it is normal to be traumatized and to be thinking about Paula. If I did not have these feelings she would be worried. Time is the great healer. It will take time.

I hear of families that have stayed together and I think that we could have/should have stayed together too. Were things so bad between us that we had to split up? Perhaps they could have been contained in the marriage. Did I push her out? Was there any choice? I am sad that we could not make a go of it. I see that sex was only a metaphor for the relationship, not the crux.

You still love her and she still loves you. But that is not enough; living together is hell. Not the hell of plate throwing: the hell of slow death, which is worse. I miss her; I miss her a lot. I miss what she represents: partner, security, home & family, odd moments of tenderness and closeness—intimacy. I also miss the things we were good at: going for walks, being on holiday together and enjoying friends together.

At the same time I feel angry and enraged. She betrayed our trust. Okay. She put the knife in. Okay. She turned it. Not okay. I will not simply turn the other cheek. I will not be trampled on any longer. I will take absolutely no shit from her whatsoever.

In the meantime she is receding into the background. She is a blurred image, almost nothing. Just another person. I am hardly concerned with their intimacy any more. I have my own. And it's good, much better than I ever thought possible; much greater than I ever thought myself capable of. And it will grow. This is just the start, man.

28 Sep 1991
I have to clean the whole house, including the students' rooms. What a drag. It's cold times with Alexa so I feel empty and lost.

I have just been for an exhilarating walk on the Heath by myself, in the rain; nobody to worry about or to have to relate to. I did fantasize about meeting Paula and kissing. It's a nice thought but I know it is total fantasy. She is poison for me. Just a weight: always was and always will be. I feel centred and strong. Confident. Things will get better.

01 Oct 1991
I feel utterly shit, empty, dead. I have no energy and no will to live. I am resigned to a lousy, dreary existence. And the worst thing is that I realize that this is me. It has nothing to do with other people, not Paula and not our marriage. I can't blame the marriage and being separated is not necessarily going to improve things.

Looking on the bright side, this has given me the opportunity to examine my life. I was exuding blackness. No wonder she left me. How can I blame her? What a terrible realization. Cruel fucking world.

02 Oct 1991
I have "broken up" with Alexa. We went out to a movie last night and had a slight argument. I said I am not interested. That's it. It was convenient and the sex was good. There will be more. I am the wild horse.

I had a session with Clive yesterday.
I have to tell these neurotic women where to get off. "Don't try to please all the time. Don't be pushed about. Fart in her face," was his message.
 I am really looking for father, not mother. The ideal father is in me somewhere. It's at the opposite end of the continuum from the child. I am naive and innocent but there is a real man in me too. "Let him come out. Stand up for who you are, man."
 By staying on in the house I have chosen to be a housefather. This has complications and is not as clear-cut as if I had left and done my own thing.

03 Oct 1991
Why do I feel so utterly shit? I am bored, depressed, dead. No zest, no energy. I just want to stay in bed and do nothing. Will I ever feel alive?
 I like what Clive said: I am in the wasteland. What I glimpse on the horizon is illusion. It's actually all right in here, not out there. My life is in tatters. Thank the lord.
 I am waiting for a big daddy to tell me what to do, to give me security and safety. Be that daddy, man. It's in you. It's all in you. Nowhere else.

I hear Clive's voice: "You are on a hiding to nothing with her, man; put down the load; draw a line under the Paula episode; cut your losses, she was only baggage; she is not your problem. Let them be and thank God you are out of it."
 I trust that in a year or two this will all feel like a brief episode; there will be no marks or tears. For me it is a wonderful opportunity, a second chance. Not everyone gets that. Next time round I might well find love.

05 Oct 1991
It's a Saturday afternoon and I am all on my own. I have spent most of the day cleaning. I feel a little strange and a little weepy. But I am fine: strong and optimistic. Even if I knew with virtual certainty that she would come back to me on bended knee on November 1st, I would say—No.
 I know what I want. I want new, different, exciting. I want it to work for me with somebody new, somebody who will love me

and adore me; someone who is beautiful, interesting, intelligent and has money.
It is Bach and a few books by the fire—the new life.

09 Oct 1991
I had a session with Clive yesterday.
I am standing at the prison door with a long, stone passage ahead of me. There is light coming in from the side, a biblical scene. There are steps at the end leading to an arched door to the outside where there is bright, Judean light—God. I can leave the prison and then return when I want to, or need to. I have the KEY. It is best to leave the prison in a metaphorical sense first and buzz off to South America later.
I must not change into another prison, i.e., another set of behaviour patterns. I need to just break the pattern when I want to: go out, get drunk, let my hair down; act differently.

My relationship with Paula has never been any good. Now I am just idealizing her. I always wanted it to collapse and when I started with Clive I was preparing myself for this. It's quite simple—I have to accept that it is over. The affair with Shawn is a symptom, not a cause. Boredom and anger were other symptoms.

I feel a little bit empty and spacey, but relaxed. I am taking it easy, going with the flow. I am adrift in the river and it feels okay. Gradually my confidence is returning. I feel I am worthy. Clive says he was always an old man. I was always young and always will be. In fact, I never really was a child as I was never allowed to be. Therefore, I am always looking for my ideal mother and father.

10 Oct 1991
I suppose part of the problem is that I cannot believe this is actually happening to me. I thought I was married forever, that I would live into old age with Paula. I believed that the bond between us was so strong that it would carry us through. Okay, there has been a drastic change. She was determined to leave and she wanted to make me suffer, to pay for the last five, ten years. I feel so sad for the kids. Is it worth it?

14 Oct 1991
I went out with Ruth on Saturday night. I picked her up at her apartment. She looked really good in a red top. Her eyes are phe-

nomenal. We went to the Bayleaf in Highgate for an Indian meal. It was very relaxed and I could not take my eyes off her. I told her I was taken by her. We chatted a lot. She said I am a good listener, that I have powerful eyes. A psychic told her she will fall in love in her forties, which is about now. She is lovely and can be affectionate but maybe too sophisticated for me—nails and lipstick. She talks of having a child, of being part of a family, of wanting more than just "having a good time."

I have been thinking about her a lot. I feel I could fall in love with her. Yet I am sort of relying on her to act, to choose, to say if I am "right" for her, that we are "right" for each other or not. Why do I pass this on to her? Can I not trust my own intuition, or is it that I do not want to commit myself, that I don't want to get hurt? I find myself thinking I should talk to Paula just to confirm it is over between us before I get involved elsewhere. Am I mad?

15 Oct 1991

I feel a bit of disquiet having spoken on the phone to Ruth last night. The point that sticks out is that I am not in a position to provide her with the style of living to which she is accustomed, or to which she aspires.

My response: in the first place, I run myself down and think that I am an arsehole for being so incapable on the money front. Then I think she should love me anyway and we will make out, or she will earn lots of money. Finally, I say "Fuck you, mate." *Take me as I am or leave me. I don't need your pressure or prison. There are many more where you came from.*

What am I offering? Not much. What prospects do I have? Few. But I am not dancing to anybody's tune, not even if she is Ruth Taub.

16 Oct 1991

After the session with Clive yesterday:
In relationships I find myself in a bind, caught between wanting a strong, dominating person and one I have power over. You cannot win sexually with a woman. All she has to do is lie on her back. The man has to do it. Whether you come in ten seconds or ten hours, you are human. You have to remember that mother was once a child, in each generation. But female is constant; male is transitory.

And to Paula I'd like to say:

P,

I am not angry with you. I hate you. I hate you with a passion. You are poison for me and I don't want to see you or have anything to do with you. As we have to make arrangements for the kids I want to keep it to an absolute minimum. I don't need to justify or explain my feeling. However, for the sake of clarity I will explain why I feel this way.

There is parting and there is parting. I can accept your involvement with Shawn. I can accept your rejection of me. I cannot and will not accept the way you have behaved over the past six months. Nothing can excuse the way you related to me. Nothing. You effectively wanted me dead, or disappeared, at least. You wanted to punish me for what you saw as the years I made you suffer. You wanted me to hurt and ache, and I did. You tried to destroy me. You shit.

Well, fuck you. I am made of tougher stuff than that. You might have lived with and left a gentleman but now you have to deal with a bastard. A right fucking bastard who is hell-bent on seeing you rot.

I am driven by the will to have you suffer and I want to see you eat your words "you stink" and "you have nothing going for you." I won't forget them. You dismissed me, you c--t.

You are a pathetic creep. From me you won't get any feeling or respect or consideration. I won't give you ice in winter. Right now I feel I would not put out my hand to save you, and you know I am capable of taking risks for others, even if I don't know them. And there is absolutely nothing you can do to make me change.

L

Not sent.

21 Oct 1991

I am at a very low point. I just want to die. There is nothing going for me and there never will be. No job prospects, no love, no joy, no satisfaction. I am useless; I am going nowhere and I can't do anything about it. I am uncomfortable about the arrangements for the kids. I don't know where I stand. I just hate the whole scene and am constantly milling it over in my mind. Horrible. All I can think of doing is running away. It's my instinctive reaction. Call it ups & downs.

22 Oct 1991
I have just been to see Clive.
He says this is the crucible of my life. In my situation my map is no good. I have been pushed out of the plane and landed, at the age of forty-seven, in a situation that is not as I expected it to be. It is strange and bewildering. The thing is not to grab for a new map but first to get my bearings, to say: Where am I? When I know that I can decide which way to go. I need to give myself a breather. I need to just shut myself off for a few hours and let my mind go blank. Right, I am lost. Wrong, I won't find my way out. I will. The old program says I can't but I can.

It's better to be away from her at this stage. She is too destructive and there is too much doubt and bad history. Just put a line under it. What I feel about the kids is largely a projection of what I think I felt as a kid, when my mother died.

Where is my anger? What does it mean to use my anger? I am totally out of touch with these feelings. I do not have the language to use them.

After all these years I realize the ladder I have been climbing was leaning against the wrong wall. It hurts. The world I thought I saw was not the relationship world. I thought that if I was a nice guy everything else would follow. Not so. I have to get in touch with the dark side, the feminine—the blood and gore.

I cry to the Corals because I am on my own. I feel it to the core: I am on my own. Alone. That is the story; that is what I am sad about. Alone in this hostile world.
I cry and I am sad but not distraught. I see a dim light ahead, very dim. I really can't see ahead at all. I just feel so fatalistic, so powerless, so useless, so pathetic. I also hear a note, a shout of defiance, of determination. I'll go on, I'll be there. *Fuck the lot of you.*

My morning of pottery was ruined by a long telephone conversation with Paula. I stood firm. She said I am here in the house "by default." I told her I am here to stay. She regrets having been away so much. Let her regret. I won't give her the time of day.

Note to Paula (sent):
Following our telephone conversation on Sunday, 20th October, during which you threatened to "destroy" me, I have decided not to have any direct contact with you. From now on absolutely all communication is to be done through our solicitors.

23 Oct 1991
I have just come back from a nice, brisk walk by myself on the Heath and a browse around South End Green. I feel fine and my body feels good. My soul is sad. I picked up *Time Out*, thinking I might find female company from the personal column. I didn't buy it.

I woke up feeling sad, wanting to dissolve into Paula and be re-born. I know that it is hopeless. I know that there was never anything really sexual between us and never will be. There is no desire on her part, no opening. I have experienced that since and I know what it is like.

24 Oct 1991
I am down in the dumps. I just want to lie down and cry. I still think about Paula though my hate is great. I see it now: Kali, the destroyer, the Third face of Eve. Just distance yourself, boyo. My heart wants to return; my head says: Not on your life, man. It is a death sentence. I think I should sell my wedding ring.

It used to be my father looking over my shoulder. Now Paula is checking up on me. Can't I just shake her off and tell her to get out of my life totally and forever? *I don't want to hear how many pairs of socks you bought Jake or where you shop for Rachel.*

I have done a bit of pottery; some bowls inspired by Koie (a Japanese potter). It feels good. I'd love to be a potter. What about going to work with a few potters in Wales, France, wherever.

I hear *La Bohème*. Sad, sad, sad.

I feel I want to wear jeans and beads and colorful waistcoats and possess almost nothing. Just my old list: bicycle, rucksack, camera and Walkman. The time feels right to opt out, to be my own person.

Given the hypothetical choice of renewing the marriage or roaming the world, without hesitation I would choose to roam. It's not just escapism. I am looking for greater freedom, ease and fresh air. They exist and I can claim them. They are my birthright.

25 Oct 1991
I went to Brent Cross Shopping Center to do the food shop and in the parking area I saw Paula's car, badly parked and dirty. I saw her in the store but I don't think she saw me. She looked good from afar but on closer observation I noticed her hair is too black and her face tense. She appeared unhappy and a bit disoriented. That gives me some satisfaction. I was tempted to go up to her but didn't. I have had my period of mourning and she is now in hers.

My private joke: how long can I not see her for? Let's start with a thousand days. Only 935 to go!

26 Oct 1991
I suppose what I keep feeling is that the quickest and easiest solution to my situation is to get back together. That would kind of relieve things "at a stroke." In theory. That is the temptation. That is why it is so attractive and why it keeps creeping in at the fringes, why I look for signs of hope.

There is loss but the pain already has a different quality. There is no fear, no abandoned child syndrome. I see that things have changed. I do not desire her any more. In my fantasy world she is not the person who comes to mind. I don't think that Paula ever wanted me as a man although I am haunted by the look she had in her eyes when she lay on the bed and said, "What if I want to come back?"

Oh! The oscillations—wanting to blend and wanting to part forever.

27 Oct 1991
I lie here on my bed on a Sunday morning, having put the clocks back. And my deepest feelings are of death, hopelessness and being valueless. I cannot concentrate properly. My mind is racing;

all sorts of scenarios go through my head, some petty, some not. Then there is this profound sense of emptiness—that I am nothing. The contrast to her apparent fullness is what I can't stand. And I say to myself: emptiness and fullness wax and wane. It feels like death but life will return.

Later I mowed the lawn and was full of energy, almost manic.

I am wondering why I have baulked at the idea of consulting a divorce therapist. I think it is because it means recognizing that the split is permanent. Up till now I have not been able to face this fully. Also, I am scared of what will happen at the meeting. I might appear vulnerable and express feelings of loss that she won't.

Will somebody please tell me the future!!!
Leo, it will be okay.

Rachel comes up to my bed. She is sad. We talk. She asks, "Are you and Mom going to get divorced?" I say, "When we are certain we are going to stay separate we will." She asks, "What do you mean when you say 'certain to stay separate'?" I say something like: "It takes time to be certain." Eventually I say, "I think we will get divorced but I am not absolutely certain." I am not really sure what to say. Should I have said: We'll probably get divorced but it won't be for a while? She asked if we are going to move house. I said: "Not for the meantime." I told her I was very sad about it all and sad for her. What can I say? It is so sad, bitterly sad. But, that's it. She wants her mother and father together—the pathos. I comfort her and give her some assurance. I say I will look after her. She will be okay. Her life will be fine, I say. I try to give her permission to be sad, angry, etc.

I was thinking that by cutting myself off from Paula I am out of touch with her thinking. Maybe she is having doubts. We might, just might, each be trying, wrongly, to second guess the other. In other words, we both want to get back together but fear the other does not. Mind games drive me crazy.

28 Oct 1991
Anything for the pain to end. Anything for the sorrow to lift. Anything.

BREAKUP

How do I play the game between trying and not trying; between doing and not doing?

I am at the stage of having given up on Paula and still thinking that giving up may actually lead to return. In other words I have only given up in order to re-gain. It's idiotic. But that is the way my heart works. My head still clearly says: Drop her forever.

Right now I feel there is not one person who has stood by me. Not one. Not only am I alone, I am on my own. I stand here on my own, tears in my eyes. What a world.

30 Oct 1991
I had a session with Clive yesterday.
We returned to the perennial theme—looking for mother. It's all inside me and I have to find mother inside. There is no point going to look for it around the world. I won't find it.

The marriage was not "good enough," so it's no good going back. We got together because we were both looking for father. It may be worth looking into what happened, after all, we gave over twenty years to it. The reality is that it is over and I have to deal with my situation. The kids, especially Jake, need to see me making my own way.

What I need is a good woman, someone who will just give and make no demands, who is not neurotic. Clive told me the story of a woman at a café on the M1 motorway. She just gave and said goodbye.

I am emotional. Rachel just came in on her way to school, looking for a sweater. She says it is terrible with Paula. What does she mean?

It is very important to drop the idea of prediction. I have been relying on predictions of various sorts. I have been handing my power to other people and I need to take my power on board, to take responsibility for myself. They have given me some hope at a time of hardship: that the road is open for me, that I will be okay and even that we could get back together. I need to give them up and deal with reality, the here and now. All there is is the present. The other picture is false, childlike and utopian.

I ache therefore I am. It hurts, but less.

It is a lovely late-autumn afternoon and I have just come back from a loop walk on the Heath. I feel so strong and determined. I feel the fire in my belly. Moreover, I want to be on my own. Either I will find love or I won't.

4: MY PREROGATIVE

31 Oct 1991
Today I met a woman about a job. I don't know whether anything will come out of it professionally but what touched me was the ring on her finger. It made me think of Paula's hands. I feel her warmth and strength—love—and I miss it. I want it and I grieve because I know I won't have it. It has gone forever. I used to think it might return. I now know it won't. I suppose I could still have it through friendship. It might be even better but I can't face playing second fiddle, getting the morsels.

Surely it is plain that there is a lot of anger on both sides. That is why the whole thing blew apart. It's not that we just grew apart. *You rejected me in no uncertain terms—adultery. It was the most powerful language you could use. It says something, so let's accept it. I do.* Clive feels I had a hand in it by not acting differently when, last September/October, I suspected it might happen. I fail to see that. You say it just happened. You were looking for excitement, not for the end of the marriage. Then you realized you wanted the marriage to end. It was your prerogative to end it and it's my prerogative to accept and say: No return.

I have been reading a lot about divorce—Alvarez, Abulafia, etc. They see it as a long, hard process that takes years. There are different patterns and different stages. For most couples it is easier to hate than to face the grief. I feel rejected, hurt, angry and hateful. I also feel relieved and free. I can breathe.

01 Nov 1991
I hang between life and death. I lie in bed and just want to die or commit suicide. I am nothing; I am going nowhere; I am a loser. I just want to blend with the earth, either in death or by living on the beach in Hermanus or Eilat. I think I will have to give up the house and the kids. Maybe they are better off with their mother, if she is in one piece.

I am not used to acknowledging this level of pain, this suffering, this mourning. I cry for my lost child, my bereaved child. My mother is dead and gone. She is just bones.

And now I'll go and do the shopping.

02 Nov 1991

Suddenly this afternoon I began to feel real contempt for Paula. To think, I feel almost nothing positive towards her after we have been together for over twenty years and she is the mother of my three kids.

I have been blinded by various people's formulation that Paula does love me. The truth is that she does not and never has, not in any meaningful sense. What she wrote in a letter to her mother that I saw is accurate: "I never really loved Leo." I see it quite clearly now; the hard bit is to come to terms with it.

My map said life should be sweet and joyful. It did not say I have to live with a deep ache. Why I should have thought that, God only knows. After all, I had a grim childhood, culminating in my mother's death. It seems I needed to create the direct opposite, the ideal: peaceful, utopian bliss. However, I still drag traces of utopia. I still want a peaceful, total reconciliation. I want the cracks to be covered over completely so that not a trace of the earthquake is seen or felt. This is the out-of-touch, idealistic, romantic boy. The man in me says: no way; it's all change, probably for the better.

What father says now:
Listen to me, boy,
Clearly you have a great need to cling to the past, to what you had and how you saw things—as a romantic. That view is wrong. It is naive and childlike. The world does not work that way and, in any case, you can see where it got you. Your wife walked out on you and you are in shit shape as regards work and the way you feel in the world. Simple, it was not working for you. Thank your lucky stars that your life is in turmoil. You needed a kick up the arse and you got one. Amen.

Now you need to regroup. Get a sense of who you are and where you are by looking into yourself. Just do nothing for a

while, just be. Let go of the sides of the pool and float for a while. Trust me that it will work out okay. You will be fine. There is no need to be afraid or apprehensive. Just take each day as it comes and live in the present. You can be confident you are lovable, talented, intelligent, caring and sensitive—the lot. You are. I see that. And you need to see it.
I love you.

03 Nov 1991
Watford Springs (swimming pool).
The weird and wonderful thing is that I do not feel jealous. He can have her and she can get her thrills. It hardly touches me. There is no going back. I am confident we will divorce, sooner rather than later. This is the way the world feels. This is it.

04 Nov 1991
I suppose I feel okay. It's the new way of being in the world—a slight ache, a sense of anticipation with absolutely no idea what is going to happen. In a way it is sad that I am alone in my bed. In another way, I like being alone. The kingdom is smaller but it is mine. My confidence is growing, though I still feel rejected and betrayed. I feel the death: the death of the relationship, of trust. I still want revenge, I want them to break up but I realize the pleasure for me would be short-lived. I anticipate a nightmare if they split up because she will be in a terrible state.

I am keen to do a counseling course, perhaps at City University, starting in January 1992.

05 Nov 1991
I went to Clive today.
I was aware that my father was "impotent." Do I feel this about myself? What is the nature of my "failure" in my relationship with Paula? I have the feeling I was "not man enough." That is bullshit. I have proved it otherwise.

I can do anything as long as there is no conflict—find a rich woman and let her support me; stay as a child for the rest of my life if I feel okay with it. If I have my mother with me I can travel around the world but not if I am searching for her.

07 Nov 1991
Tonight I am due to meet Marcia, thirty-one, a Brazilain dancer. Maybe she is lovely and huggable and interested in an "older" man. Perhaps she will appreciate me. That is what I want.

I was looking at a brochure for a Man's Group when I suddenly thought: what if I were to go to a weekend group and find Shawn there! How could I face him? He is my nemesis, my rival. He has taken my wife and caused me such agony. I feel like cursing him, even castrating him. I want to see the bastard hanging upside down. Strangely, I also feel we are bound together, part of the same fate. He is like a brother, Paula the mother. Perhaps I should warn him. Also, I can thank him for getting her off my back, for granting me my freedom. I couldn't do it myself. Moreover, I am better off with her "happy" with him than if she were on her own. Still, my heart aches. I mourn, I cry.

My trouble is that I have not, as yet, been able to see this as a phenomenal opportunity, as a break, a second chance. I have been thrown a ring, a lifesaver, only I have been slow to recognize it. I have to grab it.

08 Nov 1991
Just as I was about to leave this morning I saw Paula arriving to deliver the kids' things. Not wanting her to be in the house on her own, I went back inside. She dropped the things and then I left. I felt invaded. I don't want her snooping around in what is now my domain. It felt like a burglary.

I feel so low. Nothing is going my way and I cannot win with her. I am inclined to phone Clive but I resist. I can do it for myself.

I have this nightmare image of coming to bang on the door of the house with all of them inside, living here. I am destitute, lost, broken. I don't want to be broken.

I saw Marcia last night. She is lovely. We talked a lot at Café Rouge in Highgate.

Somebody by the name of Katznelson said: unifying is harder than separating; for separating you only need one side, for peace you need two.

BREAKUP

11 Nov 1991
The whole thing is so hard. I am going through the process again, only this time I see that it is over. I now feel it in my bones. That is what hurts. I call up my mother and father but they are not convincing. I cannot really be comforted. I am not sure it "will be all right."
    I see a little sparrow on my window sill. *Maybe you will give me life, little bird...*
    I went alone to see *Dances with Wolves* and it set me thinking. I have endowed them with an aura. Then I realized it is all in me. I am part of the romantic couple riding into the sunset. That's powerful.

12 Nov 1991
I went to see Clive today.
We spoke about the issue of martyr/victim. Paula gave me shit because I accepted it. No more. She is nothing to me, just baggage, just another person. I am still involved with her but that does not mean that I love her.
    This is pain without reward and I find that hard to accept. I have been fishing in the wrong pond, banging at the door to return to the family and security. The family was special: how lovely to have a father like me. I am unable to be the angry, passionate man. That is what I have to get in touch with, the ideal father.
    The world is not fair.

13 Nov 1991
I chide myself for "not being man enough" and then I think that I do not have to accept more than half of the responsibility, perhaps even less. In any case, who is a better husband/father?
    One moment I feel like the eternal optimist, the next moment like the eternal pessimist. Now, as Al Alvarez says, all my accounts are being called in. At one time I thought I was competent in a few areas: father, teacher, friend, potter, designer. I now feel totally incompetent at everything, deskilled. It is a case of massive self-doubt and self-pity. I have no self-confidence or belief in myself. This has undermined me completely. How fucking long can I suffer this? Life has lost all meaning, and there is no saving grace. None.

My real fear is that I will be forced to leave London, the kids, etc. I will be roaming the big, wide world on my own, penniless and depressed. I will have to come begging to see my kids. I will all but vanish from their lives and they from mine. Like a totally lost and abandoned child looking for mother, family and home. My ultimate fear is that I am actually devastated by all this. I might develop some severe illness like cancer because I cannot cope with the world. I might even have developed it already in the run-up to the breakup. I feel so vulnerable, so naked, so helpless, so powerless. I cannot accept powerlessness. I need to.

I listen to a tape of Etnix (an Israeli pop group) sing, "I will bring you a gift from the next world, my angel." It touches me, striking a note that throws me back to my childhood. It makes me aware of my lost child and puts me in touch with the poor, lost, abandoned child of nine, ten, eleven years old who did not allow himself to feel, to mourn, to cry. Now I am doing all that mourning for my mother. Only now.

I had a fantasy that Paula might be waiting for me at home when I got back from school. How I delude myself, just like I wanted my mother to come back. Now there is a theoretical possibility she will, which would make it all the harder.

15 Nov 1991
I don't know if I have ever felt so low. I see no hope. Why didn't anybody tell me?

I am just about at the point of tears all the time. The future I see is bleak: out of the house, no job prospects, loss of contact with the kids, etc. I feel a total failure; my story in England is one of failure: university, R&L Designs, marriage.

At the same time I hear a little voice inside me that I cannot ignore. It says: Leo, stay calm. Go easy on yourself. Don't give yourself a hard time. Of course it is hard but you will be okay. Your life is in tatters but a phoenix will arise from the ashes. Just breathe, just keep walking, observe.

Nobody really appreciates my suffering. Nobody.

17 Nov 1991
I feel totally different. I smile. Maybe I can cast pessimism and self-pity aside. I have been reading *Loveshock: How to Survive a*

Broken Heart by Stephen Gullo. It has made me aware of what I have been through and has given me an idea of where I might be going. There are distinctive stages; it's a process. I can heal. The pain will pass. I will be able to love again.

I have been thinking a lot about Marcia. She is special and I want to extend myself to her. I am very attracted to her and I think she is attracted to me. She does not want to get involved yet. I fantasize about going to live in France, Israel, Brazil, perhaps with her. Is this my chance to be free?

18 Nov 1991
I feel a kind of resignation: it's over, it hurts, it's okay.

I have been reading a lot on the subject of affairs, divorce, recovery, re-marriage, etc. I seem to be caught on trying to fit Paula and Shawn into one mold or another. Do they fit into the category of romantics or are they sane people who can form a stable, loving relationship? Is it fantasy with elements of maturity or maturity with elements of fantasy? And where does it leave me? What happens happens. But the child wants certainty.

I feel a fool for having consulted the witches. My response to the crisis was to panic and to look for magical answers, to want to know the future. I was lost, bereaved, insecure and terrified so I reached for something to help me, to ease the pain and give me hope. I have to live my life as if this is a totally fresh start and there is only one way to do that: to be clear that the marriage is over, it has been for years. In the unlikely event that Paula says she wants to try again I will have to consider it. Till then I go on.

19 Nov 1991
I am at the Dome restaurant in Hampstead by myself, listening to Tracy Chapman. I feel elated and light. There are tears of sadness and of joy in my eyes.

Session.
I saw Clive today and we spoke about what is close to my heart, my feelings in the world. I spoke about the child, powerlessness, emptiness. He relates it all to what I picked up from my mother.

She pushed everything on to me. She was disappointed with my father and I became her ideal. I am stopping myself from being powerful. What is in it for me?

Clive told me about Anish Kapoor's sculptures at the Tate and I went to see them after the session. The urn is amazing. I was struck by its serenity and power, the contrast of light and darkness, the depths, the void. I tried to see inside but to no avail. It was like trying to look inside my own life. God. I want to do a sculpture like Kapoor's urn. That is what I really want.

I am left wondering what went on between me and my mother. The frame was frozen when I was pre-pubescent.

20 Nov 1991
Paula spurned me, rejected and dismissed me so I'll screw her into the ground. I'll never talk to her except on essential matters. I am angry. I am rampant. I cannot believe the level of hate in me. I utterly and totally despise and hate her. And she loathes me to such an extent that it seeps right out of her. Or, worse still, she does not care about me at all.

I speculate but see she has become part of something different around work and a circle of divorced/separated couples. I think about the incidents like when she said, "What if I want to come back?" but now see them as lapses, as part of a process of letting go.

I ask myself why I am holding on to the house and the kids. Is it because I cannot let go or because I need the kids? I have so little in the world that I cling to them. They mean a lot to me and I feel I will be adrift if I let go of them and the house. And they need me now that their mother is in another world. Who am I without my kids and my family?

There must be a song about Salt Water in My Eyes. That's me.

I saw this Scottish woman in Mill Lane. She has a lovely face and feel. Her husband came to pick her up. I see him as a man. What about me? I feel like a child. Yet for a child you are doing a pretty good job managing the house and three kids after a breakup. Obviously there is something resourceful in me.

I have phoned Charli and we are due to meet on Tuesday. She sounds nice.

BREAKUP

26 Nov 1991
I feel very sad about the kids. It breaks my heart. I see Rachel's expression and her deep sadness. My heart goes out to her. And we have brought this on them.
   I am still arguing with Paula about money, past bills, etc. There are threats both ways. I feel I want to cause havoc. Open warfare, just plain vindictiveness. Be a bastard. I want a fight. Come on. Most of all I am slightly removed from it all, not really troubled. She has also tried to be decent but I don't like the contact and I don't want to get too friendly. Being friendly is an admission that I accept, that I recognize, that I forgive. I won't, I can't. Never.

I had an interesting session with Clive today.
We spoke very openly and directly, straight. What is this image I hold up? I am not a twenty-five-year-old stud and, in any case, that has its problems too. Could I accept a different pose—the more innocent, sensitive man? I have these ideas about what I should be, which come from my parents. I am cut off from myself, not recognizing who I am.
   I am still looking for the family that never was. There was no father model, nor a real family model, so I am desperate to keep my own family together. My/our sexual hang-ups relate to Mother. The ideal mother can allow the son to grow up and say, "I am satisfied by your father. I don't need you so you can go out and be with another woman."

02 Dec 1991
Feel the Fear…and do it anyway.
   I am scared to admit that it is over with Paula. I am scared that I will be alone forever. I am scared that I am unlovable, that I will lose the kids and lose the battle. I have lots of fears. What am I going to do with all of them? "Do it anyway" means to go on walking. We all have fears; some are legitimate. I can't let these fears stop me from getting on with my life.
   I just want to withdraw all my love, care and concern from her. I want to deprive her of me and do not want to give her an ounce of my goodness and worth. If I cared for her and valued her I would express my anger directly and try to get over it. I don't want or need any of her.

As to the kids, they will just have to accept that I am angry. I am not prepared to be otherwise "for their sake," nor am I convinced that it would be in their best interests for me to be so. This way they see I am a person in my own right with feelings of anger, a real person.

I hear that she and Shawn went to visit friends of ours and I wonder what the friends make of the whole thing. It's strange because she does not really like them but she might want to show Shawn that she has friends or show him off to them. I am worried that people will drift towards them because they have "status" and will forget me. Lily-livered lot. Maybe I should ask my friends to choose.

03 Dec 1991
Session.
I started off at Clive by saying, "Okay, it's over with Paula. What am I going to do now?" Then I went on to say that I want to run away. He said there is nothing wrong with that as long as I know what I am doing. At the same time, he thinks this is a "Search for the Holy Grail" when the grail is inside. There is no need to whip myself by setting ridiculous standards. I have a lot going for me.

The big question is: why am I keeping the lid on, not really expressing my emotions. I have a really cold, ruthless side to me that is obscured by a soft, gentle exterior. I am not really expressing my anger. Paula and I had a relationship that satisfied certain needs and not others. When the balance changed we began to look outside and she found an alternative. I am angry with her and jealous because she found Shawn/love. There is fierce competition between us. I said I am scared to lose the battle but he pointed out that I will not be losing it: I will just be walking away from the battlefield.

According to Clive, there are two types of "nothing." There is the nothing of being cut-off and there is the nothing of oblivion. The former is anti-life—denial—and can lead to sickness. The latter is a desirable state.

06 Dec 1991
Six months ago I took off my ring. Today I would like to acknowledge that it is over between Paula and me. I know it is over.

There is almost no doubt. There is nothing to indicate it is anything but over. However, I cannot fully accept it.
Nevertheless, there is something I can give myself today. I can forgive myself everything. EVERYTHING: being weak, being a "failure," being unfulfilled; all my shortcomings. It's all fine. I will treat myself like I treat my kids: all-accepting, all-embracing. I am here. I am me: lovable, sensitive, caring, friend, father, lover.

09 Dec 1991
I have just washed my face because I have been crying. I feel abandoned, lost and lonely. My ideal mother comes along and puts her hand on my tummy. It is total, unqualified love. I can almost feel it. A few tears run down my cheeks. Then ideal father comes along and says in clear terms: it's over with Paula, rightly so. She does not deserve you. She does not reach your bootlaces, boy. You can do better, you will. Time will come when you will find a person who is close to your ideal woman. Keep walking.

10 Dec 1991
Session.
All I have to write about at the moment derives from my session with Clive today.
We spoke about reconciliation fantasies. While going up the escalator on the way to the session I had this flash—Paula sitting with Clive, wanting to get back together. Now that the separation is certain I am toying with reconciliation!

I told him of my tears last night after she phoned, sounding so normal. There is nothing much I can do about it except to go through with it. He told me he saw his wife washing the car when he went to fetch his kids after splitting up. Similar thing—women are more grounded.

If I have this attitude that I am special I can either deny it or express it. The question is: how do I express it? By doing my own thing and by sticking my neck out. There are very few benevolent, powerful men about. I am fastidious and arrogant in my attitude to the women I have been meeting and in my attitude to my work. The women are not "good enough" for me and neither is my work. I am critical of them and of what I do but I don't do anything to change the situation.

We spoke about therapy and the bedwetting joke came up. Two men meet. After the initial niceties A says he is going to start therapy to help with his bedwetting. Years later they meet again and, after the usual niceties, B asks, "Has the therapy helped to get rid of your bedwetting?" "No," says A, "but I am feeling better about it."

Clive says therapy is not just about feeling better but about facing the issue square on.

12 Dec 1991

My feelings are mixed, both ease and disease. I am anxious about the future and have no patience for anything that does not have a direct bearing on my situation. For instance, I cannot read a whole film review in the paper. I don't want to delve into things that are not strictly "relevant." I want to start doing something new but don't know what, maybe French or mythology. The counseling course I have enrolled in might give me some focus.

I have a vague inclination to consult psychics of different kinds, as from *Time Out*. I resist. What can they tell me? Either good times ahead or hard times: I'll either find love or I won't. I realize nobody can give me the answers, the solution. It has to come from inside me.

18 Dec 1991
I went to see Clive again yesterday.

The question is: is she "missing in action" or "dead"? I think she is missing in action but any straight-thinking person would pronounce her dead. I have not got enough evidence either way. From the facts I have I would say the verdict is "dead." The complication in this analogy is that even if she is dead now she can still return to the scene.

In a deep sense I am still keeping my mother alive. Only when I drop the mode of being "pretty" and nice will I be allowing her to die. That model worked well for a time, during teenage years, in Israel, etc., but it is outdated now. It will not support life; it has no keel. I have to dirty myself in the water, the blood and gore. We are men and we don't have to look pretty all the time, nor do we have to be clever all the time.

I went to see my homeopath yesterday. Although I spoke to her a few months ago I have not seen her since March 1990 and she reminded me what bad shape I was in then: depressed, suicidal, self-deprecating, cut off, bottled up. WOW. That was the dark night of the soul. I have come a long way. She gave me hope and suggested I get interested in something spiritual, like Kabalah or Hasidism.

20 Dec 1991
I have been lying on my bed for half an hour, sad, crying, devastated, empty, frightened. I am alone in the world, scratching around for a new job. I have a very weak hold on life. I just want somebody to pick me up and cuddle me and give me reassurance and hope. A father.

Moreover, there is the ever-present contrast with Paula, who has a decent job, a good salary and a lover. I have nothing. I am jealous and angry and I want to lash out at her yet there is almost nothing I can do.

I have had a raw deal all my life: my mother died on me; my father intimidated me with his brutality and rage, threatening me constantly. Now my wife has abandoned me and wants to "see me dead." That is why I won't take one microgram more of shit. My rage is there. It is legitimate and I don't have to justify any of it to anybody. It is my dark side and I like it. I can be brutal and mad too, and given half a chance I will exercise these on Paula, in full force. I am so enraged, so affronted, so hurt.

25 Dec 1991
Xmas day: a sort of soul-searching.
I woke at about seven and writhed in agony. I just want to die. There is nothing for me. I am just a lost cause: pathetic, weak and unfulfilled. I will always be agonizing and yearning; fearful and superstitious, unable to accept it is over with Paula. On the other hand, I have phenomenal strength, determination and resources. Now I am vulnerable and severely shocked but I will reach a more stable plane. Give myself a break.

I think about Sally, whom I met on Sunday night. I was taken by her; the smile on her lips, her liveliness and sensitivity. She has nice, soft eyes. I told her I wanted to see more of her but she didn't seem too keen. I don't know how I should play it with her. I fuzz the boundaries between mother and lover.

Now I think I gave up on Paula ages ago but was scared to go outside, to have an affair. I was afraid of my sexuality or what I saw as inadequacy. It was safer for me inside the marriage. There was no risk.

Why, in heaven's name, do I want her to come back? Do I love her? Will it just be a way of restoring my shattered pride? If she wants me I'll be a man. Bullshit. I am a man, with or without Paula. She may be the worst thing for my feeling of manhood. She undermines it. Always did, always will.

This morning I was at the gates of despair when I thought: "I have to prepare the turkey."

31 Dec 1991
The last day of the year.
Paula has just phoned, ostensibly to make arrangements. Then she went on to say, "Things are hard for me" and "I feel very isolated." She was in tears and wanted to know if I was prepared to talk to her. I hesitated and then said I was prepared to talk. She says she is totally confused and that she undervalued what we had. What??? What we had together!!! She wants time to sort herself out.

I am dumbfounded. It is probably a hiccup on her part and I have to be very cautious. How should I act now? Unsure, but my confidence is boosted. I am too much of a softie. Be careful. What does my ideal father say: *Leo, you need to make your own way for a bit. Don't just get back together. She is crafty; don't trust her and think twice about speaking to her. Don't give her an inch at this stage and don't show any affection; just cold anger.*

Maybe we should get together strictly for the purpose of boosting my confidence. In other words, take her back, get her to surrender to me and then drop her. Yes. The dark side. That would do me good. Be a bit of a bastard. After all, what have I learnt in the last twenty years: that it does not work. And look at what she said about me and tried to do to me.

BREAKUP

Last night I wanted to die. I really gave up on everything and I didn't know if I would make it to the morning. Then I woke up at about four. Now I feel okay, cool about Paula. Either it will happen or it won't. Either way I will be fine. I have been through the hard bit. Now for the plain sailing.

5: THE FAMILY IS IN RUINS

01 Jan 1992
I am writing while I lie here listening to a Brahms violin sonata, having just returned from a New Year's Eve party. Paula was still in the lounge with Jake when I got back. He came out to warn me. I went into the kitchen with him and gave him some of my home-made ice cream. Paula left.

The family is in ruins. Even if the two of us get back together, an unlikely and undesirable event, we cannot repair the damage. It is massive and permanent. I guess that Paula must be feeling that too, except she knows she caused it by choosing to leave. She saw the future and strode proudly off, laughing at me and tormenting me.

If the process continues, as well it might, there are going to be a lot of pieces lying around. Am I going to pick them up? It's a question of basic human decency versus my feelings of anger, rage and revenge. And where are the people now who spoke about relationships made in heaven?

I don't really want her back, I treasure my freedom. It is wonderful at the moment; I feel strong and rejuvenated. Then I have a partial fantasy of going away for the weekend with Paula if we decide to make a go of it. The image did not jell.

Paula and I have just had a tentative conversation, all a bit edgy and nervous. She wants to know if I am prepared to consider the option of getting together again. She wants to re-unite the family. As she sees it she has a choice between her relationship with Shawn on the one hand and her life with the family on the other. She does have the choice if I say Yea. She needs time to think about it. "My feelings for Shawn have not changed," she says.

In the meantime I am in the same old situation: she wants the relationship with Shawn but she also wants the kids and the family, and I come with the kids. I said I am prepared to talk. I can see she is torn. There are tears in her eyes. She cannot stand being away from the kids.

I want her to be on her own for a bit but did not say so. I also think that we should wait for their relationship to end, to run its course. Otherwise there is no chance of it holding with me. I think we will discover that it cannot work between us, though it seems she has almost made the decision to try. In the end the attempt to reconcile might turn out to be our way of parting, a more satisfactory way.

My gut feeling is that it cannot work. It's over but it is very hard to admit it. It still seems to be a bottom-line emotional choice: do I want my freedom to be on my own and explore the world, or do I want to try to rebuild the family edifice and my relationship with Paula?

In January 1992 I decided to visit West Sussex for a weekend when my planned holiday with the kids fell through. I landed up in Arundel, from where I visited Burpham, Slindon and Chichester. I was touched by the beauty and poignancy of the places, the sense of time, life and death, and was aware of my own struggle in the world—my mother, my aloneness.

03 Jan 1992
Arundel, West Sussex.
After a walk around the town I am by myself and I like it. I can be me. I did something extravagant—I bought an Irish "down and over" hat. I like the hat and I fancy myself in it. Today I feel it is over with Paula. For one, Humpty Dumpty cannot be put back together again; for another, I look to more exciting things for myself. I see a young woman with lovely eyes and I want to look into them. At the same time I think it might not suit me to get married again or even live with someone. I feel more of a person by myself and I can have relationships with women.

It was not right to do what she did—fantasy on a grand scale that almost had me fooled. It all looks pretty turgid from here.

04 Jan 1992
Swan Hotel, Arundel, West Sussex.
I have been for a lovely long walk. I was all equipped with my new hat, scarf, rucksack and boots. It was wet underfoot and a

light rain fell. I got to Burpham Church and graveyard. What beautiful hues of the lichens on the gravestones. Maybe this is what I need: peace and tranquility to recharge my spirits and rekindle my fire. Just take in the beauty as the church bell strikes eleven. This country is beautiful. I am on my own.

On my return to Arundel I saw a pair of amethyst and silver earrings and thought of getting them for Paula in case we get together. I decided not to.

05 Jan 1992
Arundel, West Sussex.
This morning I was at the sea, where I went for a walk along a stony beach. The wind was strong. Then I went for a walk near Slindon and visited the church there. I am becoming interested in churchyards. I love them.

Back in London.
There is tension with Paula regarding the kids. She wants to "talk about" them and I am not prepared to talk until there is peace between us, whatever that means. I just don't want the aggro of talking to her. It is what you call family breakdown and it is not just in the textbooks. We are not a united family any longer. It's gone, broken, finished. I have a good mind to tell her that any thought of reconciliation is off. Perhaps I should file for divorce.

It just struck me: she made the wrong decision last time and she is going to make the wrong decision again this time.

06 Jan 1992
I am making it too easy for her. I have the major responsibility for the kids and she takes them when it suits her. I don't know if the time has arrived to make peace or even try to. As far as I am concerned I need never talk to her again. She is alien to me, my antithesis. How can I share my feelings with somebody who holds me in such contempt? I cannot share my heart with someone with whom I am so angry.

Suddenly when you start hurting you want to talk and you try to put the emotional screws on me re the kids, when for a long time you did not give a monkey's about them or me. Well, I am not such easy meat. I am doing my thing and I like it. The kids will be fine. They have both of us and they also need to see real people and real pain. This is the path we have chosen, so why camouflage it?

07 Jan 1992
I have just come back from a session with Clive.
Much of what was said revolved around the question of who I am and what I want. I may not be a husband. I am a father and I have a lot of woman in me. I have enormous compassion. I am ethereal. Perhaps I don't need a permanent woman; I am better on my own. I don't need Paula. I should show her compassion; forget retribution.

The family was exceptional and it may be worth trying to put it together again. I could then find my independence within the family. This may be a hiccup for Paula; she is having second thoughts. Clive thinks not; she has realized that Shawn is flesh and blood when she was looking for the impossible.

The most difficult thing for all of us is accepting who we are. I must not give myself a hard time about being refined, compassionate, etc. It's fine, it's me. Just find my centre and it will flow.

He had the impression from the start of our work together that I did not want Paula. Perhaps I engineered this whole thing. She is a lost child, like the rest of us. Her destructiveness and wish to destroy was not really directed at me but at herself. It is no use taking out my anger on one person. Rage against the world, pick up my dead mother and shake her. It is just destructive to take it out on Paula. I will liberate myself if I show compassion.

I also want her. We are all looking for someone else to love us, to do something for us. Crap. We need to stand on our own. It is very difficult to love and live with someone, just to be together washing the dishes or whatever. That is what life is about. The rest is illusion.

Right now I feel we have to resolve the unfinished business between us before we can go on. I expect some show of remorse like, "Maybe I acted rashly." On the other hand, I don't care what she thinks or does. Let her just piss off. *You kicked me and spat on me. Go and get lost.*

09 Jan 1992
I went out with Barbara on Tuesday night. She is very nice and I like the way she projects herself. We went to the Natraj, in honour of her Nepali connection, and sat and talked for a long time. She gave me a big hug when I saw her to the tube and we spoke about going to a movie on Sunday night.

I don't know what I think about reconciliation with Paula. I am suspicious. I still think she is hostile and angry. It doesn't seem to have receded. On balance I still feel there are bigger and better things open to me on my own, without her. But I don't know if we are just trying to communicate better about the kids or whether we are exploring reconciliation.

It is classical ambivalence: on the one hand I feel anger and rage; on the other I think that at our best we could be great together. In fact, I am far from convinced that her attitude towards me has changed for the better.

We have set up a meeting with a therapist called JH for four o'clock on Monday 20 January. The understanding between Paula and me is that we will be talking about what has happened between us and about the kids. No commitment. I feel a bit strange about "capitulating" but I could not really sustain the anger. I need to sort out my thoughts before the meeting on the twentieth.

10 Jan 1992
As I thought, it appears that Paula's feelings at the end of December were just a hiccup, a time of doubt. Because I was prepared to consider the possibility of reconciliation I agreed to meeting with a therapist. She is now saying that we are not talking about reconciliation, so I feel tricked. Her wanting reconciliation made me think she is able to regard me as a person, to respect me. Now I am not so sure. Tread very carefully, boy. You are dealing with rampant destruction.

Then I went for a short walk and I heard myself saying that maybe I do love this woman—Paula. It is as simple as that. My heart says I want her. Do I tell her? What have I got to lose?

11 Jan 1992
Firstly, I feel good. The house is amazingly harmonious and relaxed. I was thinking last night that the most painful thing is to

face up to the implications of what has happened between Paula and me in the last eleven months. For six months or more she behaved like a total shit and now, when she feels guilty and misses what we had, she comes to cry on my shoulder. Suddenly Leo is okay; suddenly the family is important. Well, Leo doesn't like it. He says: go, go from me to your world. Just leave me alone. I don't want or need to know what happened between us. I know already.

Thinking about the meeting next Monday I want to say something like: what we have between us is a mixture of intense love and intense hate. I feel them both. At the moment the hate predominates though I am in touch with feelings of warmth, tenderness, care and concern. I also feel jealous that she is giving her love to Shawn and not to me.

15 Jan 1992

I went by myself to see *Persona* (Bergman film) last night after Marcia decided she was too tired to go. I went up to Hampstead early, had a beer at the Dome cafe, read a book and then went to the movie. The movie shows the power of silence; it can drive the other person mad. Silence represents anger and hostility—my behaviour towards Paula.

She suggested buying a present together for Jessy's birthday. Maybe I should agree. What the heck. So she acted like a bastard, wanted me dead. So what, does that mean I should cut myself off from her for the rest of my life?

I had a session with Clive yesterday.

We spoke about templates and frames. I put them up and see how the women fit into them. He calls it "Auditioning for Julia." I am looking for my mother in these women—"Not you. Next please."

What do I put on the template? Unconditional love. I will never get it because all these people are human and that belongs to deity. Why do I need it from outside? I have to provide it for myself, from within. I am getting mixed up between mother templates and lover templates. One cannot begin a relationship looking for the long-term. You just have to take it as it comes. Take them and fuck them. Feel like a man.

16 Jan 1992
I am thinking about the meeting on Monday, where I stand with Paula, what I feel for her, etc. And all this in the shadow of some sort of relationship developing with Barbara. We had a very pleasant, sensual evening here yesterday listening to Mary Black. She will sleep over another time.

I have been reading a book by Leon J. Saul called *The Childhood Emotional Pattern in Marriage*. It is amazing how we live out old patterns. He gives an example of a couple where he was a loving man, good father, unable to provide for his family. She develops anger, hostility, feelings of revenge and starts looking out—love affair. Is this what happened to us? It's part of the story. There are other factors too, like looking for her father, her breast lump, adolescent rebellion and sexual fantasy.

Even if Paula were to promise me the world and offer to shower me with all her love, I would not accept. That is what I think, anyway. Life is fine for me. This freedom is extraordinary. It is the time of my life. The family has gone and the kids will be a little scarred. That is life. That is family breakdown, eruption. There must be casualties. I don't want to have anything to do with Paula because she reminds me of my pain, although this might be a reversion to a childhood pattern of cutting myself off. But I have not run away. No. I am here and I am staying.

17 Jan 1992
With an eye to the forthcoming meeting I am trying to sum up my feelings. It goes something like this:

I am angry and very sad at what has happened over the past eleven months. I understand the affair. You wanted passion and to be made to feel good at a time you were feeling rotten. It was hard, it hurt terribly but I understood and I accepted. However, you acted in a callous and brutal way. You were willing to destroy our relationship of more than twenty years as well as destroy our family unit for the sake of your relationship with Shawn.

And what was this goal for which you were prepared to pay such a high price? It might have looked like paradise, romantic love or eternal bliss at the time but anybody rational could see you were pursuing a chimera, an elusive fantasy. It's the one we all have of exciting sex and passion with some object/person on whom we project our love. You were so blinded by "love" that you were unable to see reason or to act in anything but a selfish, cruel and hostile way. You could not see that the honeymoon period would, inevitably, end. Perhaps now you see things more clearly. Maybe the fog has lifted and the debris can be seen.

I have always said that neither of us is imprisoned in our marriage but leaving it does not come easy and does not come cheap. It has implications for all of us and therefore needs long and hard consideration before jumping. The sad aspect is that we then got into a pattern of mutual hostility that destroyed any vestige of trust or affection we might have had for each other. We have the rest of our lives to live as parents of our three children and what you did, how you conducted yourself, put paid to any hope of a civil, reasonable relationship between us. You were able to vent your anger, hatred and hostility on me without any regard for the real past or the future.

And today I ask myself: how do I deal with this person? You were my partner and mate for twenty years and then became an alien, foreign body at best, a destructive monster at worst. You ridiculed me and dehumanized me, threatened to destroy me and said I stunk. And more. As if it were not enough that I had the pain of rejection, the humiliation of having my wife walk out on me, the enforced fracture of the family, my loss of confidence and esteem, I also had to bear your rampant hostility.

Well, I am here and now we have to face each other and I want to know how you answer to what I have to say. I want to tell you that I resent being a sounding board or soft shoulder for you problems. If you have any doubts about your position, as well you might have, don't come crying to me.

I would also like to repeat what I said the other day: on separation my position is clear and unequivocal. I intend to be the main carer of our three children and I intend to remain in the house at 25 Solent Road with them. As far as I am concerned

there is no negotiation on those points. I think I have shown I can manage it.
Here we sit opposite one another. Between us is a chasm. What do we propose to do about it? My view is that if you even want to consider reconciliation you have to end your relationship with Shawn, move out, find your own place for a while and think about where you stand. Otherwise, I am not prepared to begin to talk. That is where I stand. Take it or leave it.

20 Jan 1992
Ahead of the meeting at four o'clock I am going over in my mind what we have been through over the last few years. Overall we have conducted ourselves very poorly. We neglected ourselves and our relationship till it got to the point where we were both prepared to call it a day. Then it really started going downhill fast. In February '91 Paula started her relationship with Shawn and we more or less went crashing to where we are now. I don't feel it is such a bad place for me personally but for my relationship with her and for the family it is a hellhole. Questions arise: can we do anything about it? Do we do anything about it?

I steel myself in preparation for the meeting. Be cold, rational, firm and fair.

I have just returned from the meeting with Paula at JH. I did well but also expressed my feelings of ambivalence: I have love and admiration for her but I also think that we are bad news for each other. Paula just wanted to talk about the kids. She expressed absolutely no positive feelings towards me. She didn't even deny it when I said that she does not value me at all.

I left feeling rejected, once again. So I am angry. I want her to buzz off. I don't want to have anything to do with her. It was a hiccup, as I thought. There is a yawning gulf between us. She has no room for me at all and I have to accept that.

11.30 p.m.
I see that dealing with Paula just opens raw wounds for me. It reminds me of my pain, my loss. Her very presence undermines me; makes me think I am nothing. I don't need that now.

BREAKUP

21 Jan 1992
I think I have been feeling good recently because I thought that we might get back together or that I would have a choice in the matter. It was false hope, wishful thinking. Shit. I allowed myself to think that it might be on—and it is not. So, I shake and shudder; I feel hollow and nervous. I have been knocked over again but this time it feels different. It is less onerous and I know the pain will ease.

I have just come back from a session with Clive.
Whichever Rolls Royce you sit in, the ride is excellent. It is simply a matter of choosing the model. There are lots like Paula. There is no more Old Paula, so I need a new one. She might have got over her hostility towards me. She now wants me to be together with her about the kids, which seems rational. But there is no way I can do it. To share my feelings with her, to be with her is extremely hurtful to me. I have to protect myself. She reminds me of my aloneness. That she wants me as father to the kids and not as husband is castrating. I have to distance myself from her. The kids will be okay.

23 Jan 1992
We are split apart and I ache. What can I do? Just hold on. There is talk in the air, with Paula, about selling the house, perhaps when Jessy goes to medical school. Who knows where we will be then. For the meantime I am holding on to the house with the kids. We all need that stability now rather than the upset of moving, which can come later.

There is growing intimacy with Barbara. She is good company; laughs a lot and our thinking is similar. She is pretty, gentle and warm and she appreciates me. We take each day as it comes.

24 Jan 1992
This morning I felt terrible, absolutely sick and apathetic; a deep sense of loss, of mother. It's all too much for me. The house and the kids are too much of a burden. I feel everything is stacked against me. And now I'll go and prepare a meal. Soup and chicken. People are coming to dinner later.

26 Jan 1992
A short while ago I came back from the wine bar in Mill Lane, where I met Paula, at her instigation. She phoned this morning, in tears: "I have to speak to you." We met at nine and talked till about ten-thirty. It seems she is seriously considering trying to live with me/us again. She says she is prepared to give up her relationship with Shawn in order to try to make a go of it with me. "We had something and it went cold," she said of our relationship. I don't know what to make of it all.

I said I wanted to avoid further pain. I am scared I will be rejected again and also that there won't be enough going for us; that we will get into a cycle of getting together and parting. I touched her and she responded by holding my hand. She said that her relationship with Shawn is "secure and certain" but that she is torn with regard to the kids. Last time was a hiccup, now she is more certain.

She sort of apologized for hurting me and said she was full of anger as I had not valued her. She suggested we go away for a weekend but we agreed it was too early for that. It felt like a relationship with a new and strange person.

At her car, she wanted to kiss. When I touched her lips with mine she said, "Open your lips," and we kissed briefly. I said, "Still tastes good, a bit used." She replied, "What about yours?"

Anyway, I came away feeling it is the end for the two of us. This is some sort of resolution. I see her as another person and, in any case, I anticipate she will turn cold again.

She finds it very difficult to be with Shawn's kids, especially the boys, and when she is with our kids it is too intense. She said the honeymoon is over but she clearly has strong feelings for him. She also feels very isolated from friends and blames me for cutting her off from them, which is not true. I said I am not sure I want to give up what I have, namely freedom and excitement.

I noticed she had moved her wedding ring from her left hand to her right hand.

27 Jan 1992
Looked at from one point of view, she has come down to earth with a bump. The honeymoon is over. Her relationship with Shawn is okay but not worth making sacrifices for, as the simple

reality is that she wants her kids and is prepared to forgo what she now sees as just another relationship in order to be with them.

I could take it a stage further. She is actually scared shitless and is putting on a brave face but is desperate to patch things up with me. The strains on her relationship with Shawn are enormous, particularly with his kids, and she is dying to be with her own kids. In fact, I have all the cards. She needs me now. However, I am in no hurry; there is no great attraction because it will mean losing my much-valued freedom and living the rest of my life with her. At the same time I cannot deny I am drawn to her. It is the easy option and it all falls back into place—reconstituted family.

28 Jan 1992
What happened with Clive today?
I told him my story of the last week, focusing on the situation with Paula. He felt that there did not seem to be much feeling on either side; it's all a bit clinical and remote. True. He asked whether I need her. I said I do not. Then he asked what feelings I have for her. It's not clear. In that case, it would be an arrangement of convenience. Yet, maybe we need to try it. She needs to make up her mind whether she wants to come back or not. There is no need for therapists; we just have to sit face-to-face.

There is sex and there is magic sex. There is no such thing as "good sex." It's all projection, so don't give myself a hard time over this. If I put my fingers up someone's c--t, that is it unless she projects magic onto me. I used to think that Paula was magic but not any longer.

The mature thing is to forgive and to get on with life. Revenge is short-lived gratification.

29 Jan 1992
It is a really strange situation—waiting for her to decide on our lives. I want to put an end to the waiting and to relieve the pain but I can only decide in the negative. I cannot say it is on. I suppose I am excited at the prospect of getting together again and I foresee the pain of rejection if she says no. In the meantime, don't agonize. Let her decide, then react. Chances are she will decide to return. My position is strong. Just stay calm.

There are lots of thoughts and every kind of permutation is going through my head but the one that stands out is that I see clearly that she has no love for me. She needs him and he needs her. Plain and simple. That is what I have to swallow. I'll take a salt bath.

31 Jan 1992
You say you could dump me because our relationship had gone sour. Fuck you. Well, I am still standing and I might just be in the mood to knock you down.

6: THE DUST HAS SETTLED

01 Feb 1992
00:15
I have just returned home from a wonderful Mary Black concert at the Albert Hall. While there I had a feeling of strength and of valuing myself. I want to send Mary Black tapes to all my friends. It was lovely being there with Barbara, but I am holding back.

Then, on the way home by myself, I suddenly realized that Paula does not feel for me and never really has. That was the strain on our relationship. Now she wants to get back to the kids, so she is trying to find a way to love me. She can't. As she said: "You have good qualities." What a way to express feelings. It says everything. I say: "Fuck you. What am I even talking to you for? You kicked me in the balls and in the teeth. In any case, what have you got to offer me other than a mock-up of a family?" That is the rub.

Paula, let me say it for you, because you are so inarticulate.

The dust has settled. We can all see the debris now—the broken family, your torment. The honeymoon period for you with Shawn is over but there is still a lot of feeling there mixed with pity and guilt, which is a lot more than there was with me.

However, you are torn asunder by your break with the kids and the relationship with Shawn can no longer mask the pain. So, what is your reaction? Possible reconciliation. The only way back to the family is through Leo. But for Leo you have no feeling. In fact, you despise him and you are still angry with him for not being your ideal man.

I am sure it is painful and you want Leo to help you. But after what you did to him that may be asking too much. There is not even enough basis for a trial, it is just clinging to old patterns. Your relationship is no longer viable.

03 Feb 1992
It's a really strange time. I feel exceptionally good. I am relaxed and optimistic and feel I can handle anything that comes up. It was

definitely a weekend with a difference and that has left me feeling like this. It started with the Mary Black concert on Friday night. On Saturday I cleaned the house and chatted to a few people till about five. Then I went over to Barbara's to help with her party. It felt so good to see her and I could see she was happy to see me. We just hugged and kissed. I was relaxed. We worked and chatted easily.

The party was pleasant and I stayed the night. We lay on the mattress on the floor in the lounge: music, candles, incense and love. Easy. We can just be together. We stayed in bed late on Sunday morning, chatting and touching. We got up, cleaned the kitchen and I left.

Back home, Debbie, an old friend, came over for a while, brought by Paula, who had come for Rachel. Paula kissed me as she came in.

I had a nice chat with Debbie. She said Paula is in a "no win" situation. "The last word has not been said yet." I asked her if she thinks Paula can leave Shawn. She said her problem is that she also cannot be away from her kids. Later Paula came to drop Rachel. She said she wanted to talk to me briefly. She said she is torn apart. Tears. We hug and kiss. After that I had a salt bath and went to bed, on my own, with candles.

04 Feb 1992
What if Paula comes back this month and things go all right for a while and then they go sour? I need to insist that if that happens she has to leave. Can I trust her? No. In that situation she could resort to what she was like, a bastard. This could be her way of getting back her kids. It's tricky.

The session with Clive.
He said Paula is like Icarus. She tried to take a lover but is not up to it. Maybe later in life. I can show my true strength by helping her. It will be an uphill struggle. The brief in my present situation is impossible. Too much weight is being given to sex.

05 Feb 1992
I wrote yesterday after my session with Clive that she, like Icarus, flew too close to the sun and could not stand the heat. Tonight that no longer seems true.

BREAKUP

The other night we sat and chatted at the Tricycle Theatre. She virtually said she would move in in February. She said she was in a very emotional state—not sleeping, torn. She was fairly warm. We kissed a bit in the car and parted.

So, I was thinking that we were going to get together because we both felt it was worth trying. Anyway, I spoke to her tonight and she seemed more composed. She gave me the distinct impression she is *not* planning to come back now.

Maybe, unlike Icarus, she can stand the heat. It leaves me feeling compromised and angry once again. In fact, she is playing games with me. Let's go back to where we were six weeks ago. I have filled in the Legal Aid acceptance form. The battle is about to begin.

06 Feb 1992

It's hard and I am a bit shaky but I'm okay. I have been through much worse. All I have to do is hold on. Do nothing. Breathe. Barbara is coming to stay tonight and I am going to make a delicious dinner—fish. The best I can buy.

Just thinking... when Paula is with me I want her as a man. When she rejects me I feel like a child. Rejection means being rejected by my mother. My response is that I want my mother back. I want her to hold me and comfort me. I see Paula as the answer to my yearning. She is not. Nobody is. It's all in me. One hundred percent. Not Sylvia, not Sue, not Mary Magdalene.

Should I give her time? I have to protect myself. She thinks I have slept with all these women. What significance? She wanted to know where I was gallivanting on Sunday morning.

Straight Leo: do you want her back? Don't know. The witches say she loves me and will want to come back. Others say not to touch her with a barge pole. Trust your intuition.

08 Feb 1992

Life could not be better. I am alone in the lounge listening to Haydn. Saturday is cleaning day and I have been feeling good, a little euphoric even.

What do I need her for? She is unattractive and a bossy-boots. What is more, she is not too interested in me (not sure—last weekend she was running after me). I was on my bike and I saw them go past. I waved and they waved back. I rode on. I feel a bit sore. It's not easy seeing my wife with another man. Mainly, I feel sorry for her. Look what she has got—Shawn and his kids. The road is closed for her. I feel like saying to her: *your only chance was with me and you fluffed it. Poor you.*

09 Feb 1992

Things are going round in my head. I don't really want her. I just want the situation to mend and the pain to go away. I also don't want to admit that she was right to leave. And: being friends now is an admission that it was okay for her to do what she did.

Barry, my old friend who has been through a divorce, says I need another six months by myself to get the measure of things. He is right. There is no hurry. I am fine where I am and we have got the summer to look forward to. I need a new woman. Yet I still want her to phone and make up. That too will go.

How much longer can this pain go on?

Listening to Mary Black, I suddenly had the urge to phone Paula. My heart is open. I want to say: "Listen, maybe you have decided you are not coming back. Okay. All you need to do is confront me. Come up and hold me and say something from your heart. Perhaps we can cry on one another's shoulders. You have hurt me terribly and I am angry with you but let's try to live reasonably."

Can't you even find that in you?

10 Feb 1992

I don't know which way to turn. I yearn for her; I fantasize about her. I feel I want her. I was having feelings of intense anger and revenge, coupled with feelings of tenderness and warmth. Then she phoned to speak to Rachel. I said she owed me an explanation; that she needs to face me and say what she has to say. She says I rejected her! She says she wants to talk things through. She wants to be friends. She could not get the word out, or rather did not want to say it for fear of upsetting me. Anyhow, there was a touch of emotion in her voice. In relation to me she is very cold and rational; in relation to Shawn she has been totally irrational and rash.

Friends in science say it will be impossible for her to leave Shawn and continue working with him. I want everybody to know that she has fucked up.

BREAKUP

11 Feb 1992
It feels like death. I just want to die. I have no energy or interest. I feel like running away. I am scared that I cannot "face it," that I cannot deal with things. Perhaps I need to run and run and collapse on a beach somewhere.
    How can I forgive her for what she has done to me? How can she be interested in me after the feelings she has had? I don't believe she can. We can never recover from what has gone on between us. It is pure fantasy on both our parts to think we can.
YOU FUCKED IT UP, YOU IDIOT.

11.30 p.m.
I have just had the final showdown with Paula. Weird. I came back after my course and we sat down in the dining area. Turns out she thought I had made a decision when I phoned her back the other night. Likely story. I asked her if she wanted to reopen the issue. She said she didn't. In other words, she feels relieved the decision has been made.
    I made a short speech. I told her I appreciate her and that I love her smile but that I need to be left alone. Then I pulled out my piece of paper with detailed practical arrangements on it. I give nothing; she gives nothing. I said I don't want to see her and I don't want her here on Tuesday nights, as per our previous arrangement. We made a rough agreement till the end of August. There was mention of divorce. She appealed to me not to go back to where we were. The trouble is she was looking good. Smart jacket, necklace, hair dyed.

12 Feb 1992
Yesterday, on my way to my session with Clive, at East Finchley station, I almost jumped in front of the train. I had to move back from the edge of the platform to restrain myself.

Session.
I said to Clive I was scared to admit what I had felt. He said it is not a real end to do that. I have not lived yet. I need to die symbolically in a safe place. Then life can begin again on new foundations.

I told him I had been to the Mark Gertler exhibition. He had just been with his partner to see the exhibition. Gertler had committed suicide at the age of about forty-seven! Beautiful man. Such yearning. The women he painted were so complete and earthed. I said Paula looked like mother, i.e., heavy, strong and grounded. He added that she has become a crone. Once sexuality is lost all that is left is the destructive crone.

"It's over. Face it and go through the pain. It will not kill you."

I went to bed at around twelve-thirty, feeling a little numbed, not too sore. I woke up at around four o'clock and decided to phone Paula at seven o'clock and tell her what I feel. I phoned her and told her I did not want to go back to where we were and that she looked nice last night. Now, what is going on? I am still hooked! I am looking for clues that she is still interested. I noticed she didn't want to talk about divorce, for instance.

13 Feb 1992
I am excited at the prospect of seeing Paula as planned in Kentish Town. I am bubbling but I have to be careful. God, I desire her. Can I say, "I need you to lie with me?" It's almost certain she will refuse. Do I declare my love? "Tell me, do you ever have sexual fantasies about me? I love you, I want you. I want to make tender and violent love to you." Take her a present, a flower.

I need to know where we stand. Are we trying to build bridges or are we trying to part? I like the idea of starting a new relationship and seeing where it goes but I don't know if it can work. There is no trust. Where do we start?

Okay. You proved you can leave the marriage and your kids. Now let's get together. I accept breakups when it is a clear-cut case. This is not. There is room for repair.

Stop. Face the facts, Leo. It is over. This does not mean that there will be no hiccups along the way. It means that to all intents and purposes it is over. You are not going to be husband and wife. End of story. Therefore, divorce. It is hard to swallow but it is the truth. Look on the bright side. The trouble is she needs me as a friend whereas I need her as a lover. This is called incompatibility.

BREAKUP

14 Feb 1992
We met at Kentish Town tube yesterday before Jessy's report meeting and sat in an Italian cafe for about half an hour. She accepted most of what I said. She said we were great friends but, "I am still in love with Shawn." We spoke a bit about passion. I said it fades.

As we left the restaurant she said, "Don't think this does not upset my equilibrium."

I replied, "Don't think I don't want to kiss you with your mouth open." She giggled and said school kids might see us. In the course of talking she also said if she left Shawn now it would be hell for all of us. I saw her as attractive but also as flesh and blood.

I want to mend because that would mean her returning to me, her saying: I want you and not Shawn. Whether I actually want her or not is another question. My need is to mend; hers is to stay apart.

18 Feb 1992
I find myself oscillating between ecstasy and depression. I am trying to take it easy and do very little but my mind is active. I think about my loneliness and loss and I fantasize about getting back together with Paula and of real intimacy and passionate sex. I realize it is fantasy, yet there is a tinge of thinking it could happen. I even envisaged a wedding ceremony and the speech I would make. Then I thought we should rather just huddle together in a corner.

So, I feel sore but not a deep ache. I think it is over but don't yet accept it fully. At times I think she may reconsider. We are due to meet on Saturday night and then for Jake's birthday.

I have just finished a session with Clive.
A few things stand out.

The father I am to my children I should also be to myself. He is a wonderful father. Just look in the mirror and accept: loving, caring, fair, just and guiding. Secondly, take up the idea of working with families/kids. It's a vocation. Develop it in my head and then it will happen.

I have also had a weekend workshop with Clive.

It showed me I am out of touch with my feelings. She has been sleeping with him every night for a year, man. She does not want you. Look where holding on has got you. A woman there, Kate, is an amazing earth mother. "I am your true mother. I come from the earth. I am black and bloody and I can give you everything. Just take it. Come into me. Julia is dead."

At the mention of "children" I broke down. I cried for Jake, my son, my child—me. Real tears, real sobbing from inside. Then I said I still don't think I will let go of being a child. And they all said, "Stop thinking; just stay with it. You need to let go of thinking and get into feeling."

19 Feb 1992

This morning I got into the bath after Rachel left for school. It felt like death. I died. Then I thought about my true father: Leo with a smile, Leo of Israel, Leo in France at Salagou with the kite, of Bardou; the beautiful, loving, affectionate, giving man. I love it. It is my god. And I got out of the bath smiling. Look in the mirror and see that man in you, boy. Take it. It is perfect. You were looking in the wrong field. You were looking for a stern man in a suit with short hair and side parting, a man who seems to know everything and is absolutely certain of what he says. That is not your god, Leo. Your god is sensitive and strong. He guides by love and a sense of justice and fairness. He is gentle and loving and pure.

I invited Paula over for lunch and we chatted. The real crunch was talking about fucking and passion. I think she is in love with passion. We spoke about sex in our relationship. Does sex determine the relationship or vice versa? She feels sex sets the tone. I said sex is a metaphor for the relationship. Can we do anything about our sexual relationship? Not sure. I say we can but she is unsure (though I think not).

She feels she is in a "no-win" situation. Whatever choice she makes she will lose out—fear is stopping her from making a decision. She is having great difficulty with his kids. When she is with his kids she wants them to be her kids. His boys destroy everything.

I kissed her and held her and said I want to melt into her. She was a bit tickled but pushed me away. Was she scared or was this a rejection? And I fantasized about getting drunk and spending the night together. Earlier on, on the phone, I asked her if she was asking me to give her more time and she said she was. When I asked her to say something nice she said, "I miss doing things with you."

20 Feb 1992
There are all sorts of permutations going through my head about our compatibility/incompatibility. Can she live with me and maintain a relationship with Shawn? Can I meet her needs and can she meet mine? She has discovered an energy in herself that cannot be married with her need for family, friendship, etc. I fear that if she were to give it up it would be catastrophic. For her to keep her relationship with Shawn while we were living together would be a disaster.

At ten to one in the morning I find myself trying to sort out which comes first, sex or the relationship! She says there was no ease in our relationship because the sex was not good. I say the sex was not good because the relationship was uneasy. Who is right?

Can a relationship be repaired? What if we live together and get sex outside. Or she gets it on the outside and I get spiritual sustenance. Maybe this will relieve me of the burden of sex. Is it possible? Is that a better solution than the one we have or is it the road to hell? Leo, plain and simple: if you found a "rightish" woman now, where would you stand? There is not much doubt. You would tell Paula to piss off. You would tell her where to put her passion. Well, tell her now.

21 Feb 1992
It was a very strange morning. Paula brought Jake and Rachel here as they were due to be with me and I planned to take Rachel to Madame Tussaud's. Anyway, she arrived at about nine fifteen. I felt thrown into that situation we were in last June when she was sleeping out and returning home in the morning. Here is my wife, the woman I desire, dropping my kids off for me to look after. The pain has remained with me and I am worried. How long can I go on like this? What do I do? I am giving her the power to decide whether I am a worthy person or not. That is bullshit. It is all within me. I am not dependent on someone else

granting me life, manhood, etc. I grant it to myself. I am tempted to phone her for re-assurance. Don't. Reassure yourself. Accept the pain; it will ease.

22 Feb 1992
I want to consider agendas, hers and mine. What is my real agenda? Do I want to mend and put my heart into reconstructing and loving, or do I want to win her back so that I can conquer her and then tell her to piss off? I think it is the former. And I speculate about her agenda. Does she want me to drop dead so she can take over the whole scene with Shawn? Does she want me to be a nice little boy and look after the kids while she fucks her arse off with him? Does she want to live with me and have Shawn on the side? Don't decide. Just do nothing, man. Live.

I am having quite a lot of contact with her lately. We spoke on the phone yesterday and this morning we accompanied Jake to tennis in Muzwell Hill. He won the final. Tonight we are due to go out for a meal. Today we chatted in the car. She talks of her love with Shawn growing, that she misses the family terribly and thinks about it 90 percent of the time. She admits it is easier to fuck a non-Jew.

24 Feb 1992
Paula and I went to an Indian restaurant in Kentish Town on Saturday night. I gave her a red carnation, which she seemed to appreciate. We joked about her being quite tall; me being quite short (meaning shorter than Shawn). We spoke a lot. She told her side of the story: how she felt unhappy and angry, particularly about my lack of involvement and my inability to live in the present. She said Shawn is pressing her to give up her past—the family, me, friends—and move on. She thinks she can. She also feels her anger towards me is justified, that she had supported me in R&L Designs but not in the way I dealt with my partners. I was weak and she could not respect that. I told her that her anger was with the world and it was convenient to have me to vent it on.

To celebrate Jake's birthday we went to the Jubilee (a Chinese restaurant) with Jake and Rachel. I felt tense. Paula was hostile and I had the feeling she looks down on me. Certainly there is no warmth there. However, at one point she did start talking positively about what could happen between us. It was the first time I heard her say that she would like to build and love, etc. When she phoned to wish Jake happy birthday I spoke to her. She was very upset and said it was the closest she had been to deciding to come back.

In the car now, by myself, I was soaring with Etnix. My heart is big; I have magic in me. I feel loose and easy. I want to tell Paula: if you want to walk with me, great. If not, I'll find somebody else. I am not scared. I have strength and beauty and magic. I feel it in my gut. There is a loosening up. I feel the energy returning.

26 Feb 1992
I had a session with Clive yesterday.
Clive: Shawn represents her sexual liberation. He is the key that opened her lock and she has mistaken that for love. Of course, she is torn. I can do nothing for her; just have to look after myself, which means making my position clear.

What I am saying to her is: a) I want you and will devote myself to you, and b) If you don't want to come then we have to cut the tie and we need to create some sort of emotional space between us. That is the voice of the fair, rational, cold man. It is a voice she has never heard and does not want to hear.

There is the harlot/mother polarity. If she chooses the harlot, as she has, then the mother is compromised. It has already been: she deserted her children as she deserted me. For the children, who see things in archetypal terms, she has abandoned them.

When I came home after my course last night Paula was still there, sitting in the lounge with Jake and looking troubled. I said I wanted to speak to her. After a few niceties I told her what I have been thinking re affection, etc., and then stated my position as per "a" and "b" above. She did not like what I said or how I said it. She said I was cold and remote and hostile. She thinks she can live with and love Shawn and be mother to her kids. "Everybody says so." It was tense. She said I had a hidden agenda—wanting the kids—and that I was blackmailing her.

I asked what she was scared of about mending with me. She said of being trapped and not being satisfied. It seems to me she is trapped with him. She was very upset and regretted that we cannot be friends. She left in tears. I was tense too but managed to fall asleep, feeling strong. I had done the right thing. I had a feeling of power and control. I need it.

It is as clear as daylight that she does not want me, so what is she carrying on for? When she said she has a love relationship now, I said, "Then go for it." She replied, "Don't tell me what to do." Afterwards she said she has not made up her mind yet.

On the question of "leaving her kids," which occupies me at the moment, she justifies her infidelity and leaving by claiming that I could not fight for the family against my business partners. But what does she do? She runs off with her boss in the full knowledge that the family will collapse. I wonder if their relationship will last. After all, she worked with him for five years before "falling in love." She could surprise me.

I need you to say, "My beautiful man, just relax and melt into me." She could never accept my masculine assertiveness. She had to be in control.

28 Feb 1992

After another long, torturous day. I sit here by myself in the almost certain knowledge that it is finished. She came over to the house after we had been to a concert at Rachel's school because she was anxious to hear what I had to say. I said that no decision is, in fact, a decision. That from now on if there is to be any talk of reconciliation she has to move out from Shawn. We cannot proceed on the present basis. She said she was emotionally unable to decide. That's it. She wants everything and she can't have it. I feel calm. Give her an ultimatum.

What does the father say? He says:
Leo, it is a hard time for you but not as hard as you have been through. Look after yourself and don't let her push you around and dictate everything. It is all very well being a nice guy but it won't get you anywhere. Find your voice as a man and don't be shy to use it. Most of all, don't be afraid to alienate her. If she does not like it, that's it. The other way is futile. You have power man. Use it.

BREAKUP

29 Feb 1992
I cannot remember feeling better. I am buoyant, my body feels and looks good—thin, lithe and energetic. I lay in bed for a long time and had a great sense of warmth for Paula, a sort of spiritual warmth radiated out of me. I had a relaxed bath and shower. After I came back from food shopping at Waitrose Paula came to fetch something. She came into the kitchen and I kissed her. She responded, seeming emotional. She says she wants a special relationship. I said I feel very close to her. She asked why I do not show it and I said it is hard. I put my hand on her bum as we kissed and pressed her lightly against me. Exciting. Dangerous. I sensed a bit of excitement in her.
 Question is: Do I do anything about it or do I just leave it? Is she open to persuasion?
 And now for breakfast—melon and yogurt.

02 Mar 1992
It is just amazing how my moods fluctuate (although yesterday I was quite steady). Paula was at the house when I came back from a walk on the Heath with Joe. We chatted and I could see she was cut up. I mentioned that I had been thinking about her since the kiss the other day but was not expecting a future together. She said she may still move back, that she did not just leave and then forget what happened. She was particularly upset about her day with Rachel, who was unhappy. I suppose she feels guilty.
 I put on the Lambada to dance with Rachel while Paula was upstairs with Jessy. She came down and I indicated I wanted to dance with her. She came up and held me and we moved a bit. She asked if I knew the rest of the dance! She was tight and cried on my shoulder. I felt a bit of power. I felt good when she left and we made an arrangement to meet on Saturday night. I said I see no sign of real interest from her. She says she is in a difficult situation. "You don't have to choose," she said to me.
 I had a quiet night with the kids. Later I had a shower and just lay in bed listening to music.
 She talks of coming back. I don't think it's possible. In any case, what do I want with her? What is the attraction, tell me. So, it is a thrill to kiss her. I can get that from hundreds of other women.

03 Mar 1992
I was tense when I woke up and generally angry towards Paula and Shawn. I felt like going to their apartment and tearing the place apart, or perhaps just shitting in their bed. I felt this incredible anger and desire for revenge. I fear my deeper need to get my own back is greater than my need to reconstruct. I want to conquer her and tell her to piss off, or maybe to have her as a wife and then do my own thing.

You have to climb a mountain and really show you want me; that you are prepared to commit and forget the anger. I need to see some willingness to do that before I agree to your moving back. You cannot just decide you want to move back and that is that.

Well, I have never seen anything so clearly. It is totally plain and obvious: she wants him. Amen. That is the whole story and there is nothing I can do about it. What I say is: you want him, fine. If and when it is off with him, let's talk. Until then I don't want to know.

I find this easy to write but difficult to carry out.

05 Mar 1992
After the session with Clive yesterday.
If I am not for me, who is for me, and if not now, when?

I have to find the man in myself and listen to what he is saying. It's there. Right now he is saying something like: Paula, I want you to come back to me. It is going to involve pain but we will work through it together. If you don't want to come back there can be no friendship between us. I cannot hold on because it will prevent me from making my own way.

Right now she is drawing me into her neurosis, into a closed situation. I have to break out. There is a complete role reversal. She is like the philandering man who pops back and says: "You look nice today, dear. I miss the kids so much but I just have to get back to these *shiksas*. They wear stockings." But Paula is not a proper man. I am the real man. My femininity can be either my strength or my weakness. I have to make it a strength, and find the masculine.

I said, "The world feels heavy." Clive replied, "If you think you are Atlas. Put down the load, man." I said, "I need to collapse." Clive answered, "You have never said a truer word."

07 Mar 1992
I am painfully aware that things with Paula are over. She is due to come to dinner tonight and I think it will be the farewell dinner. How weird—I am going to spend this evening with my wife, who lives with another man. We meet every two weeks or so. I will make dinner for us—salmon. I am apprehensive and anxious. Their boat is going in a different direction. I am looking at it. Stop. Look ahead.

I had to stop writing because Paula arrived for dinner. We were both tense and angry. Afterwards we smooched on the couch. Then she went on to tell me that last Sunday she told Shawn she was leaving! I saw her pain and told her. Strange that she should wait until the end of the evening to tell me. Anyway, she is trying to live with it, which explains why she is feeling so terrible.

I am not sure what I feel. I don't think she has made the break yet, and I don't know if she can, although she seems to be moving in that direction. Overall, I am glimpsing success but don't know if I want it. Maybe she is on her way back! When I think I've got it I don't want it and when I think I haven't got it I want it. Is the same true for her?

08 Mar 1992
This morning we had some time together after taking a friend to the airport. She looked tired and haggard. She said I am pressuring her and she cannot decide now. In the course of talking I asked her if she saw a future with Shawn. She said, "No. Not with him and his kids." I think they are going nowhere. She took offence when I said she needs the "sweaty fuck." She went on to say that with the two of us the problems start when we get into the bedroom. With them they start when they leave the bedroom. It hurt but I can live with it.

I stopped near Queens Park to drop her off. She took out her cheque book to write a cheque for me. I noticed it was from their combined account. I was angry and refused to accept the cheque. She said she would put the money into my account. I told her to leave.

I am not going to be humiliated by her/them. Let them go their way. Why struggle with her? If they want their little relationship, let them have it. I don't need to put my head into a hornet's nest. Let her stew. Let her go, for at least six months.

09 Mar 1992
As I was walking into Westmoor School this morning it suddenly struck me: she sees no future with this bloke. How long is it going to last? Do I give her time? Do I go my own way without too much animosity? My gut says it won't last and I want her back. That is the only way to redeem myself, to reclaim the inch I lost.
    She doesn't want me. I am not man enough for her. She rejects me sexually. I give myself a hard time. Just face it and go through the pain. It will ease. In any case, an experienced woman like Alexa says I am A1. She will write me a recommendation. What more do I need? It is very simple really. My wife feels that I am good for everything but bed and that Shawn is good for nothing but bed. So, let her have it. Let her go. Let them find their way.

You have no reasonable right to be going on like this while you are married to me and mother to our kids. It reeks of exploitation and manipulation, of selfishness and lack of consideration and respect. I won't tolerate it any longer. It also puts a different complexion on having the kids over and going on holiday with them. I feel very uncomfortable with them going with your current fuck. If we are divorced and our relationship is declared over that is a different matter. Then you can do what you like. But you are still married to me and talking of possible reconciliation. I cannot acquiesce in this.
    I feel like squeezing them so that it hurts. I feel like applying absolutely all the screws. Bring in the kids, the lot—friends, phone calls, money and divorce. I want them to scream for mercy. Divorce, not separation. I want: use of the house for seven years, the kids and financial support.

7: TAKE THE NEXT STEP

10 Mar 1992
I am more or less where I was eight months ago, only it doesn't feel quite as bad. I feel anxious and vulnerable but not sick inside. I feel angry with her. She is in fact saying: hang on while I sort things out with Shawn. If I don't manage I will be forced to come back to you.

And what does father say to that? He says: tell her where to get off.

I want to shout and scream. I want to express my rage and I cannot. I am mad at her for leaving me, for betraying me, for rejecting me. I am mad at her lack of concern. I am mad at her for what she did to me in a time of crisis. And then I feel compassion. Why should I do the same to her? I want to act decently. I am not a brute. Just let her be. There is a middle path, which I have not been able to follow, of acceptance and respect, of being a gentle, caring man.

I just want things to get better. I am impatient for recuperation. I was on the mend and then I allowed myself to get contaminated again. Why? Last night on the phone when I spoke of divorce she said it is not what she wants. I can't understand this. Is it that she wants to keep all options open?

11 Mar 1992
After the session with Clive yesterday.
TAKE THE NEXT STEP WITH ME, SON.

The scene is an accident. My mother is lying on the ground, dead.

My ideal father is holding my hand and urging me away. "Come with me, my boy. We have to walk on. She is dead. There is nothing you can do for her, so come with me. This is the way. It is hard but it will be okay. I can show you. Follow me. I am with you."

And I say, "Dad, it hurts. I want to go back to her. Maybe I can make her come to life again. Maybe if I fuck her in the right way, in the way she wants, she will come to life again. I can't leave her."

Dad says, "Come, my boy. This is the way of the world. This is where you'll find your manhood. I'll take you to where you grow up. Just take the next step."

In relation to Paula and mother I think: love her in the right way; fuck her in the right way; please, satisfy. That way I can revive her/them. I think I have the kiss of life.

And with Paula it is doubly confusing because she is not physically dead. She is showing signs of life. In fact, she has chosen to get the kiss of life from Shawn. She has rejected me but I hope that if she drops him for one reason or another she will choose to get the kiss of life from me. And I think, with some trepidation, that I can give it to her.

Clive is saying, and I went along with him, that Paula is dead as far as I am concerned. I have to recognize and accept that. She never really was alive. We never really had a marriage. The centre never held. For things to work for us she has to make a psychic somersault of which she is incapable. She needs to project her love onto me. Impossible.

As to me, I need someone who appreciates me for what I am. I am a pure tea, not a blend. I am a thoroughbred, not a mongrel. I am a type. I need affection and intimacy and some fucking. I am not a thick dick, hairy chest. *Ah-so!*

Call it a day with Paula. She will come in and help with the kids. Something has been revealed in this time to both of us. Recognize it. It cannot be put back together. We can do a botch job but it won't be satisfactory for either of us. Pack it in.

I left the session thinking quite definitely that this is what I have to do and I phoned Paula to tell her to stay on at the house to talk. She couldn't stay. We made an arrangement to meet later in the week.

When I look at where I am through that central image, the accident, it all seems to make sense. I feel the pull backwards. I hear the voice of father calling me on. I then phone Paula and feel warm, warm. I feel a stirring in my groin and I am pulled back. Ultimately I have to go with father. That is the greater truth.

I am blinded by the past, by my relationship with Paula and my love for her when what I have to do is listen to father: You have to take the next step. It is not a place we are going to; it is a journey we are embarking on. This is the start. The next step is the beginning of your real journey in life, your adult journey. Take it, my boy. It is safe.

I'M COMING, DAD.

At this point I have to recognize that between us it is dead. Not dormant, dead. And, yet, I am not entirely convinced. Perhaps I should hang on a while. What have I got to lose? Be practical. Set a date. You can't go on like this indefinitely.

Try something else—a fawn. You may be pleasantly surprised, beyond your wildest dreams. She has given you a ticket. Take it. You have a whiff of freedom. She is off your back. Fly. You might just soar.

Get out of the trap, man. Cut the knot; it is strangling you. But it's strangling me and holding me up at the same time. I am scared to break free.

Yes, Dad, I can come with you, but don't drag me now. I need to look at the body again to make certain there is no life there. You say I will never be certain, that I'll always see some sign of life. You may be right but at the moment I need to look again.

12 Mar 1992

I have to walk away from the wreckage. I was walking away until she called me and said, "Leo, maybe we need each other." And I said, "Maybe we do. Let's explore." But the exploration is too painful for me. I hear the voice of father saying: walk with me, son. But when I say I don't want to leave any stone unturned, to see what we can salvage from the wreckage, he agrees. We are colluding with each other because we cannot face the terrible truth. These are all death pangs.

I fall on the floor, contrite. I hear the voice of mother saying: I love you and of father saying: come with me. Then I conjure up the voice of Paula saying: it is not over; I am moving out from Shawn, and I feel easier. I am kidding myself. It's dead. Dead until declared alive.

13 Mar 1992

We had a chat last night and I have a deep sense that there is no life in the wreckage. Even if she stops getting the kiss from him we will have moved too far apart. There is a void in the middle.

They were also tears of joy because I was having happy and warm thoughts about myself. Tears of sadness, tears of joy.

15 Mar 1992
Sunday.
I woke very early and lay around thinking. Then I found myself in a crouched position facing Paula/mother between the legs, entering as a whole body, staying in for a while and then being reborn again. Maybe I should ask Paula to let me do this with her. Then I can be a total child and from there become a man.

I am realizing that things take time. Patience—my dad's message. How do we hold our lives together in the meantime?

16 Mar 1992
I am reading Sam Keen's *Fire in the Belly*, and I think he is right. I have to exorcize the demon of woman. I have to drop the awe. Who is she to me? Just baggage, no more. She is not my mother or my sister (and not my lover). Amen.

18 Mar 1992
I can see why she wants to keep in touch with me. It eases her guilt and allows her to stay in touch with the kids—an insurance policy. What is in it for me? Sand! Nothing but angst. It's overs kadovers. *Fin.* End of chapter. Let a new chapter begin. There is no sign she can give me what I need: love, affection, caring, acceptance and sex. On the contrary, it is blatantly obvious that these are precisely what she cannot give me. Thank her for revealing it to you. You could have gone on for another twenty years kidding yourself.

The session with Clive yesterday.
In a sense we rehashed the same ground. I leave him determined to call it a day with Paula. Then, with time, I become less and less convinced that I should. At the next session I look for confirmation again that I should... Looking for father.

There is the ideal mother: the all-beautiful, all bountiful, totally giving and loving mother. All things; everything I want. The pain, the tragedy is that she does not exist in the real world. What I/we want most is not of this world. It only exists in the imagination, in the realm of ideals. It didn't exist in Julia either, only I thought it did and I am now searching for it again. Auditioning for Julia: Line up Everybody!

Yes, be the child if you want to. But you have to find a woman who is prepared to play mother. No conflict. You can have fantasies of crawling back into mother but recognize them as such and don't try to act them out.

There are plenty of women who like men like me. I am not everyone's bowl of chocolate. I am not Paula's. I can get what I need much cheaper elsewhere. Break out man. All that is keeping me tied to her is my need for revenge, for redeeming myself, for proving I can be man to her. In other words, for all the wrong reasons. There is no good reason for me to be with her. There is next to nothing that she can give me. There may be life in the wreckage but it's not for me.

I need to remind myself that it is *all* in me. I am the wild horse, the lover riding into the sunset. Outside is the wasteland. Look inside. Get rid of the demon that it is not happening for me. It is, in a big way.

While watching a Carl Rogers video at the course, I hear him ask: What is it you want? Is it in your power to achieve it? And I find myself saying I want the new, the different. I can do it.

Amen sela. I have cut the knot. I am free. I lay in the bath at about half past six and I realized my manhood is on the line here. I am not going to continue as martyr, as servant, as page boy, as eunuch. I am a man in this fundamental divide. Accordingly, I will act like one. The male principle is cut and thrust. It is firm and clear. I can do it and I don't need to wait for x, y or z to help me with it. I have the power, here and now.

I will celebrate by going to see *Raise the Red Lantern* by myself. Le'haim. She is not worth the candle.

20 Mar 1992

Well, well, well. I am sitting at Trinity School, much like yesterday, except that all has changed. Yesterday I was thinking it was all over and should be; today it is on in a real way!

When I got home yesterday at around six thirty Jessy said that Paula had phoned at around four o'clock, which seemed strange. I had a shower and phoned her. She was very cheerful and asked me to hold on briefly while she moved to the bedroom. She told me she had been trying to get hold of me and that she had reached a decision—she has decided to return. She had thought about it, decided, and will not go back on her decision

I was shocked but I took it calmly. Now I have to think what is involved. Suspicion wells up in me. Is this a plot of hers to get the kids? It is not out of the question. Anyway, my internal response was excitement and arousal. I felt turned on, expanded. I feel I have to go ahead even if it doesn't work out. It is going to be a struggle. WOW.

Later I went to meet Sacha at Delancy's in Camden Town. She was waiting for me. She has a lovely face and lively, green eyes. She had turned forty-eight the day before. We had a good chat. She is extremely nice and seems to be a woman of passion and love but is going through a bad time at the moment.

This morning Paula came over to deliver the kids' things. We smiled at each other. I said it felt like an arranged marriage. She said something about not knowing how we would do it. I feel much more sober about the situation and will take it as it comes. This has to be a new relationship. Same people, new basis. What are my anxieties? They centre around sex. She will constantly compare me to Shawn and be drawn to him and even carry on with him. The old question arises: am I man enough? I am. I am also worried that the familiar emptiness will return. What was that all about? I am worried that she is not interested in me and just needs to be with her kids. I'll soon find out. I am scared we won't make it and that we will all be worse off in the end.

I walked away from the wreckage and now I am returning again. She wants me to join her. I am coming, Paula.

22 Mar 1992

I went for a walk by myself to Golders Hill Park, feeling I wanted to be on my own. I don't want to share my life with anyone. I want to get a small house in France and live with a dog or two. Maybe the Cape. Then I think, no. I am bound to be with the kids now. That is my responsibility. Later I can buzz off.

Getting back with Paula is going to be paralysis. I will stop growing and that is a high price to pay. What for? I ask again: what is in it for me? She shows no signs of real interest. Yesterday we chatted briefly when she came over. I asked her what had made her change her mind. She said she could not be away from the kids and she could not stand the life-style she is being forced to lead. I told her we cannot just get back together. I have to be accepted and valued. She said she wouldn't give up what she has got if she didn't think we would have something together. This is not enough for me. Her whole mode puts me off.

I went to see *The Prince of Tides* with Charli last night. It's a real Hollywood tear-jerker, but good. I nearly cried at the point where his daughter says he can't hide from her the fact that he is not getting on with his wife. There are interesting character contrasts: he, Tom (Nick Nolte) is animus; she, Susan (Barbra Streisand) is anima. She needs his bullishness, he her softness. He finds himself in his relationship with her and is then able to go back to his family. At one point she asks if he loves his wife more. He says, "No, longer." Later he says a man needs two lives. He is torn but decides his destiny is to be with his family. Tom has his wife and family on the one hand and romantic love with Susan on the other. He does not realize that the romantic love cannot last although for both of them it is wonderful while it does. Can it be transformed into everyday living? Interestingly, his marriage has deteriorated largely because of his own crisis. The notion of tides is intriguing—all life gets its rhythm from tides, he says. And I hear Derby (astrologist) saying, "All waxes and wanes under the moon."

Not surprisingly, I was touched by the whole scene and more and more I am thinking that Paula needed a holiday.

23 Mar 1992

I had a brief word with Paula when she called this morning to speak to Jake. I asked her if I could rely on her. She said, "Of course." However, I feel strange. The whole thing does not feel right. Maybe I need to give her the feeling that I am not waiting with open arms. Right now I want her back but, at the same time, I know I am "better off without her."

Who is this woman? Who is she to me? Is she attractive, interesting, stimulating? Can she give me what I need? Is there anything to show she can? No. On the contrary.

24 Mar 1992
I cannot decide whether I want her back or not. We are getting into a competitive situation where she is telling me about all the things she has been doing, short of lurid sexual details, and I told her that Marcia came for dinner last Friday night. She wants to know what is happening there. What's between us? I told her I wasn't sure. She asked if I'd be prepared to give it up and I said I needed time. How much? "Ten minutes," I said. She said I should trust her!

She is still confused. And I have this nagging feeling that now that I have the chance I don't want it. I feel anxious about being with her, the uneasy silence, her oppressiveness and overbearing manner. I wonder how I will feel with my freedom curtailed. I see the attraction; I see the repulsion. I try to weigh them up. Where is my heart? It is in mending. After all is said and done, I love her.

25 Mar 1992
Paula wants to come back. Kicking and shouting, mind you, just like an adolescent who cannot stand the place. No remorse, no regret: still justifying her cause and defending what she did. She is laying down conditions and prescribing how things will be. The main condition has to do with my having a job. She says she is not prepared to come back to a situation where I am not earning, like the Rob & Leo Designs days. She says that I cannot expect any warmth or affection from her as she is in mourning.

All in all, a heavy load. My response: Ugh! I don't like it.

Just accept. She is lost and distraught. Be calm and things will probably settle down. She will realize it is her only option.

What do I need this for? I admit to being emotionally involved with her but she cannot admit to being involved with me. I think: She wants Shawn without his baggage and my baggage without me. She can't have the one without the other but it doesn't make me feel good. I don't want to be with her. She bores the arse off me.

BREAKUP

After the session with Clive yesterday.
The desert. I need to go to the metaphorical desert to see that God is within. Perhaps I should rebuild with Paula as there are kids involved. She is lost and I have to help her. We may find each other this way. You don't have to grow in a marriage. You can grow outside or not all. Marriage can be other things: refuge, relaxation, kids.

I have to realize the strength of my position. She has to make the running. Getting sexual satisfaction is her problem, not mine. She has to make it work. My looking at Paula and Shawn became the wasteland for me. It is utterly destructive. I have to look inwards. It's all in me. Imagination is everything.

27 Mar 1992
My mood is black. It's a false peace. I should not accept it and, instead, trust myself to the deep, uncharted waters. In turbulent times don't run for the harbour. It might be safer out in the open sea.

So, last night I had a long bath and then got into bed with a book by Sam Keen and Radio 3. I wanted to be by myself. I need solitude. All the old thoughts came up: it's not the time; I am better off without her. Why suffer? More than that, I am angry. Why can't she behave reasonably? I don't want to see her. I don't want to have anything to do with her. I want to cut her out of my life. I have to say: STOP.

You can't take the chance of her coming back now. Once she is back she won't leave. Next time she won't leave as hastily. Don't be in a hurry. Time is on your side. I don't have to be reminded every second of the day that she cannot stand the sight of me, that she despises me and cannot accept who I am. I don't need to have my ego slashed to bits every time she appears on the scene. She represents the absolute antithesis of what I need. And it will never change. Pain. I can't stand it; it's too much.

You are your own person now. Don't surrender that for the promise of family harmony. It's a chimera, man. She might want to come back but she cannot leave Shawn or love you. Amen. Face the pain. It will cleanse and pass.

My moods are dictated by whether I think it is on or off with her. Now I think it is off so I feel down. A week ago I felt it was on so I felt high. Shit. I am ready to file for divorce.

28 Mar 1992
I am listening to Bob Dylan singing *It's All Over Now, Baby Blue*.

What can I say? My marriage ended on March 28, 1992, just nine days after she said, "I am coming back, for sure. I won't change my mind. Of course you can rely on me, I have decided."

She phoned this morning and the conversation deteriorated pretty quickly because she went on about how much pressure she is under. She said she needs to see how we are together. She is putting me to the test again. What will she be testing next? How can I allow myself to be rejected every ten days? Am I off my head?

Father says: Leo, you have to walk away. Leave the scene of the accident. She is using you. She is in a mess; don't get sucked in. If she ever sorts herself out there may be room for talking. Till then, stay away. Leave her, not in anger but in peace.

And even now I want her to phone, or to appear at the house. Every time the doorbell rings I think it might be her. Is this the process of parting or of getting together? It's hard to admit but I think it is parting. The odds are heavily against it working.

29 Mar 1992
It may be a false dawn but it comes after a walk on the Heath together this morning. She phoned at about nine forty-five to say she wanted to see me. We arranged to meet here. We walked and talked. She says she has not changed her mind. She still wants to come back, only she has first to end her relationship with Shawn. It is difficult and she is torn. She wants to clarify things with me regarding practical arrangements. She is concerned that in the past we did not stick to allocated divisions. Can she ever be satisfied, I wonder.

At one point, while walking up through the wood above North End, she put her hand in mine, which was in my pocket. It was a lovely touch and I felt she meant it. Later I told her I felt she showed almost no interest. She didn't really deny it. She said she is restraining herself! I asked if she can separate from Shawn while living with him. She is not sure she can.

BREAKUP

30 Mar 1992
Well, well, well. I never thought I would get to this point. I feel like letting them stew in their own juice. What do I need a big, fat, angry Paula for? Thank the Lord I have not got her on my back. The load got off. Thank the load! Say that prayer a thousand times.

Speaking to Mala, a close mutual friend of ours, yesterday makes me think what an irresponsible thing they did. He wanted to get away from his wife and kids so he used her. Mala said, "He came on strongly to her."

Last night Paula came into the house. She said she could only stay a minute. She went on about how I did not do enough for her fortieth birthday! Earlier in the day she ranted about how I had not done enough when the kids were young. How many nappies did you wash? My fuck! What is it all about? All she is interested in is how the chores will be divided.

01 Apr 1992
I have a very strange, blank feeling. Paula is so remote. When she phones she is cold and removed. She is just aggro. My inner voice says quite distinctly: there is virtually no chance of harmony. You are caught in a fear trap.

The wise father has some questions:
1. Are there sufficient grounds for getting back together? Not clear.
2. Do you think there is more than an even chance of establishing a reasonable relationship? No.
3. Do you want her? Yes.
4. Does she want you? No.
5. Can she make a real break from Shawn? Not sure.
6. Can she stand by her commitment? Not sure.
7. Has she done anything to date to show that she is either committed to change or has any feeling for you? No.
8. Is this just a romantic notion; a soppy, sentimental wish? Possibly.
9. Would you prefer to be on your own? Yes.
10. Is your response simply one of fear; fear of being alone and facing the pain of divorce? Yes.

Your overall score is a big negative. The conclusion is clear! You are searching the wreckage in vain. However, my final conclusion after all this is that my responsibility is to the family, so we have to give it a try. We have to give it our best shot. That is what I *feel*. I *think* we should not even try.

What do you want, Leo? I want it to work with Paula. So, go for it.

The session with Clive yesterday.
He said I was hysterical when I came in. "What is this wanting Paula?" he asked. I said, "Partner, mate, etc." There was such a strong bond between us that I still cling to her. I have to assert myself. I am too giving, forgiving and accepting. She wants the refined, pure me but she also despises it. I want her dark femininity and I also despise it.

02 Apr 1992
I woke up this morning feeling free and unburdened. Last night I phoned Paula and said to her, "If and when you end your relationship with Shawn, you can talk to me." She said, "I am still in love with Shawn." So I asked, "Well, why don't you stay with him?" She replied, "I know it can't work."

Then at lunchtime while doing a crossword I thought I saw the word "areola" and it threw me. I immediately had an image of Paula and I could not stop thinking about her. I have to control myself. God, I'd like to meet somebody now, a woman who will appreciate me as I am; who will want me to hold her and who I will want to hold. Is there such a person? Imagine not having to think about Paula. And she is off to Italy soon.

03 Apr 1992
I am all in a tizz. When she came to drop off the kids' things this morning I said to her, "Don't give up on me." She said, with a smile, "I haven't, but you give me a hard time." I told her I had thought about her yesterday when I saw the word "areola."
Well, I am laying myself open. I am playing the naive Fool. Will it get me anything or just bring more pain?

04 Apr 1992
P,
To be absolutely candid. I love you, I desire you. I want to get the family back together. But I think we have no chance of doing it

in the present circumstances. We have to have a transition period.

If you are genuinely interested, go and live by yourself for four to six months and in that time we will see if we can establish a relationship. I will commit myself to you if you are prepared to do the same to me. Perhaps we can consider going on holiday together in the summer and maybe weekends before then.

If you cannot do this it is a clear sign that you do not want to go ahead.

L

I wait for her to phone from Italy and say "I love you." I must be mad. It is equally likely that Princess Di will phone to say that. I have a strong sense of the gap between us. And I still listen to Mary Black singing *Love is Just Around the Corner*.

And I imagine being in bed with her. Build up of energy, release, intimacy, blending. One. We are healed.

14 Apr 1992
I have almost lost track of what has been going on. Paula is back. It all happened when she returned from Italy last Thursday. We had dropped a friend at Kings Cross and as soon as we had said goodbye to him she said, "I want to come back."

By the next day she had moved in all her things and we were in the same bed—no pyjamas, but not too relaxed. I thought we needed a transition period but it was a question of seizing the moment. Now we have the task of building up again. Overall, I feel good though I am tense about the lack of intimacy. She does not want to be too close. We have touched and fucked once. Now we are wearing pyjamas until it feels easier, if it ever does. We have tea in bed in the mornings.

The look of relief and delight on Jake's face when she got out of the car outside the house said everything.

The session with Clive today.
I have to accept things as they are. "Pass the jam, please." She cannot combine her sexuality and her morality. She has to work on being satisfied; it's her problem, not mine.

15 Apr 1992
I feel very low and depressed. I think it cannot work. We have different and conflicting needs now and for the foreseeable future. Again I say: It's not worth the candle.

She has come back as an act of will. She could not make it out there so she has returned. She says she has decided to end her relationship with him but she still yearns and feels guilty for leaving him and wants to go to him and comfort him. In other words, she is still in love with him. So, instead of being with him and longing for the kids, she is now with the kids and longing for him.

She is angry with me for causing her breakup with Shawn. She cannot touch me, pushes me away and is hostile and distant most of the time. The only thing she gets excited about is her arrangement with him. She wants to see him next Tuesday. I don't mind that, but it's not kept in reasonable proportion. It seems like the highlight of her week.

How long can I let this go on? I could just let it be and keep away emotionally; keep it low-key and place no demands on her. Let's sleep in separate rooms and see what happens. It is too painful. Her conduct is saying: I want to be here but I don't want to be with you. It's a mess. A bloody, fucking mess. Yet again.

I have a terrible feeling that it will slide downhill and she will start seeing him again.

I feel bad that I have reverted to type. In relation to her I have become who I was a year ago. We cannot break the mold. Bring out the textbook, man. You have let her in. The man would have said: stop, wait. Go live by yourself. You said: take the opportunity.

17 Apr 1992
There has been turbulence. We had a row yesterday morning, triggered by her asking for the Royal Academy card to go to the Calder exhibition in the afternoon with Shawn. I was angry with her whole tone and wanted her out, and started moving her stuff out of the room. She remained calm and I calmed down. We went for a walk and talked. We agreed we would see what happens till the end of April and then decide. She went off to work.

I tried to phone her at work to discuss the arrangement further. No luck. After an Alexander lesson I tried phoning again.

Two people at the lab said she had not been in and I was getting suspicious.

When I got home Paula was there. She had a smile on her face. I was trembling like a frightened child. She assured me she had gone to work and said that she had chatted to Shawn and that she was going to stay with us/me. He is gong to help her. I was greatly relieved and I put my hand on her shoulder. Mother had come back. She goes, she returns, she doesn't return. That is the fear.

Last night I slept on a mattress on the floor. In the morning I got into bed with her and we held each other for a while. I touched her body gently and said a little of what was in my heart.

Yesterday, even when I felt really anxious and actually thought it was over, I was not nervous or sick. I did not have that deep fear that I have had in the past. I felt strong and determined. That is a change for the better.

20 Apr 1992
Easter Monday.
This morning Paula said she was "cracking up." She wanted to see Shawn. We had a chat. I said this is what she has to face and she should go out with a friend instead. No. She needs him, so she went. I was not upset and asked Elaine to come for a walk to Golders Hill Park. It is a lovely, warm day. Spring is in the air. We spoke easily and a lot, right across the range of kids, house, her, me and Paula.

She feels Paula is unable to make any decisions and has not been able to for the past year. She went on to say that Paula has been shocked by how I have handled things and not cracked up.

For me there is only minimal involvement with her, like ships passing in the night.

22 Apr 1992
It is still school holidays and I am sitting in the graveyard with Rachel. I have no expectations, just keeping body and limb together. I have reached a new stage in my life: I am not looking for anything, particularly not with Paula. I am still clinging to the idea that it might happen though I am not too bothered if it does not. Any residual interest I had in her is drying up fast; there is such a

gaping chasm between us. She cannot bear the sight of me, almost. She certainly cannot touch me or kiss me.

Times have been grim but I feel fine. Nothing can shake me now. The night before last she was in a total tizz, just about on the point of breakdown, absolutely neurotic. She woke me at three o'clock in the morning and I couldn't get back to sleep. I tried talking to her but it was hopeless. She cannot listen to me because she sees me as part of the problem. In the morning I took her some tea. She smiled and later we talked. She said she may be on the way back to Shawn. She has not decided to leave him yet. I indicated acceptance, adding that she needs to consider my feelings as well.

The session with Clive.
I need to limit the damage to the kids and to myself. She will either work it out or she won't. Fineness and compassion can be either strengths or weaknesses; I have to see them as strengths. That is me. I originally went to him trying to be the big fuck. That is not me. I am the eagle, not the elephant. The easiest and the hardest thing is to be yourself. It is so easy that it's almost impossible.

Clive says he and I are opposite Jewish polarities: he is the mystical kabbalist; I am the rational, refined Talmudist.

After a walk by myself I sat in the garden with Paula and we chatted about little things. She has contacted a therapist she saw last year, who has given her some advice. Again she said she might eventually leave, I said I accept that. No decisions.
I made dinner for the five of us and then she left to see Shawn. I did some puzzles with Rachel and then had a long salt bath. I fantasized about Kate. She is young with bright eyes. Paula feels peripheral to me now. If she wants to make the running she can.

24 Apr 1992
I feel apathetic and depressed. There is tension. She does not want to be here and does not want to be with me. We wake up in the morning in the same room but she refuses to be touched. I feel rejected. It's not terrible, but who needs it? Why can't I just accept that the two of us live under the same roof and don't func-

tion as husband and wife—just two people, parents to our children?

My urge to cut and run is great. That is me. I tried and it has not worked out. I don't even know if I am interested in her or not. I see nothing in her any more: a neurotic, destructive hag. My mind is racing. Pack a few things and go as a free man in the world. Wow. Problem is my responsibility to the kids.

25 Apr 1992
I woke at about five and lay around till six. Paula was up, having slept on the mattress on the floor. I leaned over and said, "Sad day." "Why?" "Because it's over." She agreed and then got into bed with me. We lay together for a while. She wants to go back to Shawn and wants me to be nice and to support her. I told her she was making the wrong decision again. She says she is not the right person for me and that I'll find someone else. People have successful second relationships. I said that in some ways it is a relief. "Let him bear the burden." She laughed. Anyway, I feel strangely calm. What will be, will be.

In talking to her I felt I was fighting for our life as a family. At the same time I also felt that it would not make any difference because she cannot listen to me. Defying me might be her strongest drive; defying the world, more likely. She is defiant, like Winnie Mandela.

I agreed to her coming back too early. What can I do now? It seems that she is capable of leaving again. She now says she panicked. She came back for *Pesach* (Passover) because she didn't want to be excluded.

27 Apr 1992
Last Sunday morning, much to my surprise, Paula, who was sleeping downstairs (middle floor), came to my bed at about six. She said she was very sad and wanted to lie with me and "do nothing". We lay together for some time. I felt the sexual tension mounting but resisted it.

28 Apr 1992
I am close to letting go. Whatever happens will be fine. The totally new could be wonderful. She is angry with me because I am

forcing her to choose between Shawn and her kids. If I were out of the picture everything would be so much simpler. Thing is, I am here. I am a force. I am father.

For the kids the best solution is for us to repair; for us the best solution is to go our own ways. For the meantime I am saying I'll do what is best for the children. Obviously, for her it is more difficult to compromise.

29 Apr 1992
The session with Clive yesterday.
Her wanting to cuddle but not fuck is a denial of me as a man. In other words I am sacrificing my manhood for the chance that this will help to repair things. Is not the "wanting to get the family together" the Holy Grail? Is it the wasteland? Clive says it is.

I am still on the edge of the void. I have not let go properly. I say I have let go of the sides in my own quiet way. He says I have not fully let go—of my mother either. My mother is dead. She is just old bones. To all intents and purposes, Paula is dead to me too. She showed signs of life but now she is dead again. Amen. Everything has to die before there can be new life. I have a sense now that she will die for me and I will find new life.

I have to see the writing on the wall. She does not want me. When people fancy each other it is mutual. There is no such thing as unrequited love. In this case it is simple. She is in love with what she cathected onto Shawn.

I am father, friend; gentle, loving, intelligent man (with no money). Any offers? My pattern: denying myself; denying my talents; denying my sexuality. Stop. The lid has been on for too long.

30 Apr 1992
Paula was back from Dorset when I returned home yesterday. She greeted me perfunctorily. "No kiss," I said. She kissed me lightly. "Feels heavy," I said. Yes, she said, she has decided she wants to be with Shawn. Boom! We chatted. I told her she had not given it a chance. She says she feels like a caged animal and wants to go for a walk with him on Monday.

Anyway, it doesn't feel too bad, all things considered. I sense I am going to fly a bit. All I have to do is let go—of everything.

Trust yourself and resign, deeply. Let her explode, or not. Just keep a safe distance. There is nothing quite as destructive as a forty-four-year-old, 160-lb, neurotic Jewish woman with a severe case of hard-headedness in a defiant mood.

01 May 1992
What we have learnt from this little episode is not that it cannot work between us but rather that she could not commit herself. She could not leave him. I have to recognize that. The nature of their relationship and how long it will last is irrelevant. My task is to let go. Move away from the wreckage. And stop looking at their boat. My boat is fine.

04 May 1992
There is lots of tension surrounding the barbecue I am having tonight. Paula had said she was not coming, which I was happy about. Then she decided she wanted to come and she started making a potato salad while I was out. Later she phoned (from S's) to sound things out. I said I would prefer her not to come. In the end she barged in and it was unpleasant for everybody. She cannot accept the implications of separation and cannot stand being excluded. She wants to be part of the fun.

There are lots of small incidents where she just vents her aggression. She sees a book and says she'll be taking that. Someone calls for the student who is staying with us and she thinks it was a call for her that I took and did not tell her about. Why do I have to deal with this kind of behaviour? I am getting to the point where I can almost say: I want nothing from her (except her financial contribution).

05 May 1992
I have not felt like this before. I have a sense of anticipation, of floating in the unknown, and it feels vaguely exciting, also worrying. I have no idea what will happen. About her I have mixed feelings. At times I see her as plain Jane, at others she seems very attractive. Last night, for instance, while sitting with the Coles, Paula was holding the tea pot and fondling the spout. For me it was a powerful, sexual image that was hard to bear.

06 May 1992
Paula is tense. She told me she intends staying for an undefined period. She said, "I haven't decided anything." What? She then tried to lay down some conditions. I don't know what she is up to. She says we will have to find some way to live! She has now moved into the back room of the middle floor and set herself up there. In a way it suits me. We share the practical burden and she does not limit my style too much. I am letting her act now but she is establishing herself here again.

The session with Clive yesterday.
In the ideal world: ask for anything and take nothing; in the real world: ask for nothing and take anything on offer.

    The overall message of the session was: untie the knot. Get out of the neurotic bond. I can live the second half of my life with integrity if I break with Paula; she is not my problem. It is an exercise in damage-limitation. She is abusing the fact that I want the family together. Getting together with her is like two one-legged people tied together. They can walk but it is not good. I spoke about my thoughts of going to France and Israel. He says, "The inward journey is the only real journey."

07 May 1992
For the first time I feel I don't want Paula. I am better off without her. It's inside me, not just in my head. Let's move on. Make this my France. I feel my focus has shifted away from re-uniting the family to doing my thing.

10 May 1992
I have been walking in Holland Park by myself. It is a time of solitude and it feels okay. I do want somebody to walk with me in the world, somebody who will say what I now say to myself: Leo, you are lovely to be with. I want to walk with you. You are beautiful and fine. I want you as you are: your smile, your silence, your intuition and your blandness. I want it all, complete and untrimmed. I feel an intense sadness at the passing of a world, the world of my little family. That fucking idiot stuffed it up beyond repair. Maybe we both did.

BREAKUP

This morning Paula was in tears, frustrated, angry and distraught. She looks terrible, torn and bewildered. She says I am trying to isolate her. She wants me to leave; no she doesn't. She gripped my throat and hurt me. She threw tea at me. I kept calm. She is out of control. Earthquake is not the right metaphor. It's more like wild cow or injured rhinoceros.

13 May 1992

There is talk about going together to see a therapist couple, the Zs, and I have reservations. Paula is here and we are going our own ways. There is minimal talk. I don't know what is going on in her head. I fear she has plans to stick it out for the next year and then to press for the sale of the house and share the kids. Wait and see.

The session with Clive yesterday.

He was angry at the suggestion that we go into couple therapy with the Zs. He said he felt undervalued and that we would be surrendering power to them, like two children going to mommy and daddy. He thinks there is nothing between Paula and me that needs to be resolved. I need to get away from all that. Perhaps we both need the neurotic bond and will go on fighting for the rest of our days. Bad news. She needs me as a piss-pot for her guilt. Little else.

The nub of the session was Clive's observation that my inability to get in touch with my anger is connected to my anger with my mother for dying on me. Once I admit my anger towards her, I am admitting her death. I have not done that yet. I am aware of the theme of being out of touch with my anger running through my life. That is the repression, the lid that is being kept on.

17 May 1992

The thing is I fluctuate. One minute I want her, the next I don't. Then I realize I cannot have her.

Yesterday morning I went into her room and sat on the bed. She was lying in the bed reading, not wearing pyjamas. I said, "Can I touch you?" She said, "No." So, I offered to make tea. We chatted for a bit and she suggested going to the flower market. I agreed. She wants us to see the Zs but not right away. I think we should not go into couple therapy while she is seeing Shawn. I now regret having gone to her room yesterday.

18 May 1992
Last night, in the bath, I had the feeling I want it to be over. I am beginning to lose all feeling and respect for her. In any case, it's not our relationship I grieve for it's the breakdown of the family. We both can't let go of the family.

It is totally unacceptable. She got in by the back door, decided to leave, decided to stay and to continue her relationship with Shawn, all with utter disregard for everybody else.

20 May 1992
I really don't know what will happen; it's all unknown. I think she wants couples' therapy to placate me, so that we can be friends. Nice little Leo—look after the kids while I run around with my Shawn.

We have arguments about the phone. She wants him to be able to phone her here. I refuse. She smiles when she sees my hurt. She likes to see me wince. Fuck her. It is horrible times. The kids hear us argue and they don't know what is going on. Rachel clings to her; Jake is pretty cool; Jessy gets upset.

The session with Clive yesterday.
I spoke about my lack of anger and fire. He suggests I need some impetus, like a breakdown. The almighty kick up the arse I got last year was not enough. I rely too much on stimulus from the outside. I need a family, a community or a cause to draw energy. This is not healthy and not reliable. It has to come from within.

It is a lovely evening, now eight forty-five. We have just had a barbecue. Things are absolutely terrible. Never has there been so much hatred and anger. Let it all come out. When I came home earlier she was throbbing with anger. She had been to see her therapist today. She had learnt a few things from him: that she has just as much right here as I do; last time she was a fool to leave. This time she is not leaving, and if she does she will take half the things and the kids. Real anger. I said I wanted to discuss money. She said she is not willing to talk. I owe her for all the years she supported me, she said.

Maybe this is just what I need: real confrontation. *I have had enough of your anger. You want to be angry. Right. I'll also be angry and I will match you pound for pound. I can feel my power and I'll match you anytime. Your anger does not threaten me. I'll show you anger. For one, I am canceling the direct debits on my account. Chaos.*

We are just where we were a year ago, except that I am not cringing now. She says our relationship is dead. It is. She says she does not need me; she can manage. I say the same to her. She says she wants to pull a knife on me. She just might.

21 May 1992

I am tired and empty. All I know is that it is over with Paula— and I can't fully accept that yet. It takes years. De facto, it's over, yet bits of me cling. It is very reminiscent of a year ago. Only now I have been through it before and survived. I won't die. The tide will come in again. There may even be new life. Give me the hills with a dog.

8: I DON'T WANT HER

28 May 1992
Bargemon, Provence, France.
I feel a different person here. After a week I have almost lost track of the days and the date and I can barely write. The church bells strike eight o'clock (in the morning). I came down to help install a kitchen in a friend's house and have just about finished. Today we walked to Clavier and I have been sitting above Bargemon. It is a most beautiful spot; the area is spectacular. All the superlatives apply. I really like this part of the world and want to live here. I need to learn French, find a woman, sell up and come down here. This is close to what I am. Fuck London and psychotherapy. Paula is a million miles away. I don't want her. I want someone new, a soul mate.

01 Jun 1992
London.
What have I come back to? Nothing.
   London is not as bad as it seemed from far away but I feel terrible here. I am thinking about myself and my situation all the time. I think about Paula and what she will or won't say, what we'll do—finances, practical arrangements, etc. She is in Finland at the moment, with Shawn. When I was in Bargemon I knew definitely that I did not want her any more but when I got back I fell into the old pattern. It is hard living in the same house as her in this way. It grinds me down. I could leave. I have come to the point where I have to choose between being with the kids or leaving them. Jesus, this is painful. I don't want to give in to her.

02 Jun 1992
I have just had a strange experience. I was in the house on my own and I went to look through Paula's letters. It amused me to see all the fuss and bother. She clearly does not want people to keep contact with me. I now know that our close friend Nancy wrote to Paula in July last year saying she could have kept the whole thing quiet and just carried on!

BREAKUP

The session with Clive today.
I am so passive. I just take what she throws at me. She is sitting on my face and farting and I do nothing. What can I do? I feel powerless. Stop feeling powerless and I won't be powerless. Do my thing in London.
    I have rage and energy but it is suppressed. I have never had what I wanted and life is short. Do it now and for the rest of my life have what I want. Make the dream come true. It can be done. Be authentic. That is the basis of power. I am not a Don Juan or an earth mover. I am a nice, spiritual guy. Not an artist, a designer, a writer or a potter. Be a man without qualities. Just be.

03 Jun 1992
The imagery of the puzzle I am doing with Gary at school has a strong sexual association for me—one piece fitting into another. My mind drifts to having sex with Paula. With other women it works but not with her. Why, why? Hunt in the right field. Maybe Tracy. She is petite and sexy.
    A ray of hope is creeping in. This is your moment. For god's sake, take it.

04 Jun 1992
There is general anxiety because Paula is due back from Finland today. How will she relate? She is chronically angry and needs to take it out on me. All that remains between us is a lingering feeling from the past and my attraction to her sex. I feel I could just stop working from September.
    When I told Barry of my intentions he said with a laugh, "That could cause a crisis in the relationship." And then went on to tell me the joke about the anti-government protester in a South American banana republic who is about to face the firing squad. The commanding officer says, "You have time for a few last words." Seizing the opportunity, the protester starts remonstrating against the government. Says the officer, "You can get into serious trouble for saying things like that."
    Paula would be raving mad. Maybe that is not a bad idea—raise the temperature a bit.

05 Jun 1992
Paula has switched herself off from me; she cannot allow herself to feel. Can I do the same? Perhaps it is time I took the initiative. I'd like to write a letter like this:

Dear P,
It seems that we are not going to make it together. Let's call it off properly and give a thought to divorce so that we can go ahead with our lives separately.
I think the time has come to say finally—it's over.
  Love
  L

James told me that Raya, a friend of his who he likes a lot, is coming to London at the same time as him, at the end of June. He thinks she would be a good match for me. My mind starts whizzing. I am smiling, not just because of Raya but because I am optimistic, excited. I'll be okay. I am looking forward to the rest of my days. What is more, Paula looked a bit fragile this morning. I would like to be able to refuse her.

07 Jun 1992
I am just back from a "fathers and sons" weekend in Wales, where Jake and I went up Snowdon with Jamie and his dad Chris. I felt a little bit sad thinking about having been there with Paula all those years ago. Then we went to visit Abi at Rhiw Croch, a beautiful spot; real paradise. It was lovely being there and we had a good time. Last night Chris and I told the boys stories of our youth and growing up, including the *Iron John* story by Robert Bly. We said we are still trying to define our manhood. It's a long struggle.

At home Paula is moaning that she has always borne the financial burden. I told her that is only partly true. Later she apologized and mentioned that she still thinks we should see the Zs together. She thinks there might be something in our relationship! I said I thought there wasn't.

I am really getting the feeling that: a) She does not know what she wants, and b) I want the new and the different. She was not happy with things and her answer was to have an affair. Simple. She stopped liking her husband of twenty years, so she got into bed with the boss. Then she screams and shouts at her husband!

09 Jun 1992

I really feel different. I am not concerned about Paula. I don't feel for her, I am not interested in what she does, where she goes or who she has a relationship with. It hardly touches me any more. I feel strong and centred.

Last night we had a fight. When I started filling in the remortgage application I put my name down as the first applicant. After all, she had shown absolutely no interest in the mortgage and a month ago she said I should put my name first. She started ranting and raving, "You are home at three thirty while I work till late." That made me mad and I tipped up the table with the tea on her. She wanted to attack me and I sort of contained her and we pushed each other around, shouting abuse. I went easy on her when I saw I could overpower her. She threatened to bite but didn't.

We calmed down and went on arguing. She said, "You act as if you own the house; you don't work. I, at least, have achieved. When you go shopping you shop for yourself." Utter madness. She said I called her "wife." "You don't possess me," she screamed. She was in tears when she said I don't appreciate her work.

Maybe divorce is the only way. We have nothing to gain from the therapy she talks about. Why should I live with her? I see that last night she was just as she has been for the last umpteen years—angry, frustrated and unhappy. We are right back to where we were fifteen months ago, except this time she won't leave so quickly.

10 Jun 1992

She looks grim and unhappy, while I am on the verge of doing something stupid. She is going off to the States at a crucial time without consulting me. I feel like destroying her passport as she is due to leave tomorrow.

The session with Clive yesterday.

First of all I have to recognize we are stuck. Then we can try to deal with it. When I told him about Paula's anger yesterday he said it seems we feed into one another's bind. She needs to vent her anger and when I am passive she tries to provoke me more. If I respond she feeds on it. We have got nowhere.

11 Jun 1992
Paula left this morning for the States. At seven forty-five she came to ask me if I would take her to the tube or should she take a taxi. I hesitated and then said she should take a taxi. I am not going to try to please her. As she left I said, "I'll see you." She smiled, trying to be pleasant. I was worried she might be thinking I cannot tolerate her traveling again. Not true. It's a relief. I am happy for her to be away. I feel lighter.

I saw pictures of her and Shawn yesterday. They look good together, even though he looks like her child. I feel they should be together. She has got more with him than she ever had with me. I feel enough for her to say, "It's good for you, have it. I know I am better off without you." In fact, I am giving them my blessing. Somehow I think that if she had come to me and we had cried on each other's shoulders it would have been so much better. But she had to reject me and blame me and vent her anger on me.

The effect of her relationship with Shawn on the kids saddens me. What am I if I am not good enough for their mother? It diminishes me in their eyes. They see that she is prepared to leave them for him so they are devalued too. Maybe I have not spoken enough to them. I don't know how to approach it, to tell them what I feel.

14 Jun 1992
Sunday.
Yesterday while talking to the Kings I took another step in the long, hard process of breaking up. I said in a clear voice, "I don't want a relationship with Paula any more."
On the phone James talked again about Raya coming to London and contacting me. He says, "There aren't many like her," but I feel I am nobody and I have nothing to give.

15 Jun 1992
Yesterday the four of us—Jessy, Jake, Rachel and I—had lunch together on the deck. It was lovely. No one was missing. Maybe

that was a turning point. I realized that we are a complete unit. They were relaxed and so was I.

I came home today to find a letter from Paula, written in Boulder. She feels bad about leaving under a cloud and says she thought about our "conversation" most of the flight. Why am I so angry? she wants to know. *I am angry because of the style of your US operation. You planned for us to see the Zs before you left for the States. Now the first meeting has been delayed by more than a month. It's easy for you, perhaps.*

16 Jun 1992
I have been formulating a letter to her in response to hers from Boulder...*Your letter is of the apologize-after-the-fact genre, which I have had from you before. You cause a blow-up and then say you overreacted. Well, I have had enough. I think you should use this break as an opportunity to leave. We should look to getting divorced as soon as possible, so I'll start proceedings immediately.*

17 Jun 1992
The session with Clive yesterday.
I told him of my feelings and of events over the past few days. Clive said in my position he would get out. Her mode is anger; mine is fear/sensitivity. Anger is more powerful. She is like a rampant tank and all I can do is run for cover. Is there still a marriage? Is there anything to be salvaged from it? I always leave a door open for her. I don't say: get out of my life. This is a mixed message.

I walked out relaxed and just ambled to the station. I am all right as I am. What a relief. I don't have to change. Something special happened between Clive and me for about ten minutes. There was truth in the air. As he said: "We have a better marriage than you have with Paula." Have I ever had anything with her? I must have had if it lasted twenty years. We had a close bond and we functioned well together. We built a good family. Tears came to my eyes. Loss. I hardly think about her sexually, though I miss aspects.

18 Jun 1992
In advance of the joint session I have an appointment to meet Mrs. Z this coming Monday, and was thinking what I would say to her. I feel guilty about my conduct in the marriage—I didn't pull my weight financially. Does Paula feel I pushed her into having an affair? If she was unhappy she should have dealt with it. It's too late now. I fear that she might use the forum to make the break final. And, I ask myself again: what do I want? Don't know. I think I want the new. At least I have to try. How can I even consider going back to Paula after what has happened between us? The marriage is over.

19 Jun 1992
I am still smitten by her. I can't help it. I see words that have a sexual connotation, like "passage," "entered," and I am taken. The problem is that she is the only woman who is real to me sexually. Alexa and Barbara are great to be with but are not embedded in my psyche, are not as real as Paula is. Pity. I obviously need to find somebody who will become real sexually.

21 Jun 1992
I went to a Tai Chi lesson in St. Albans with Fu, a Chinese master, yesterday. The whole experience was good: meeting Pamela, the train journey, getting out of London and into a different world, Fu himself. I need to persist.
   Of course I love her. So what?

22 Jun 1992
I am going to see Mrs. Z at 5:15 p.m. Can I be honest with her? Can I admit my true feelings? If she asks me straight out how I feel, what do I say? At the moment I feel terrible, dead. I feel I can't go on. A year on and we are still warring. But, all discussion has to be on the basis that for the next year, at least, I am staying. I am here for now.

23 Jun 1992
Mrs. Z is a rather cold and lifeless lady, sharp perhaps. I did all the talking. She seemed understanding and offered a few comments. I told her my life story in brief, keeping much to my point of view and saying little about the nature of my relationship with

BREAKUP

Paula. In that regard she said Paula was clearly uncertain but that I was too. I said that my feelings change from warmth to anger and hatred; the child in me wants to blend but my adult self wants other, a new relationship. I am absolutely sure of that.

Cecil came over for dinner and we chatted openly. He cannot understand why I am not angrier. We spoke about our partners seeing/not seeing our magic. He went on to say that women cannot be satisfied because they want contradictory things: they want us to be strong and to be gentle. They want a hard fuck and gentle love. I want the same: mother/harlot.

Recently Paula said to me, "The marriage was not working so I got out." *Well, fuck you. Get out then. If that is your message, live by it. Go, go, go. Who says we have to get on? I've had enough. Why should I tolerate the sight of you? You betrayed me and did your best to hurt me. Get away from me.*

24 Jun 1992
The session with Clive yesterday.
His message is clear and simple: stop trying to be Vlad the Impaler and be the Christ child. That is who you are. Find the Paula who is right for you. This one is finished. Accept. Recognize it is over.

He went on, "Paula could not accept who you are/were. That is her problem, not yours. Find this other woman and go to her. Worship her as representation of the female principle. Let go of everything: of giving yourself a hard time; of devaluing; of searching; of looking for integration. Just be yourself. Let it happen. There is nothing else. She has this beautiful midriff, nothing above and too much below; just this cave, this orifice of womanhood. That is her attraction. That is what you are drawn towards. Only, you can't have it. Go elsewhere. There is better. Your mother had feet of clay. Paula has legs of clay."

The point I really latched on to was Paula's inability to accept me for what I am. I am 100 percent and have to accept myself fully. That is the one real truth for me, the one area of certainty. The rest is padding.

We have put our ladders up against the wrong wall: pragmatism, the past, etc. We should be putting them up against symbolism: what the past represents. Don't be trapped by its immutability. Transcend it.

Elaine thinks Paula may be able to use the forum with the Zs to explore what her anger is really about. Also, we might be able to build up some trust, which is what is missing between us. They could provide a safe environment for us to say things we are not able to say on our own, and to listen to each other.

25 Jun 1992
I do not accept that we should live together. By any standards of reason or fairness she ought to leave. There ain't room for both of us in this town. I should make her moving out a condition for further (four-way) talks.

How can I let it go on? I'm mad. ENOUGH. It cannot go on.

And I hear father say: This is not the time to blend with Paula. Keep away. Whatever you do, don't go back to her now or allow her to try to get back with you.

26 Jun 1992
Part of my anger is because I see no remorse or sorrow in you. There is no sense of: Leo, I am sorry I hurt you. I am sad about the breakup of the family. I have broken up the family and it is painful for me.

I have been sitting on the deck by myself. There is only one dream I have. It is of making tables, sculptures out of wood, metal and marble and pots from clay. It is a rural scene and I am at peace with the world, though it would be nicer if I had a partner.

29 Jun 1992
I finally met Raya. Speaking to her yesterday convinced me that Paula and I cannot get back together, and summarizing my work situation showed me I have got nothing going for me. She told me about the relationship she had with her ex-husband. It boils down to her feeling it was too much of a brother/sister type relationship. What she needed was a hairy fuck, and she got it for a while from a man who was all body.

So, naturally I felt inadequate because that is precisely what I think Paula wants. They cannot do without it—women in their early forties. This is the Zeus syndrome.

I feel like crying. It is so painful. This is what I am faced with. It seems to me that the real issue between Paula and me was that the sex was no good. I did not give her what she wanted and she did not give me what I wanted/needed. End of story. I am here now. What do I do? Just die. Get into a hole and fade away.

30 Jun 1992
I feel much better today, having spoken to Raya again last night. She values me and finds me attractive. We spoke about anything and everything. She feels I am bound to continue identifying her with Paula, which would spoil our friendship. She is attracted to me but does not want to sleep with me because she would get involved and she doesn't want that with her living in Israel and me in London.

She also said that in the early stages of her breakup she was obsessed with the situation and everything represented something, was significant. That is no longer the case.

I felt very comfortable with her and we have only known each other for a day and a half. We went to Marine Ice, to a pub in Camden Town and then to Hampstead. She wanted to hold my hand.

01 Jul 1992
The session with Clive yesterday.
There is no point going on a heroic journey to France or Israel. It is all here, inside. I have not "gone down," not broken down. I have been incapable of descending into chaos. Also, there is no such thing as the hairy fuck. There are only a certain number of things you can do in bed.

We need to incorporate what the devil represents: the dark side, desire. Where is my dark side? I have to love every aspect of myself: the anger, the crude sexuality, the failure, everything. That is me. That has to come out and be exposed. You like it, okay. Not, not.

I have to use the crisis to get in touch with my real self, the authentic core. It is hard and sad but it has to be gone through. The relationship ended for a reason. I can't fight that.

This is radical, dangerous stuff. Can I go along with it? Can I collapse? Somehow I have to let it happen but I find myself baulking at it. This is Clive's kick and I am wary of it. I don't think breakdown is the answer and, in any case, it is not a matter for contemplation. It either happens or it doesn't. Why go mad? There must be other ways. Go on a long walk perhaps, or a bike ride. Go and live in the desert for a while. Maybe this summer.

I listen to the Corals. I cry. *Mother. Leave me. Fuck off, woman. Get away. I don't want you; you hurt me so much. Have pity on me. Go, for god's sake.*

Do I phone and tell her or do I wait for her? Do I do it in anger or calmly and firmly?

I think of my deep guilt in relation to my mother—that I could not save her. I was not good enough. I am not good enough.

03 Jul 1992

Listen, Leo, I hate to tell you but it is absolutely simple. She is not interested in you, so no matter what you think or feel it won't make any difference. Don't even bother. Not only that, man, you can do better.

The process of separation is slow and difficult. The end of a relationship is like a death. Nevertheless, the writing is on the wall—your marriage is over. The bottom has dropped out of your world. Just float and life will return. Don't expect or anticipate anything in particular. Just let it happen. This is a bit of a revelation for me, not holding on to a picture of the future or what it may hold. Whatever happens will be right.

05 Jul 1992

I am being made all the more aware of things because James is here and we are talking. His general impression is that we cannot perpetuate this situation; it is intolerable. Therefore, we have to separate and possibly even sell the house now. That hurts me.

I am mad because she fucked up our relationship. James asks: Why are we beating each other? He says, "She should not be punished for taking a lover." I say, "That is true but in a real-life situation decisions have to be made. She left this place and has less right to be here under these circumstances. We are not equal."

He feels I am not as angry as I was. More to the point, my feelings about Paula do not upset me as much. I am not as thrown by things as I was. I was hardly affected when he told me that Shawn (who hardly knows them) had visited them in Jerusalem. I feel I am a little further along the road of accepting and that pleases me.

06 Jul 1992
James thinks that my relationship with my kids is fundamental to me. I can't give that up and if I try to I will suffer, like Paula did. I am not sure about that. I still think I can do something drastic, or go away for a while. At the same time as all this is going on I find myself thinking that Paula has broken up with Shawn. It is totally irrational and wishful thinking but it comes up all the time.

07 Jul 1992
Paula sent a letter to Jessy from Madison, which I happened to see. I am shaking. The writing is on the wall. What hurts about the letter is, firstly, that it is all over, that the parents are separating. Secondly, the calmness, the hardness and the lack of sorrow or remorse. She even tried to make capital out of my relationship with Jessy. She says some things still have to be resolved with me. What could that mean?

Can I control my rage? Should I?

I went to Clive this afternoon, came home and had a beer. Fuck the world. I'm okay.

The session.
The family is over. Finished.

I have cathected all onto Paula but I need the new. She is just a neurotic woman trying to cope. I have to leave her. It's only because of my Pan-like appearance that I have been able to stretch it out this far. Time has come to call it in. How? Act out the dark side. Do something drastic. Tell Paula to get fucked. Let her decide between mother and lover. Play the big card.

As to the kids, I need them too much, which can't be healthy. They will survive and value what I do. I have been cuckolded and messed around. Get out, man. I cannot patch up any more.

The abiding message was: to move out, to go and be by myself and be a bit of a bastard. There is nothing worth holding on to. And I feel easier for it. I like the idea—I want to disentangle myself from her.

Napoleon said: As long as I am in touch with my destiny nothing can harm me. I ask: What is my destiny?

08 Jul 1992
Draw a breath, Leo. You left Clive yesterday with the absolute conviction that it is over and that you have to leave, for a while at least. Paula comes back this morning and expresses ambivalence, looks attractive and you start thinking, Well, maybe. Get your head straight, man.

When she came back yesterday I was cool. Later she asked if I was going to speak to her. She tried to be friendly but I remained remote, unsure of what line to take. I felt like kissing her but resisted. She said she is not moving out yet. I asked her if she wants to live with Shawn. She said she is not sure. She does not want to see this family break up. She feels terrible about it. She is going to finalize the date for us to see the Zs. She feels we must not rush into anything, like divorce.

10 Jul 1992
Raya leaves tomorrow. We have been out two nights running. It has been relaxed, easy fun. She likes me as I am, vulnerable and confused. She says my fantasies of France and mountains are farfetched. I have to come down to earth.

12 Jul 1992
I have just returned from taking James to the airport. His sense is that we are parting; Paula is not interested in me. She wants the kids and the house but not me. So, fuck her. I say: when push comes to shove we don't really want each other, however, neither of us can accept the implications of separation.

Now that both James and Raya have left my world is empty but I feel fine. I wonder if I'll ever meet anyone as nice as Raya.

13 Jul 1992
I am really restless, having read Paula's correspondence while she was in the States. She leaves it lying about as if she wants

me to read it. Okay, I am impressed, as well as amused. But I pity them, too. It consisted mainly of love letters from Shawn, most of which are pleading for her to be with him, harking back to the good old times, and declaring his complete love for her—body and soul. It's real and I accept it. It hurts, but not too much. What I cannot stand is her duplicity; she is deceiving me, again. Why is she even intimating to me that there is a possibility for us to get together? She is stringing me along. Her sojourn here is an interim measure and she has no intention of making it long-term. *You want him—go. It's fine by me.* It is over and I need to use the meeting with the Zs tomorrow to make it clear.

It is interesting how the letters have affected things. They are windows onto the truth. Without them things are left to my imagination, whereas they make things real. But, is she telling *him* what she really feels? Maybe she is leading him on too! Keeping her options open.

Pamela arrived downstairs. We talked. She feels strongly for me. We went for a walk on the Heath. She is "in love" with me. I am restrained. We talked of France and India. Romance is there for the taking. Do I take it further? At least it gives me a little more confidence ahead of tomorrow's meeting with the Zs. My intuition is that Paula is running scared.

14 Jul 1992
Bastille Day.
I received a surprise call from Raya in Israel. She was so nice on the phone and said how much she enjoyed being with me. She made my day. Later on I wrote to her saying I would like to come and spend time with her over the summer. Maybe we could pick up from where we left off here in London, though I am worried we will never recapture the joy we had together here. I sent the letter to her express mail.

15 Jul 1992
What a time. I feel so strong, so centred, so unneedy. Yesterday I went along to the joint meeting with the Zs after a short walk on the Heath. They represent the establishment and, it seems, are generally in favour of keeping families together.

Paula spoke first. She said she was torn because she could not decide between Shawn and her family. I said I was not sure why we were there and that I have come down on the side of separation, now. We sort of wrangled on. They wanted to talk about what had happened in our relationship. I felt it was a waste of time at this point. I spoke about my discomfort and humiliation and the need to sort things out for the kids.

I said Paula knows what she wants—Shawn—but cannot face the implications. She insisted that she is torn. Maybe she is a lot less certain about their relationship than it appears. Mr. Z says the fact is she came back home and she wants these sessions. He also said that it is better if things could be agreed, rather than one party deciding. We agreed to meet again next Tuesday.

I then went to my session with Clive.
We spoke about the Zs and the need Paula and I have to keep wrangling. She has a vested interest in obfuscation and does not want clarity. She is still trying to use me as an anger-absorbing machine. She married me as the perfect vehicle for her anger and she left me because I got filled up, or wouldn't absorb any more. I have a talent for taking other people's anger.

Clive used the image of a volcano to explain what had happened to us. The volcano has erupted. It changed the landscape irrevocably. What I want to do is put the lava back inside. It's impossible.

The time has come for clarity and for decision. I said I go away thinking I am clear in my mind and then I hit up against the real world. He says that the real world is that the marriage is over. I have to face that. What is her anger about at the moment? That is the question. From what she says she is still punishing me for what passed between us years ago. Fuck her.

One of the things I came out with from Clive is that her affair is her neurosis (and his). There is no need for envy, jealousy. On the contrary, don't be blinded. Okay, so she prefers his cock. Don't eat yourself up about it. Find a better c--t. You can. You will.

This morning I went down to Paula and told her we need to separate. She asked if I thought we could have a relationship. I said yes but it would be difficult. She said she respected my coming to talk. She feels both doors are open for her despite what I said about separating.

16 Jul 1992
I am nearly forty-eight and I'm ready to die. There is nothing I want to live for. Nothing. I cannot go on any more. I am finished. I have to give up. The hardest thing for me to accept is that their relationship is not an affair, that it might last the rest of their days. I have not accepted that yet.

18 Jul 1992
She was out with Shawn last night, which I found a bit hard. This morning we had to make arrangements for tomorrow night and the car. I was a bit up tight. She taunted me by saying: "You can't tolerate my relationship with Shawn." I saw red and told her to "Get fucked." I then cleaned the house, went to Camden Town and now am on the Heath, calm but excited.

My pain is not that I "cannot stand" their relationship, as she says. It is what their relationship implies, i.e., the end of our family as we knew it, and it also means the end of any friendship between us. I would feel better if she were capable of saying something like: let's bear it together and go our own ways in a spirit of sad togetherness. She isn't. I have to stand on my own in the world. I am strong like the tree in the face of the flood, as per the *I Ching*. I will prevail and the waters will recede.

Let go of the fish that got away or it will eat you.

22 Jul 1992
It's the end of the school year and I am not sure I have a job for next year. Paula met Pamela and is now trying to arrange my love life for me! "I am happy for you," she says. At the same time she was fascinated to hear about Pamela's feelings for me and wanted to know if I entertained women here. "Perhaps you go upstairs at lunchtime and fuck." She says she has "moved" in her feelings about us, away I suppose. Each week I get an update on where she stands in relation to me. Crazy.

Session.
Clive is angry on my behalf. He feels I go to him because he is in touch with anger. I am not. What we discussed is a blur. The

overall message was that I should leave. Get away, do anything, but do. Stop thinking and act. I am the calmest and most placid man he has ever met. And, I won't have difficulty finding a woman. They are already flocking.

What is there between Paula and me? Marriage is an ordeal that you go through together. She has chosen to go through her ordeal with Shawn and not with me.

I have this deep, overpowering sense of the end of our family. There is no other way but to go through the pain. I see Paula getting used to the role of being a single parent. It is the role she has always wanted to create, like her mother. We might be able to stay in the same house together but there is absolutely no way we can have a relationship. We need to arrange the house differently and we each need a car.

23 Jul 1992

Last night the head of Soul School phoned to offer me the job. I now have a job for next year: half-time at Soul and half-time in schools in Barnet (London borough). I am thinking of doing a course in psychotherapy in order to integrate it into my work with children with emotional/behavioural problems.

In the meantime there is tension with Paula over my forthcoming trip to Israel. I am due to leave this coming Sunday, with an open ticket for three months. She was in tears when I said, "Work starts for me on September 1st." She said I did not discuss dates with her. The truth is that she could not bring herself to discuss details with me. "Why don't you go for the whole holiday," she shouted. I remained calm.

24 Jul 1992

I am in Golders Hill Park and have just been through a complete transformation. I came to lie down here, feeling heavy, nervous and sad. I looked into myself and my feelings for a while. I then had this lovely image of a beautiful young woman lying feet to feet with me. I saw the line of her legs, thighs and bum, no head. She receded into a line of trees (a la Sisley). I have this ideal woman inside me.

And now I feel the world is a wonderful place. I feel at peace. It will last a while and then the feeling will change. Ebb and flow;

wax and wane. That is the pattern. Live with it and enjoy it. Recognize all the feelings, even fear, and stay with them. I have felt that I needed a fixed approach in order to cope. I now think I need to be more flexible. I have to be able to handle contradictory feelings. They are all part of the picture.

26 Jul 1992
Victoria Station.
Charli gave me a ride here. I saw her last night. She is very keen on me and I am still holding back. Why? She says I am very sure of myself, deep down.

Well, well. Here I am again, going off on my own to Israel. It was sad saying goodbye to the kids. I was emotional and the atmosphere was tense. I kissed Paula on the cheek. Earlier, she had wanted to talk. I told her to get off my back and went on, "If at some point you feel able to treat me as a person, let me know."

27 Jul 1992
A moshav near Jerusalem.
I slept well till about six. Then dozed till eight and woke up with kids all around. I didn't know where I was. The air is lovely and the light bright, the sky is clear. I strolled around the farm. It's hot. I must get myself a pair of sandals—for the next ten years! I am relaxed; no strong feelings or profound thoughts. Let's see how each day/hour goes. I'm thinking a bit about my kids and London seems very far away.

30 Jul 1992
Tel Aviv area.
I am with Raya, who was warm and welcoming, but is feeling low. Perhaps she needs space. We went into Tel Aviv, walked around Dizengoff and went to see *Strictly Ballroom*, the movie. Nice. Then we returned to her place. We talked and later went to bed together.

It's been a quiet morning—beach, home, love. She went to work. I stayed and read and listened to old songs on the radio that made me nostalgic. Raya says I need to use this time to make decisions. I think I can't force it. For the meantime I will definitely stay on in the house and at work, Soul/Barnet, as planned.

I do need to look at my professional direction. Perhaps a return to doing/making is on the cards; getting back to using my hands will establish a better balance. It's all about balance.

Raya was shocked to hear that I even considered leaving the kids. "Promise me that you won't," she urged. I think I need to accept that. It's a big step but it feels easier.

Right now I have almost no ideas, no philosophy. I am beginning to love myself. I want to be me and nobody else.

02 Aug 1992
Bible Lands Museum, Jerusalem.
I have a sense of dislocation. The line is broken. I am not part of a civilization and I would like to be. I need to tap into something ancient. Perhaps pottery is the key. I am obsessed with finding a balance between mind and matter; between pottery and poetry; between psychotherapy and carpentry.

I went to see the Abel's on Friday night. They were warm and friendly. Aharon said, "Why mess up her whole life for a stupid mistake," referring to Paula. An affair is an affair. He also thinks I should be a carpenter, a simple cabinet-maker. Forget the rest.

04 Aug 1992
I spoke to Deena this morning. She asked if this is the separation that is not going to happen. I said I think it will. She said their relationship had "gone dead." I asked how she recognized that. She said the sex had died. "For me there was no more juice." I said Paula and I were not sure it was completely dead though it seems there was no juice in our relationship anyway.

Slowly but surely it is dawning on me that it is over. Wow!

06 Aug 1992
Mt. Zion.
I am sitting under a vine canopy, on the steps, in what feels like the most beautiful place in the world. I have never been in the here and now like this. From here I can travel back and forth. It's all unknown, the future, that is. Right now I can float; I can go with the current. I have a vague sense of myself as a doer/maker. I cannot visualize myself as anything else. Off to the Jewish Quarter.

BREAKUP

19 Aug 1992
I spoke to Raya. I was expecting more from our relationship but it was not a good time for her. So be it. I think about Paula a little—another woman? Not quite, but if I never see her again it would not bother me. The kids need me so I will stay in London with them for a few years and then piss off.

20 Aug 1992
Jerusalem is beautiful. I see an old man and I want him to give me advice, to lead me. I am the wise old man. What does he say? He says: Take it easy. Do nothing. Be patient. Things will work out. I am not sorry what happened to us/me. It has been hard but I needed a kick up the arse. I was stuck, so stuck. Now I feel good. No watch; just a bathing suit.

23 Aug 1992
Moshav Amirim.
I have been sitting above one of the loveliest sights in the world: Galilee mountains and the Sea of Galilee. And I thought: just love yourself, value yourself. You are 100 percent. Not the sexiest, not Vlad the Impaler, not the cleverest. Just you, Leo. That is all you have to be and fuck the rest. Nothing else counts. Nothing. That is the message. When will I feel this free again? I want it to go on and on.

28 Aug 1992
London.
As I got on the train at Gatwick I started feeling my London self: jilted husband, father, teacher. How different from my Jerusalem self: free spirit, friend, beholder of beauty. Fucking hell.

However, this is the real life and I am not afraid to face it. Paula was tense when we met, though she did say hullo. She feels I am leaving her out of the Israeli friendships, so she responded in the only way she knows—anger. She attacked me. I just laughed at her and told her to piss off. She gave me such a look of hatred. The kids were happy to see me, especially Rachel.

I lay on my bed with Jake and Rachel for some time. We just talked. By the time I went to bed I was sad, sad at what depths we have again descended to and thinking what our kids face from now on. I took a long time to fall asleep and woke up early. Paula came up to apologize then got nasty again.

Hill Garden

Yesterday evening Paula and I talked while making dinner. She wanted to know about my trip, especially about people's relationships. Every now and again she said something hostile or bitchy. She is living in the past, trying to confirm how bad things were between us. I felt that all the tensions between us have been exacerbated. She clings to how we used to be. In the end I told her she was a destructive witch. When Elaine phoned to invite me to a movie Paula made some remark about me "getting in there." I told her to lump it. Later I went over to see Charli and came home at about midnight.

Now I am going to clean the kitchen to the sounds of Gypsy Kings. She is still telling me how and what to clean and then criticizing what I do. The difference is that now I can laugh at her.

31 Aug 1992

Paula made a conciliatory gesture yesterday—she came up and held me. I just remained cool. Perhaps there is a way, but she is fucked up. Am I prepared to get into a relationship? Not really. I want to go skiing.

04 Sep 1992

Paula does not stop talking about how bad a parent I am compared to her, who will do anything for her kids! Tomorrow she goes to Germany for ten days and she has just informed me of her planned trip to South Africa in December with Jake and Rachel.

The time has come for me to do what I want and I have been out every night this week. Charli is putting pressure on me to give more but I don't want to be committed at this stage. Paula has been trying to be reasonable and even suggested we go to a movie together.

I went to the Royal Academy with Elaine on Sunday. We had a nice long chat. She says Paula is trying to cut me off from my kids and Shawn from his. Paula hates Shawn's kids. I wonder what he feels about that. Elaine also feels that Paula is where she is for her sake and not for the kids. For the kids she would cut it clean.

Later I went for a walk on the Heath. When I returned I was standing in the kitchen and Paula came up to me and held me. She cried on my shoulder and wanted to hold on to me. I held her and kissed her cheek gently. I felt she was accepting me and acknowledging who I am. Emotionally, I felt it was a step towards reconciliation, though I have to guard against that. When she slept out on Sunday night I was hardly upset about it at all.

She resents my going out so much and doesn't want to leave the kids on their own. I suggested she could stay in. "I am going out," I said. We need to share time equally. I am exploring… all different types. I need to find a place in the UK to get away to as much as possible, say for weekends.

07 Sep 1992
A bench in the cemetery.
I am smiling, despite everything, and shedding tears of joy. Paula is away in Germany. Yesterday I went for a walk on the Heath with Jan. She says it was expected for Paula to leave her first husband. The adolescent in her needs to say that the "parent" is all bad in order to leave and establish independence. In her view, the rage in both of us is part of the grieving and is to be expected as well. Now we need to talk in order to take care of the children. She feels Paula has a lot in common with Shawn and believes that an affair usually signals the end of a marriage. She indicated that Shawn is suffering and suggested I should befriend him. All very instructive, and I feel the weight of the breakup.

In the meantime I am being chased by two women I am not very keen on while Paula and I are like Punch and Judy—we can't be together and can't be apart.

10 Sep 1992
This morning I feel the full whack, having read a bit of Shakti Bahia last night about relationships. I feel I have nothing and she has everything. It may be the "right order of things" and I may ultimately be better off without her but right now it hurts. The one consolation is the lesson that relationships are in me, as is everything. My real relationship is with myself. I should move out

of London and go somewhere where housing is cheaper and where I am removed from the memory trap.

It is so lovely with her away. There is no tension and the kids are warm. We talk and read in my room.

13 Sep 1992

I feel apprehensive about the future but surprisingly self-contained. Walking along the Sandy Path yesterday I realized that she is not going to give Shawn up. He means too much to her and does too much for her ego. She cannot give that up. In any case, why should she? The problem for me is that it is still infringing on my world more than is comfortable.

16 Sep 1992

Paula is back and we are fighting. She came up to my room while I was reading and said we should talk. I felt invaded and asked her not to disturb me and not to come up here. She wants to take over the room in six month's time. I told her to leave.

Yesterday I had a nice chat with Valery, an old friend of mine, who thinks I should get into something practical. As chance would have it I went out to King's Langley to see Rael, a very old friend of mine who has just arrived in England, and we spoke about my learning to make musical instruments with him. I was excited about the idea. It feels close to who I am—gift is material; mind is poetic. This is a craft with an aesthetic side—that's me. Also, I could get back into pottery. It is time to do my thing. Take small steps and see where they lead.

I went to see Clive for a chat, after not seeing him for two months. I might not see him again. The message is: tell Paula to get fucked and find myself a *shiksa* who will love me plain and simple. What is it with these neurotic Jewish (South African—few examples) women trying to be men? Don't give them room. Express your anger, cold anger, not the cattish, feminine type I have been showing. "Not even you can be so nice."

18 Sep 1992

Paula and I were both home last night and we managed to talk about a few practical things. Being together and her slight softness made me feel warmly towards her but I tried not to show it.

BREAKUP

Unfortunately the way we are living means I cannot distance myself from her, which I need to do. So I took a long bath and felt the pain, the pain of rejection and of grief for the family and the end of a relationship. I called up my ideal mother and father and I knew the pain would pass. It is just another stage in the process.

I have started making harps with Rael. We are using beautiful wood, like cherry. Is this the start of something? Another voice says it is all futile, including harps. Okay, now do it.

19 Sep 1992
Last night I had the strangest feeling of power and strength, resulting from a small tiff with Paula over a mango, at the end of dinner. She was livid and started swearing at me. The upshot is that I do not want to eat her food and I don't want her to eat mine.

21 Sep 1992
I don't want you around any longer. Get out. You chose "out," now act on it. You said you could not be with me for another day. The marriage was over eighteen months ago when you started your affair. I don't need to tolerate you and your anger. Go and vent it elsewhere. You need to leave.

23 Sep 1992
It is a generally relaxed and quiet time with the kids, looking at books and listening to records. I am trying to cut my contact with Paula to a minimum, though last night she came to eat with us because I did not want to exclude her. I am prepared to live with her under the same roof if she does not give me shit.

24 Sep 1992
She is off to Cambridge, looking good. I don't want her but it still hurts. I took myself to see *Howard's End* last night and really enjoyed it. England looked beautiful. At one point in the movie someone says that nine out of ten people who love each other just can't live together. It made me think what it might mean if they cannot live together. Stop the speculation.

I have powerful images of turmoil in my head. I feel like throwing out everything of hers or getting up at the Rosh Hashana meal and slinging the food out. Wild anger. I am scared I am capable of doing it.

Rachel and I went for a walk and chatted about dogs. She wants one and I think of living in the country one day with dogs.

27 Sep 1992

I feel sorry for Paula. She is in a horrible place and looks it. She was crying when she came back from shopping and appears to be on the verge of tears all the time. Maybe this is her crisis. When we are both around I get turned on by her and I think she feels a little bit excited by me.

28 Sep 1992

We had a day of relative harmony and I don't know what to make of it. She was due to take the kids to a movie and asked if I wanted to join them. I hesitated and then agreed. It worked out that I sat next to her. It felt really strange. I wanted to touch her but resisted. We came back and worked in the garden together and then went for a walk and spoke about various things: her trip to South Africa, seeing my family there and so on. My sense is that she is sad, but determined to stay with Shawn. We can all see the debris now.

29 Sep 1992

I woke up early this morning, feeling quite relaxed. I was tempted to go down to her but, instead, fantasized about her coming up here while I was in the bath, and lying seductively on the bed. All I have to do is survive. The rest will follow. I feel a million dollars and I believe I radiate joy.

30 Sep 1992

When it comes to filling out the mortgage application Paula gives me the impression she is not planning to sell up in the near future or even in a year's time. Maybe she is having second thoughts. And I find myself lapsing into thinking that we will be together, that the pain will ease.

01 Oct 1992

Gradually, ever so gradually, I will let go. However, it is damn hard when she is around. In relation to her I will always be the rejected one. She is trying to restrain my going out all the time. I have just picked up on the edge of something growing inside me: I don't want her. I want my freedom above all else. Leo, whatever you do, go now for freedom. This is your chance. My need for freedom exceeds my need for re-acceptance and reunion.

03 Oct 1992
Another harrowing Saturday morning. Just hold tight, boyo. All will be well. Paula was out last night and I had a good time with the kids. She came down this morning full of hostile talk, accusing me of "taking over" her friends and saying, "You are not Mr. Nice Guy." Later she put her hand out to me saying, "I don't want to be bad friends with you."

Why do I still think we will mend? It is the child in me and it is fuelled by chats to certain tarot witches. *Enough already. Get out, man.* I am trying to, Dad.

04 Oct 1992
She is trying to be warmer and is talking to me decently. As Rachel and I left on our bike ride this morning I offered myself to be kissed as Rachel had. Paula kissed me on the cheek. It felt good. I sense she is not untouched by things between us. There is a change in her, though I am not sure what it signals.

05 Oct 1992
She looks drawn and worried. What is going on with her? Flash thought—it's over with Shawn. Shock. Would she tell me if it were over? No. Let her be with him. I am not far from not wanting her. I am almost there but it's taken a year and a half. Right now, I don't want her back. Simple.

07 Oct 1992
Yom Kippur.
Paula asked me to go for a walk with her to Parliament Hill. She was hostile all the way there. I saw she was distressed and I felt I needed to say something, so I asked her: "How are you finding this arrangement?"

"Wonderful," she said sarcastically.

Then I said, "Separation is difficult."

"No it's not," she said. "It's leaving the kids that is hard."
I said, "That is part of separation."
She didn't reply.
She says she is in pain. "I don't know what I want."
She was in tears. Obviously she is very troubled. When I asked her if there is anything I can do for her, she said: No. She looks as if she is facing the prospect of breaking up with Shawn. Why should she? We are miles apart though I sense she wants to be closer. I must hold tight now.

My star is on the rise.

Graveyard.
Ironically, this place has given me life. It is beautiful and calm. I sit here on a stone, thinking. I feel good. I also want her with me. I feel deeply for her, not just habit, not just mother. It's in my heart.

08 Oct 1992

I feel very light-headed, out of touch with reality: sort of hallucinating. I woke up early, my mind all over the place. I thought about my anger over my mother: I am ten and she is alive; I am eleven and she is dead. I remain ten. I am angry with women. I want to rape Paula. Perhaps I can explode inside Roxanne tomorrow night. She is hot but I wonder if it's for me. Why not? I am as sexy as the next man. Allow yourself to be a forceful and potent man.

I cannot figure Paula out. She is all over the place. This is a dangerous time. The whole picture could disintegrate now and she could go crazy. Her illusion has been shattered. My gut feeling is that this is another one of her crises, like she had at Xmas and *Pesach*.

9: WE NEED HEALING

14 Oct 1992
Barry S, my life-long friend, is to be buried today at noon. How close can you get? I am shocked, numbed and frightened. His heart gave in; my broken heart is about to fragment. I feel fragile. I look at myself and wonder what is going on. Actually, I am too stunned to allow myself to feel properly. I am just trying to keep my bits together. I find myself in the position or organizing the funeral for Barry. It's bizarre. I thought of saying something at the funeral but won't. My heart aches. How much can I stand?

Later.
My world without Barry.
 The rain that falls now falls on Barry's grave. It was a fitting ceremony in every sense and I was moved to tears. He was a person of integrity. It feels frighteningly close—he was my age and we took the same path, so I feel very vulnerable. How could this have happened? It doesn't seem possible. Barry is in the ground. Who will cry for me? What will they say about me when I die?
 Things are delicate with Paula. She agreed we need a dose of healing. I am in the process of giving up my anger but she will not give up on Shawn. At the funeral she put her head on my shoulder briefly while we were standing next to the coffin. There is an easing for both of us but I cannot kid myself it will lead to reconciliation, even if I want it to.
 On the way back from the funeral she said to me, "Could we live together again?" I said, "We could if you want to but I am not sure we should." She asked what I meant. I said we need to take stock and see what each of us wants. She said there is no point in delaying it, but I am not sure. Since then we have been together more, especially over Barry and related matters. We need healing—what sort, I don't know.

22 Oct 1992
I am feeling low because there is nothing going for me. All the women around me are of little interest. Paula is hostile at virtually

every turn. Now and again she softens; a mixture of hostility with little bits of tenderness. Anyway, she can scream till she is blue in the face, I will not shift until we both move out.

26 Oct 1992
Last Saturday morning I was cleaning my bathroom, not giving anything else a thought, when Paula came in, obviously distraught, and said something like: we can't go on like this. "What do you mean?" I asked. In short, it is all too much for her. She wants us to try to live together! I was shocked and wanted to leave it at that. She seemed anxious to conclude something. But I had plans. I then went to see Everton vs. Arsenal with Jake and to see *Husbands and Wives* with Charli at night.

On Sunday morning I was reading the newspaper downstairs when she came in. Straight away she wanted to clear things up. She fears the split and cannot contemplate the possibility of not being the major parent. As she said, it is a defeatist attitude but the alternative is too painful to face. We, therefore, have to try to get together. She says we had something and we need to try and build on that. Unlike last time, she says she can make the break from Shawn and now realizes what is involved in being with him—the price. She says their relationship is already suffering because of the prospect of the breakup of the family.

She is putting on a brave face but I think it is tickets for them. I asked her what is different this time. She replied that she has changed. She now realizes more fully what family and all its associations mean, friends, etc.

We have sort of decided on a trial from now until next spring. Why am I letting myself be sucked into this again, especially in light of the fact that she has cried wolf a few times before? It may be different this time. Can she break from him? I think she can. Am I prepared to give up what I have got—freedom?

I am thinking about her. She is not beautiful or interesting or of like mind, yet I am drawn to her. What is it? It's the attraction of opposites and I am still on the border of fantasy. In the ideal world ask for anything and take nothing; in the real world take what is offered. She is offering reconciliation. Try it. Is the healing we need, sexual healing (Marvin Gaye)? Go away for a weekend together and just lie together. Get drunk and get into bed together. It's going to take time. I want to hold her but I am resisting. She needs time. This morning I put my hand on her gently. When I left I kissed her goodbye and she seemed to respond. She says I can trust her in relation to Shawn. I am not bothered; I'll be fine either way.

28 Oct 1992
I don't really want to live like this. I want a life of leisure and ease. It's my life, why not grab it? I don't think it will work with her anyway. She is not interested in me and resents me too much; she is just too frightened of a future of separation. I feel for her but there are plenty of other fish in the sea. And even if I don't catch any I'll be okay. I should press now for a separation, including the sale of the house. I want to be in Israel or France. My head is full of ideas. Buy a place with potential and develop it slowly. Yes, yes, yes. I need to start preparing myself by finding out all I can about moving to France and learning French.

30 Oct 1992
On the train between Carmaethen and Fishguard (Wales).
It is an extraordinary time; another magical moment. I am on my own and at peace with the world. I want nothing more than I have. I am content, relaxed. The countryside is pretty, the sun is shining. Can you leave a family as she tried to do? It can be done but it does not come easy or cheap.

Hotel in Wolfscastle.
I just went for a walk in the area. Lovely light; lovely colours; absolute calm and tranquility. I feel wonderful sitting next to a fire in the hearth. I'm me. I have been thinking of Paula and bonding with her. Either it will happen or it won't. It seems to me the overall direction is towards getting together, but I don't know if we will sustain it.

31 Oct 1992
On the Welsh coastal path.
I am looking out over the sea and I have never felt so good in my life. I am walking at the edge of the land, where it meets the sea. It's

life on the edge: land/sea; heaven/earth; sky/earth. I am on my own at the memorial to the French landing here in 1797. It is totally beautiful. This is the life! I don't want anything else. I am perfectly content and in touch with the universe; at one with the world.

On the beach.
I have picked up ten stones and a shell to remind me of the best day in my life. I'll keep them in the bathroom.

01 Nov 1992
On the train from Swansea to Bristol.
I am inclined to go on seeing other women. What the hell. Maybe I need to try the alternative before I decide. Time is short; take your chances. There is more to life than Paula. Maybe I should wait for her relationship with Shawn to end. If it doesn't, okay. If it does, we talk. Right now I feel we should split up in summer.

I had a beautiful, short walk with Phil, a friend who lives in Wales, this morning. The trees and the river were such exquisite colours—sheer beauty.

02 Nov 1992
When I came back from Wales yesterday Paula looked worried. Later she told me she had ended her relationship with Shawn and it was hard for her. I don't know what to think. When I said that a chasm had opened up between us she said she understands if I don't want to get involved now. However, she feels it is time for us to try it out but added, "I am not getting into bed with you."

There is general uneasiness. She wants time to herself but also wants to do things together. I said it would be easier for me if she wasn't so angry. She replied that she has a lot to be angry about. Just before going to bed I went up to her and said, "Let me look into your eyes." We held lightly. She seemed to convey warmth. I kissed her on the cheek and went up to my room. I think we cocked things up. We should never have allowed things to deteriorate to such an extent. Now it's gone too far.

03 Nov 1992
I am at home by myself on a beautiful day, dreaming about France. The house here is lovely but I can give it all up. Take a

few things and go off for a long time. I cannot believe that this is fantasy. I am not answerable to anybody but myself, not for anything. If I had guts I would tell Paula to piss off forever. It is only fear that is stopping me, fear of the unknown, of being alone and of losing contact with the kids. Kick the lot, mate, and free yourself. Do your thing, Leo, you are a dreamer, a romantic. Live it to the full. She opted out and by so doing handed you your freedom on a platter. It is not for you to correct her monumental cock-up.

06 Nov 1992

I don't know where to start. Two days ago it looked like things between Paula and I were at their lowest point ever. I was wildly angry because she had come home and announced that she had decided to remain with Shawn. She said it was too difficult to part from him and what had passed between us the other night had made her decide. I remained calm.

Then followed the most extraordinary series of events. I went upstairs and she went down to the lounge. I felt a fantastic anger and rage welling up inside me. I wanted to destroy everything between us. I went down to tell her what I felt. We went for a series of walks. I told her I would make life impossible. I was absolutely clear, "I want a divorce here and now." I was furious. She pleaded with me not to mess Jessy around now and she would be happy to split in June. She won't leave; I won't leave. I will bring the temple down with me. I just could not rest.

She went to bed and I went up to my room. I wanted to get a bucket of water and throw it over her. I hesitated and then went down to her. I could see she was frightened so I just sat on her bed and then kissed her. She warmed. We really kissed and I could see she wanted me in her bed. We caressed passionately. I wanted her and she wanted me. It was wonderful. There was an energy between us and a barrier was shattered. We lay together for a while, unable to believe what had happened. I went up to my room feeling good and went to sleep.

At about four thirty she came into my room and got into bed with me. We lay together for two hours, talking and touching. A wall had come down. We realized we could reach each other. She said she had had a fixed idea about what sex could be like between us. That seemed to have changed. I just loved being with her and felt very relaxed. I told her about my various relationships and she asked who I would choose. I said Raya. Her fantasy is to combine me and Shawn. It was a rare time, tender and easy. When I left to go to school I kissed her goodbye. I knew she was going to face him.

In the evening she said she had spoken to him and she had not made any decisions. She can't give him up.

I cannot stand idly by. I feel like telling her to go and have her Shawn. Yet the other night, taking the words from someone, I told her we were "fated to be together." It is frightening to think we may be moving inexorably towards union.

It is time for me to take a stand. *You want to "see" Shawn, fine. Then don't expect to have any relationship with me. It's time to choose. If and when you are properly finished with him you can contact me. I am not interested in friendship. It's all or nothing. It starts now. I will do what I feel like. I won't be cleaning tomorrow and I might sleep out tomorrow night.*

08 Nov 1992
I felt ready to die this morning. Then I felt something very powerful inside me—there is only one decision for us: to get together. I have to compose a note to her.

P, my love,
Something very powerful inside me says we have to get together. I have no doubt that this is the only real decision for both of us and we have to go with it, difficult as it might be. We both have to accept that one cannot have it all. Choices have to be made, even agonizing ones. There is no point prolonging the pain.
I am willing to commit myself to our relationship. Come with me.
Yours,
L

I left the note in her room. She saw it and we talked. She is still deeply in love with Shawn and cannot leave him. That is the message; all else is irrelevant. She says she has spoken to Rachel and Jake. They are both very sad. All I can do is give her a clear message and let her decide, which is what I have done. Any bets on the decision?

09 Nov 1992
I have sexual power. Get in touch with it. It's there. I want to blow her apart. I also want to melt into her. I feel tremendous compassion for her. It is terrible to see her suffer so much. My heart aches, almost to the point of saying: "Don't."

10 Nov 1992
My biggest demon is that I am not man enough. I am. Another myth is that some magical quality is required to conduct a relationship. It isn't. It just requires the two people to say each day, "I want to be with you," and go on with their lives.
Getting back to the mechanical metaphor: the car has broken down. Do we repair it or not? Both have to agree to get it done. Possible answers: yes/yes; yes/no; no/no. I don't think it's repairable.

11 Nov 1992
Last night after my bath I felt wonderful. The world was beautiful. I just felt light and easy with myself. I wanted to be on my own, then and in the future. Paula is down in the dumps.
    I don't mind splitting up. It's the rejection I find hard to take. So, do something about it. I am hurt by her detachment and hostility. Why should I be made aware of it by living with her? She cannot touch me or be with me. She is pleading with me about going out. She says, "We should not both be out on the same night. The kids need us."

12 Nov 1992
I woke early because I was cold and lay quietly for about an hour. Then I got the urge to be with Paula. I hesitated and then decided to go. I went down to her, condom in my gown pocket, just in case. She moaned as I came in and again as I got in the bed, so I got up to go. She stopped me. We lay quietly for a while because she did not want me to touch her. I thought I should be more forceful. I wasn't. I kissed her lips, her right nipple and then left.

13 Nov 1992
I feel empowered. I am tense and excited and a bit scared. This morning I decided I know what I want and I am going to go for it—to put the brakes on; to force us to stand still for a while. I have told her what I want. She panicked as this is exactly what she does not want to hear. Once she responds I will have to react.

This all follows from when I let my gut feelings take over. I went to a lecture on "Infidelity" and one of the things that struck me was what the lecturer said about passion being linked to both joy and torment. It suddenly struck me that Paula is using me to inflame her passion for him.

Leo, finally you are in touch with your gut. Stand by your feelings and face the consequences.

17 Nov 1992
I have just about given up on her. I have thrown her the life belt and she does not want to take it. *Ah-so!* In my heart I want her but other factors have come into play, like seeing reality. I have kidded myself all along. I am convinced she can't do it. However, my attitude has changed and I won't tolerate the situation any longer. It has already gone too far. Enough is enough—that is what I feel.

Paula suggested we go for a walk to talk. She said she is prepared to try with me but that it has to be done at her pace. She said she needs some time. "How much?" I asked. "Weeks," she said. In the meantime she wanted to go out with Shawn again. I asked her how this fitted in with our agreement that we won't see other people. She wormed and squirmed. In effect, she does not know where she is.

18 Nov 1992
Last night at the cinema I was prepared to give it all up. Then, when I got home, Paula, who came in a few minutes later, told me she had broken up with Shawn. She had tears in her eyes. She asked me to hold her. I held her briefly, not saying anything. Later I said, "I am here if you need me." She said she didn't. I had a bath and went to sleep. Jesus, am I stuck with this now? I really don't know which way it will go.

BREAKUP

19 Nov 1992
I feel sick to the core. This morning's incident made me realize we are at a dead end. She has got no stomach for getting together, or even doing things together, not now anyway. The look of horror on her face when I suggested going to the seaside said it all; everything about her points to her not wanting to be where she is. More frightening, she says she has broken up with him so she will be in bad shape and will probably blame me for their breakup. Hostility reigns again.

22 Nov 1992
And I wonder what I am still doing with this woman. Are you still hooked, Leo? I tried going down to her this morning but she was not interested so I left. I am not too bothered. We talk every now and then and every now and again she vents her hostility.

23 Nov 1992
I have just come home from my musical instrument-making class and I feel so strong, so sure of myself. I am centred and I know I am okay and will be. It's a nice, mild night so I went for a walk.
  Meanwhile the saga continues: she moans at me for something, I tell her calmly I don't like the way she is relating, she starts her aggro and I blow up. Eyeball to eyeball. Maybe she engineers these scenes to provoke me, I rise to the bait and she says to herself: I told you so, he is impossible. No win.

24 Nov 1992
Is it death throes or signs of new life? Don't know. Just stay at the edge.
Last night we had a fierce argument. This morning when I left with Rachel our eyes met. We kissed on the cheeks.

27 Nov 1992
I had a long bath with lot of voices going through my head. The voice of father is absolutely unequivocal: tell her to get fucked. Then I hear the voice of my other (female) advisors who say I should give it time; pursue her. And my own voice is an echo of theirs.
  I woke early with a strong urge to be with her but didn't go. Later I went down and got into bed with her. She protested a

little. We just lay together and I felt relaxed. I wanted to penetrate her but didn't even try. At six she said she wanted to be alone. I kissed her on her neck, burning with desire, and left feeling good. I have a strong sense that we will get together by next summer, but I could be wrong.

29 Nov 1992
Paula, in the plain light of day it is clear that there is nothing between us, nor do I want there to be anything. There is no mileage in it, not now and not in the foreseeable future.

I went to see *Peter's Friends* last night. One of the characters in the film says, "I can't live with a woman who hates me." Absolutely right.

08 Dec 1992
The whole of last week Paula reeked of Shawn and I smell a rat. She told me she was not seeing him any more and I am mad. I won't have her here. I am thinking of cutting off the electricity. I am shaking with rage but I feel strong.

I have to believe this is the end of the road, it's intolerable. The phone bill arrived and Paula was looking at it. For no obvious reason, she broke into a fury and shouted at me, "I hate you and despise you." It hurt, I was angry but what could I do? Later she apologized by saying that she had not meant to say what she had said. "I didn't even know I was saying it." I said she was making life intolerable.

I am in touch with my anger and I won't be pushed around: *you don't have to like me but right now that means chaos.* I really think she does despise me. AND IT WON'T CHANGE. I should say to her, "I am giving you two hours to get out of this house. I have had you up to the eyeballs. I want to be shot of you. I want an immediate divorce so let's agree on it."

Why do I still feel for a woman who treats me like this? That is what kills me. She spits in my face and I still tolerate her. Where is your pride, your manhood, your self-respect, your dignity? Indeed, I have not been able to generate and sustain real, long-term anger.

BREAKUP

09 Dec 1992
She has asked me not to come down to her room. Maybe she is scared I will harm her. I, for my part, will not give up my room for anything. This morning at about five o'clock I really felt the shock of breakup go through me like a bolt of lightning—the shock of loss and abandonment I experienced as a child. Then I felt easier and now I feel fine.
The common pattern: you want what you have not got.

10 Dec 1992
Kiddos, you are caught in a horrible situation and I cry for you. I am so angry with Paula I feel I won't do anything for her. If she goes away, I'll go away too. I won't cover for her. I will do anything for you but not if she stands to benefit from it; I'll choose what to cover and what not.

I have come to the conclusion that it is over and there is no chance of recovery. I have yet to accept that fully in my heart; it's going to take time, probably till we separate and go our own ways. I am determined not to take this into 1993. Surely we have had our fill.

God, can you be so horrible as to let my mother die *and* let our family break up? Yes.

16 Dec 1992
Paula, Jake and Rachel leave for South Africa today and I am relieved, though I am left with a feeling of anxiety and nervous anticipation at what is to come. Last night I had a wonderful fantasy about starting a relationship with a woman I met recently and hiding it from absolutely everyone.

17 Dec 1992
They must be in South Africa already and I have been thinking a lot about Paula. I want her, plain and simple. I want to lie with her in harmony and joy. I would like to go away for a weekend and spend time together, reading, watching TV, walks and gentle sex; or not so gentle. I throb for her, thinking of that night in November when we reached each other. Can we get there again? She was passionate and I could match her. I've kissed better! Being more sober, it is a well-known phenomenon that people who are splitting up still have sex with one another.

Strangely, I don't feel angry towards her. I am hardly aware of the rage I once bore over the abandonment, the breach of trust, the intense involvement with Shawn, the venom she poured out, etc., etc. We are almost at square one—clean sheet—and I feel for her as lover, as partner. I just do. How can Paula and I decide to separate, it's too painful. We need something to blow us apart. Something already has. Amen.

26 Dec 1992
I have made a little corner for myself, my own space in my bedroom: a shelter to survive the storm. I don't expect that we will have it in us to go through this decently. She is my one enemy in the world. What we have now is just a temporary ceasefire.

27 Dec 1992
I sit here in my corner, having found new peace. Forgive myself everything and give myself unconditional love; nobody else has or will give it to me. Beautiful, nice guy—love it; deceitful, dark shit—love it.

According to Peggy Vaughan in *The Monogamy Myth*, getting back together requires a commitment to honesty. There are two stages: 1) Recovery and 2) Re-building. It takes time but it can be done.

31 Dec 1992
It is the last day of the year and I feel fine. I think our problems are too great to be sorted out. If you give me the slightest hint of crap I'll throw you out of here on your arse. You had better believe it. You can hate me if you want but don't dare to act it out here. Furthermore, I will not move out of this room till we all move out. I am breathing fire right now. Then the anger recedes and I feel calm again.

I look in the mirror and what do I see? A lovely, smiling man. That is you, Leo. Don't let anybody take it away from you. I hear Chris de Burgh singing *Lady in Red* and my thoughts turn to Paula. After all is said and done, I love her.

But maybe we shouldn't try to live together.

01 Jan 1993
New Year's Day.
It is a beautiful day and I got up late after lazing in bed for a while and then went for a walk in the cemetery after a light breakfast. All sorts of ideas are floating around my head. For one, the world is extremely beautiful; for another, it is over with Paula and I feel the fear of post-separation scenarios.

04 Jan 1993
Jessy and I went to fetch them at Victoria Station. They were all smiles and tanned from the South African sun. Paula just about managed to kiss me and an evening of tension filled with her aggression followed. I wasn't expecting much but this is ridiculous. I felt sick; my heart ached for the kids.

The next morning Paula and I talked about this and that while we walked. Then I broached the subject: Where do we go? She says: Don't know—general blank, dead, vacuum. I suggested we need to go forward, either with a therapist or on our own and she sort of agreed, with little enthusiasm. We walked a bit further and she said, "The problem is Shawn. I have to work with him..." I kept calm, unsure what she was getting at. I reminded her of her commitment in November to break with him.

Back home I thought things over. I think it is finished but I will give her a last chance, till the end of the week. She has to do something positive by then. If not, it's over and I will start divorce proceedings.

Leo, couples do break up.

Today she was decidedly more friendly than she has been any time before, so one can discern a gradual thawing. Still, I am not sure what it indicates, though it is certainly healthier. Here am I, looking for crumbs; it's pathetic. At this rate we might even kiss in six months time!

06 Jan 1993
Little incidents mounting up to sustained tension and hostility lead me to think that it is irredeemable. At the same time, this is the cutting edge of our relationship and last time we ran away from each other at this point. Are we going to do the same again?

When she came home from work she suggested we all go out on Saturday to a movie to celebrate Jessy finishing her A-level mock exams. I agreed but I don't feel like going out with her.

08 Jan 1993
I am nervous this morning because Paula told me that the course she is due to attend next weekend lasts two days, whereas I noticed on the receipt she got that it lasts for only one day. Is she genuinely mistaken or is she deceiving me in order to "have a day off"? I doubt she is mistaken. I am suspicious; my antennae are up. But I am smiling because if it turns out that she is "cheating" it will finally be over and I will be free. However, it is all the more curious as she is definitely warmer at the moment. Of course, she could have a whole other life and I would not necessarily know about it.

09 Jan 1993
Today I phoned and checked—the course only lasts one day. And tonight Paula and I are going to the cinema to see *Tout le Matin du Monde*.

10 Jan 1993
This morning I was agitated and wanted to confront her about the course. Before we got to that she said she was "not recovering," whatever that means. When I told her I had found out about the course she was offended. Anyway, she admitted that she was planning to spend the "second day" with Shawn, adding that she had not spent much time with him. I said this was dishonest and devious and I began to get angry. I said to her, "Will you go peacefully or is it going to be war?" She replied, "I am not going." I went downstairs, switched off the electricity to the whole house and locked the kitchen door.

Then followed chaos with the kids; they have to accept that this house will not function while she is here. I also took her handbag and hid it in my room although she thought it was in the kitchen. At one point she came up to my room and pushed me over. I let her. She then tried to lock me in the room but I forced the door open before she could lock it and grabbed her, threatening to throw her down the stairs. I relented.

BREAKUP

We have come nowhere in eighteen months, only this time I am not going to be pushed around (literally). My stand is that our situation is impossible, we cannot continue like this and the relationship is over. I have been scared to admit it and I intend to force her out. I will do whatever it takes by making life impossible for her. It is time to be fierce and utterly ruthless. Catastrophe looms. So be it.

I have got the keys. As I was about to go out of the front door this morning she pleaded for them and tried to stop me leaving. I said, "You do as you want and I'll do as I want." She said: "I am not doing anything I should not be doing." I cannot stop her having a relationship while she is in this house; I can stop her being in this house while she is having it.

I am free. Bloody marvellous.

11 Jan 1993
We are hovering on a knife-edge. Late yesterday afternoon she demanded the keys from me and I refused to give them to her. She grabbed me by the neck and squeezed hard. I restrained her and felt like I could throttle her. She said she is phoning the police. I said I would, and I did. A tall sergeant from West Hampstead police station came round and gave us a lecture. By this time Jake was crying outside, Jessy was on the way to a friend and Rachel watched the whole scene. Terrible. Eventually I opened the door and she took her keys. Anyway, I have made my statement—it's time for separation. And she thinks likewise, only she says it's because I acted like a madman. In other words, she blames me.

Perhaps we had to use this explosion to keep us apart forever as we can't do it rationally. We took a decision in the heat of the moment but it is the right decision. The thought of splitting is quite a relief, the air is a bit clearer. We even started talking about selling the house.

Oh, my kids, I weep for you. I weep. I haven't actually cried for some time. Tears, my old friends. We have wasted all this time and forced the kids to suffer. I also latched on to people who had repaired, thinking we could do the same. Obviously not.

Leo, you are free; you have got a second chance. You can do better; better head, better body, better fuck. I am ready to welcome into my life the woman I really desire. I have to do something about weekends. Who can I see?

Yesterday we hit rock bottom.
I feel hurt, injured, scarred, mauled, damaged and fragile. Just breathe, man.
This is not just a case of dishonesty. She is cheating on me even now. That is not acceptable. She has not been able to sustain any arrangement since 1991. What angers me is that by making this arrangement she effectively killed things off. And what does that say about her feeling for the kids? Essentially it is similar to April '91, when my wife admitted to cheating on me. Then I curled up, now I say: fuck you. Dishonest is the least of it. It was irresponsible, capricious, possibly even highly aggressive and hostile.

12 Jan 1993
I want her out—she upset the cart and has to leave. She does not want me to start divorce proceedings immediately and would prefer to wait until we have sorted certain things out. I feel we should get things moving. She does not want to sell up now and cause disruption for Jessy. I agree, but how do we live together for six months when she has been unable to sustain any of the agreements we have made in the last two years?

As to this last incident, the one thing you don't do in a Trappist monastery is talk. The one thing you don't do when you are trying to repair a delicate situation with your husband is arrange a clandestine meeting with your lover. *What level of irresponsibility are we talking about here, to me and the kids? You have a record of deceit and dishonesty from the start of the affair until now. It is a long catalogue, not a one-off.*

Think for a moment what planning this deceit implies in terms of relating to me. In this one incident we have a microcosm of the whole situation: Paula wants to be with Shawn; she is prepared to do anything that suits her to be with him; she is prepared to shit on me to do so and is prepared to risk a nasty incident and breakdown in doing so, which is what happened. In fact she answered the question I have been asking her: are you in or out? In the meantime Elaine told me that Paula has decided to separate from both Shawn and from me. That is a sensible idea and I am relieved.

13 Jan 1993
Yesterday alone there were three incidents of outright hostility on her part. Today she is playing games with me while pretending to be reasonable. It's screaming at you. There is no way forward in this situation. She has the gall to say she rejects me on the basis of my response to her duplicity. Is she stark raving bonkers? You should be livid, absolutely bristling. Why aren't you? Where is the real anger, where?

This patient is sick. Let's kick him to death. You are right: he's a gonner.

10: Do I Want Her?

14 Jan 1993
The one thing this blow-up has done is push me to find a new therapist. It is some months since I last saw Clive. Max was recommended to me by my good friend Cecil and I have just come back from my first session with him. He is lovely: sharp and just right. He asked why I had come. I said I was in a crisis and went on to tell the story of our relationship.

The key themes he pointed out were:
1. I talk as an outsider, as if all these things are happening to somebody else. Where am I in all this?
2. I have power and strength; I have achieved an enormous amount over this period.
3. Go by my feelings and not by my thoughts. Take them on and own them. Heart, not head.
4. Let go of the past. What's been has been; learn from it.
5. It's okay to be the child. We all want love and affection but the child has to know how to look after himself.
6. Learn to love the child in me.
7. At the moment, do nothing. Be caring and look after myself and don't try to hurt anybody.
8. We'll regard last Sunday as the witches coming in, in Macbeth.

Towards the end he asked me why we shouldn't just be able to live reasonably because we can't part now. I replied that I had not fully accepted the separation. He said I have to stay with that. From my description of the family he felt there must have been a lot of love and affection around. He then asked me what I want. I said, "To stay together, definitely."

Now that I am home I am not so sure. The lesson of this session is that I have to be a bigger player and view myself as such. I have value; I am able and determined. I count. It seems strange to wake up at the age of forty-eight and realize that all this time I have been guided mainly by what I *think* and not by what I *feel*. Get in touch with your feelings, man.

BREAKUP

15 Jan 1993

I woke up at five this morning with one question on my mind: Do I want her? Do I want her lying next to me? The answer: I don't want her as she is. At the same time, neither of us is ready to let go of the family and neither of us is prepared to leave. It's simple: we both want the family and home; we don't want each other. In fact, when Max asked that crucial question about what I want, what flashed through my mind was a picture of a harmonious family, which is what I want. I want Paula for what she represents, not for what she is.

At a time when things between us were at a low ebb Paula fell in love with Shawn. *Finita la commedia.* The rest is history. There is no going back. But it has taken us two years to get to this point. So what? Don't make a disaster out of a crisis. Except for a few hours back in November there has not been a single moment when she even allowed herself to think of me as her man. She is not turned on by me. I see it plainly. Shit.

No more agreements. I have been invited to a singles party and I am excited by the singles scene again. She keeps asking me what I am doing and I am on the verge of feeling I want her to get jealous, but I don't want her back. Take the plunge, boyo. Let go of the sides. I love it here; it's painful but instructive. I have tears in my eyes. And we will separate and I will long for her. Maybe not so much, just maybe. Smile.

17 Jan 1993

This morning I acted on impulse, overcame my fear of rejection and played her Chris de Burgh's *Lady in Red*, a reminder of her in a red dress. I asked her if she got the message. "What message?" she asked. I said, "How much I care for you." She did not respond so I got up and left.

Later she suggested we should cancel the people who were due to come and see the house. What she said was, "We are not ready and Jessy is uneasy about the sale." I hesitated but agreed. Then she got all hostile about arrangements and started moaning about how much I go out and neglect the kids. I went for a walk with Rachel and then took Jake to Chinatown and the Jubilee Line exhibition.

I have seen softness in Paula's eyes before but now there is none at all. Her eyes look vacant. She will never drop her hostility towards me while we are together and perhaps even after. It's endemic, chronic. And I feel stupid for having played her the song this morning, though it was done with strength and honesty. I am not scared.

18 Jan 1993
I was distinctly aware that I was hardly perturbed by the thought of her being with Shawn last night (if she was). That is a change. It was almost a feeling of letting him have her, surrendering her. I am finished with her. Not entirely, but for now it is no big deal. Every day I seem to come back from death and life starts afresh, my energy starts flowing. I genuinely felt I could give up on her. I want it to work but if she chooses not to, so be it. I'll be fine. The trouble is we face the prospect of being under the same roof for some time.

19 Jan 1993
She is like a tank on the loose. Run for cover, boyo. She is totally crazy, just rampant.
   This is an explosive situation, worse than it has ever been because now I am angry and there are no restraining factors. She had outbursts yesterday and today, both unjustified and both expressions of anger and a disproportionate response to a situation—defiance, confusion and probably pain and grief too. On Sunday last when we spoke about openness and honesty I cared for her. Now I feel hostile and enraged. Maybe if I smashed her face in she would have some respect.
   Anger: how to get in touch with it, how to express it and how to control it. This is my anger here, these words.

20 Jan 1993
It's the same battle being fought out every day. She is trying to portray me as being irresponsible on the kids issue, when my whole thrust has been that we have to settle things largely for the sake of the kids; that we can't all be so insecure and that we have to stop bickering. When we split up in 1991 I was hurt to the core but I supported her fully on the kids. If I see sense and integrity I

can respond but in the face of deceit and dishonesty, at this stage, I have to put my foot down.

Let's not forget that initially I did not go crazy on Bloody Sunday. My first reaction was to say, let's talk. She went crazy and attacked me three times. After that I reacted.

It seems we have stepped back from the brink. We were nearly there.

21 Jan 1993
I had a session with Max today.
We spoke mainly about whether I want Paula or not. What are my feelings? It's all confused: I can't stand her but I desire her. There is something holding us together. He asked, "She is hurting you by continuing her relationship with Shawn. In what way are you hurting her?" I could not come up with an answer. He suggested that it's my anger. I am giving her a mixed message. I need to make clear to her who I am, what I feel and want.

The situation has to be resolved for everyone's sake. We cannot go on hurting each other. The relationship is parabolic, going up and down, with no meeting point. We need to talk, stabilize and resolve. At one point I said, "I want her to be 'how she is with Shawn'." He said, "That is fantasy." I have to drop that. I have to put things in such a way that she can make a rational decision. There has to be negotiation and compromise. I need to ask her where she stands, not whether she is in or out. Whatever happens we have to resolve things. We cannot go on inflicting so much pain on one another.

Paula and I have spoken, sitting at the kitchen table. I was very emotional; she seemed calmer. I told her that I love her and that I desire her, that I want it to work with her. Her response was considered and low-key. She basically said what she has been saying for some time: she is torn. She is emotionally involved with Shawn and she wants her family whole and full-time. She is not attracted to me. She says her hostility is a front, a defense. From what? From getting too close to me? She says I do not hurt her; she is just hostile and she does not like it in herself.

She asked, "Why should I give up a loving, meaningful relationship for one that is not that?" I replied, "Why have you not left, then?" She sort of implied that it was because of Jessy. She admitted that we were both still holding on—we can't face loss. She said that when we were married she was unhappy and now she is pained. She does not know if she is better off or not.

We spoke about sex. She said she needed a passionate relationship and it didn't seem we could have that. I said, "You don't know as we have never really allowed ourselves to be passionate." And I mentioned November 5, last year. She said she had thought about that and went on to say she had been prepared to open up then.

We talked for about forty minutes and afterwards we hugged briefly. I think I made her confront things. Her overall response was far less certain than I anticipated. She wants it all. I laid my cards on the table and nothing she said surprised me. My gut says I am in with a chance and we might move towards some sort of resolution. Let's wait and see. I am astounded that she has made absolutely no progress on the central issue for her: she cannot give up on Shawn and she cannot give up her family. The rack.

Right now Jake and Rachel are acting out what we went through last Sunday. They had an argument and he wants her out of his/their room. I pointed out to them that they are doing what we did.

Paula and I are precisely where we have been all along, though now it is clear to me that she is the one who is suffering. To me, it doesn't feel like such a big step for her to give up on the family (as it was), share the kids with me and live with Shawn. Yet, she cannot. Why?

11:45 p.m., after my bath.
Something has shifted in me. She cannot continue with this balancing act at my expense, wanting the best of all worlds. It is too destructive and it's intolerable. It has to end here and now. I have to say: You cannot live here and have a relationship with Shawn.

22 Jan 1993
This has been a really interesting morning. I came home, read the paper and then, on my way up to my room, decided to snoop. I found a piece of A4 paper folded in the back pocket of Paula's jeans—the worksheet from her Saturday workshop at the WPF.

She had written on two sides of the paper. On one, a list of attributes, other people, future hopes, etc. Shawn is top of the other people list, above the kids; I do not feature. Under future hopes she has listed: 1) relationship with children remains intact, 2) relationship with Shawn is not pulled under by the separation, 3) manage to maintain a relationship with Leo.

The other side of the sheet deals in more detail with the points on the first side. The question must have been: What would you feel if you were to give up those things? Interestingly, on Shawn her initial response was, "I am not sure." Then she says, "Sense of terrible loss." On her relationship with me she says, "Very difficult; wish he would vanish into thin air."

All this was written on 16 January 1993! Leo, to say she is not interested in you is an understatement of gigantic proportions. The thrust of what she is doing is taking a break from her living arrangement with Shawn to be with the kids for a while. She hopes it won't destroy their relationship and believes he will wait for her. Or, can all this be interpreted just like you would interpret a page of mine that said: Fat and ugly. Who wants it?

Despite it all, or perhaps because of it, I feel powerful and energized. It's not that I can necessarily achieve what I want; it's just that I have a strong sense of who I am and what I want. I cannot go along with this torrid setup. She is in a neurotic malaise and is dragging all of us with her. It's not on.

24 Jan 1993
I sense we are heading for a complete breakdown. She is acting like a stern matron, a headmistress, unable to relate to me. We went for a walk to Shaw's Corner with friends. On the walk I asked her whether she could handle a situation where she was living with Shawn and we shared the kids. She said she couldn't accept that yet. I am beginning to think that she will never be able to decide one way or another. Maybe she wants me to make the decision. Would changing our living arrangement improve things, say if we eat at different times and each had time with the kids?

25 Jan 1993
I woke up this morning at about six, feeling like death. I felt nothing for anybody in the whole wide world, so I lay there let-

ting the pain go through me. It was bad. Loss, emptiness, grief; there is no hope. Yesterday she said she does not think we should divorce now. We should separate first. What does that mean? After all, we have already had a trial separation.

I need to speak to Max about what to do next. Having decided it is over is not enough. I need some sort of bolster to reinforce my conviction. Maybe the best way is to go out and get somebody else. That will seal things.

26 Jan 1993
I want to stay in this house. I am happy here and the kids are happy. When I am ready to move we will sell. That clear thought suddenly surfaced last night as I lay on my bed for a long time without any definite ideas. It felt right and still does.

This morning when I left I wanted to kiss her goodbye, partly out of warmth and partly because I feel her slipping away. She offered her cheek, so I did the same and then withdrew and smiled. She smiled too. Just old friends. We are both scared to get to a place of peace because it means recognizing the end of the marriage and it is too painful. At least I am at peace with myself.

At some level I can see that this breakup was inevitable because we did not address our problems at all. We just expressed our anger in different ways and are still doing so. Divorce is marriage by another name.

27 Jan 1993
That it's over I can deal with; that it's acrimonious and unpleasant I find difficult to handle. I can't seem to find the right line between simply accepting and standing up for myself. This is the issue at the moment. I have not found the right level of anger. I am either raving mad or placid. There is no cold, hard anger, the so-called masculine type. Perhaps we should see Max together!

I hesitate because I am scared he'll say: It is as clear as daylight that there is nothing left between you. So, why don't I come to that conclusion myself? I have pretty well done so. I am prepared to let it die though I still think something might arise from the ashes.

BREAKUP

I saw Max today.
The message is simple: cool it; get my own life going and let her go her way. Let her say and do what she wants; she is not my affair. She knows where I stand and there is nothing to say until she wants to talk seriously. She can say anything and be hostile. For me it should be like water off a duck's back. The way I have been reacting is a childhood pattern, trying to prove to my father that I am better than he thinks I am. Her aggression is, in fact, a defense against feeling close to me. She is protecting herself as she is afraid of that and I have to break the pattern.

28 Jan 1993
I feel fantastic. I have not felt like this for a long time; there is an inner peace and appreciation of myself. It has to do with the greater ease with Paula following the session with Max yesterday, as well as with the fantasy of going away with Janice, whom I am due to meet. I am buzzing and confident. *You are losing out if you don't want me, Paula.*
Last night in bed I opened a book for the first time in about a month. It was a wonderful feeling, just reading a few pages.

Later.
I am shaking with fear, having just seen *A Few Good Men*; not a film I would like to have seen with Paula. I am scared to admit my lack of feeling for her, the hostility and the awareness of the chasm between us. Right now I feel it is unbridgeable and I don't even want to try to bridge it. The fear arises because admitting this means admitting the end of the family, and that it is over between us. We have reached the point of no return.

31 Jan 1993
Paula is all bark and no bite: a lot of bombast but no substance. I can feel myself letting go and being in bed with Charli this morning gave me the feeling of the other world, a bit of freedom. Also, on Friday night I managed to call up my ideal lover. It was absolutely beautiful—she was everything to me and I to her. I have never been able to evoke such a strong image before.

02 Feb 1993
I am having strong fantasies of up and out, of being elsewhere, living a different lifestyle with a good enough woman and even of having more children. I have this image of a workshop and a tranquil life.

Is the truth that we love each other or is it that I am holding on to her, that it is all one way? She tries to deny that November 5 was a landmark but she cannot. I feel there is something powerful there though it has looked flimsy of late. Am I living in Cloud-Cuckoo-Land? I realize something interesting about November 5: my passion was greater than hers. She reached her limit; her fire was weaker than mine. I am not sure what that indicates, because she was not holding back intentionally.

03 Feb 1993
Last night Paula was out. I had made a nice dinner for the four of us and later Jake and Rachel came up to my room but I felt down, angry, vengeful and embittered. This morning it is almost forgotten. I am reading about erotic passion. It's me, I am the wild horse.

04 Feb 1993
I saw Max yesterday.
According to him it is a confused scene: what I want; what she wants. We need to get it sorted out. I have arranged to see him together with Paula on Monday next, February 8.

Max says we need decisions, which we can always change later. At one point he said, "It is over; she is a boarder. That's it. *Fartik.* You have to get on with your life." He asked how I can love a woman who shows no care for me, who won't even let me do what I need to do—pottery. He wanted to know if sex was all that was keeping us apart. I said: essentially, yes.

We spoke about a Sackville-West situation, of each of us having outside lovers, but I don't think it can work. We really do need to resolve it. My life has been on hold for long enough. Says Max, "Your real gesture of love to Paula is to let her go and to give her your blessings."

I have the feeling that Paula will want to separate and I'll have to agree. In fact, I will be disappointed if she does not want to because I have the possibility of having myself a good time. Tracy has suggested we go to Scotland together.

Maybe Paula and I will separate now and get together in the future.

06 Feb 1993
Today I realized it is over. The old life is ending; new life is beginning. It is made up of many strands. I am allowing myself to reject her, at last. It's a dark, dark time for us.

07 Feb 1993
Yesterday afternoon I went for a walk with Tracy from Green Park through Kings Road to Chelsea Harbour. Just being with her and talking to her made me realize that I am getting to a point of acceptance with Paula. There is another life and I can have a good time. You have a second chance, boyo, take it.

08 Feb 1993
We have been to Max together.
She was dead, absolutely dead—dead to me and dead to the world. I think she was scared to be honest for fear of saying something she might regret or that would make it impossible for us to continue living under one roof. Even if she didn't say it she expressed it through every pore. She did say she was very angry. She knows not why. I fear the worst.

She said she feels independent, which I respect. Trouble is she is so fiercely independent that she cannot compromise on anything and living together requires a compromise. "Adolescent" is the best way to describe her behaviour. I said I wanted to move away from the adversarial mode and I don't want to continue the pattern of unilateral decisions. Max remarked that I wanted too much finiteness. I need to be flexible, especially now.

Now for some truth. As I sat next to her on the couch at Max's I looked at her and asked myself: Am I really interested in this woman? She is dead to me and has nothing to say. You know what, she might even think of coming back again. That is the danger for me. We need to divorce to put an end to it. There is

no life left in the body. Fighting with her is holding on; not talking to her is holding on; staying in the house is holding on, too. I feel incredible anger. She is dead to me. I don't want to have anything to do with her. It has gone too far already. Mourn and move on.
    I am on my own. Ultimately, we all are.

09 Feb 1993
I want to lash out and hurt her, make her yelp.
    Stop. Recognize an end and accept it. Clive told me and I did not listen. I had to examine the wreckage again. Now I am satisfied there is no life. Something that Sylvie said about getting back together has just passed through my mind: There is a brief moment when it is possible. It cannot happen before or after. That moment came for us in November and it didn't happen. I tried my best and she was not able to try, not able to let go of Shawn. Now it is too late.

11 Feb 1993
I now definitely see that things were over in June 1991 and what has gone on since then as simply death spasms, induced by the inability of either of us to let go and the forlorn hope that it might mend again. I am mad at the tarot ladies for leading me on. Had it not been for them I would have given up a year and a half ago. How could I have been taken in by them?

17 Feb 1993
After the session with Max.
A few things are clear:
1. It's over. He does not see how I could even have wanted it not to be.
2. We have to find a way of living, for all our sakes, particularly mine.
3. Stop dreaming. I cannot go to Hermanus (South Africa) or even France. I have to be here for six to eight years. This is not the time to leave the kids.
4. I need to get sorted out with Paula and to decide how and where I will live.
5. I need to start finding myself and expressing my creativity.

BREAKUP

6. We should start exploring what happened in our relationship and learn from it. I need to look at myself, which will be hard.

I said I cannot stand the thought of being a lone, divorced man. He said it does not have to be that way. I am attractive, sensitive and intelligent, so I should have no trouble having multiple affairs or finding someone permanent if I want to. He said he did not detect hate in Paula. Anger and irritation, yes.

It's all simple, and bloody hard.

19 Feb 1993

It's quite late but Jake and Rachel are in my room with me. We are listening to Capital Gold radio. Paula just phoned from Paris (she is there with her cousin) to speak to the kids, as usual. I could not bring myself to ask what they have been doing.

I have replied to about sixteen ads in the *Guardian* and *New Moon*. I wonder how many replies I'll get. If it does not work I will put in an ad. It is hard work but the prospect is exciting. I am gradually leaving her.

21 Feb 1993

I have been reading *Creative Divorce: A New Opportunity for Growth* by Mel Krantzler. We all have these feelings of hanging on and hoping all will be restored. It won't, it can't. Not in our case.

Last night Rachel came to sleep in my bed and Jake was up at two thirty, crying. He said "everything" was worrying him. Unsure of myself, I comforted him. It is wonderful not having Paula around. Charli, who is divorced, said to me that this is what it will be like once we have separated and I have the kids on weekends.

25 Feb 1993

Yesterday morning Paula was in a state, partly because Jessy was unhappy as well as a few other things. Suddenly she wants to talk. She is now blaming Max. The woman is crazy, desperate. My feeling is that I want to file for divorce and keep on the house.

She said she realized how destructive the meeting with Max had been. "He's unprofessional," she said, blaming him for I don't know what. I kept quiet. Later, on the way home from Jessy's report meeting, she blamed me for Bloody Sunday. I lashed out at her, verbally. Anyway, we are talking about talking. We have decided to meet on Saturday from four till six.

27 Feb 1993
Saturday.
There was talk of talking but it now looks as if it won't happen. Paula has just walked in to say that she has arranged to go out at four forty-five. Fuck her. I won't be treated like this. No consultation, nothing. I see it all collapsing around me and I am unable to do anything about it. It feels like the end of a civilization. This is the destructive phase *par excellence*. The heat is on. I feel like letting rip but I won't. The same tendency has allowed her to go on dismissing me: the original infidelity, the dishonesty, the duplicity, the clandestine arrangement in January. She is a self-centred, neurotic princess.

More to the point, I have got two replies to my sixteen letters and I am due to meet Kathy next Thursday.

01 Mar 1993
I feel peculiarly okay. Something has freed up in me. My mother is dead; my wife is dead to me. Amen. The world feels like a wonderful place.

Maybe I need to signal the end and not wait for her. I have been putting it onto her, just accepting her decisions. It's getting closer. Take the plunge, Leo. Buy yourself a ticket.

Oh, Leo, hard time. Paula has just "gone out". Shawn is back from the States and she is full of fuck and smells of his place in Kempe Road. What can I do? I want to do something drastic but don't. And yesterday she was on the verge of breakdown; such pain and agony over the kids. She called it Day 1—a fresh start. She was all apologetic about breaking our arrangement to talk on Saturday and wanted to talk immediately, to "Save things before they go down the sewer," in her words. She also said that the basis for functioning now has to be that we are not going to get together. That sent a shiver through me, although I agree.

She came across as a woman in real trouble, crying out for help. "Let's talk and make things better for the kids," she said. I am saying let's talk first and then move on to the kids; she is saying the reverse.

BREAKUP

She wants me to ease her way and I don't feel like complying any longer. She can have her relationship but not in my face.

Leo, stop. The truth is you don't really want her. You want a monkey and she is a buffalo, a wounded one at that.

Four women have contacted me so far and I am due to meet all of them over the next week or so. It's not the end yet; it's just starting. You can do a thousand times better. AND YOU WILL.

02 Mar 1993
I have been behaving like an abandoned child. Stop. I am a fully-fledged, powerful, resourceful, determined adult. I am a grown man. Grant myself the power to be that and stop acting like the hurt child. It's hard because I see her wobbly bum and I melt. If only I did not have to face it so much.

I came home, had a lovely shower, accompanied by strong fantasies of Nadine, from whom I have had a tantalizing reply, inviting me to stay over in Cambridge. Then Paula returned unexpectedly and spoiled it all. She went to rest, preparing for being "out" tonight. It makes me sick. There I was in seventh heaven with Nadine and she comes home. How do I get rid of her?

04 Mar 1993
The message I got from Max yesterday was that I am depressed and sad. I see no future for myself and I have no centre. Mind you, he was more positive. He said I have to start finding it—work, lifestyle, relationship. Find my centre and the rest will follow, wherever I am. This is the opportunity.

If I want to win the pools, at least take a ticket. I have to start getting a ticket for myself. As to the relationship with Paula, it is at an end. There is no reason to think differently, except for the witches.

Acceptance for me comes in very small increments. That's fine, because trying to kick it in one go is useless, as she did. We have to get on and work towards a reconciliation and being there for the kids. Max told me about his daughter, who insists on having her ex- around for a meal once a week.

The session was a vision of acceptance, of loving and caring after the breakup. Also, I have to stop looking at them. It's their business/problem/affair. Let them be. Look at my own ship. I am a romantic, an idealist. It's a strength. Why try to live with a woman who does not want that. In the meantime I have to forget the beautiful workshop in the country, a fire and dogs and come down to earth.

08 Mar 1993
Nadine, Nadine, Nadine. All I can think of is you. You are different, other, exotic, attractive, sexy, bright and interesting. Your smile, your poise, your walk. God. A French (lapsed) Catholic, thirty-four, lecturer in Economics at Cambridge and there seems to be something between us. It's incredible.

I went up to Cambridge on Saturday, not knowing what to expect. Nadine had arranged to pick me up at the station. She arrived a bit late, in her left-hand-drive red Renault 5. She had sunglasses on, black tights and a black top. She has a good body and an angular face. I kissed her on the cheek; quite relaxed but excited. She apologized for coming late and then we tried to decide what to do. She said she was not a good driver but she did well.

In the end we decided to go to a pub in the country. We sat in the sun-room and she wanted to tell me her story. I was riveted by her; her bearing, her eyes and her sharpness. I listened intently and asked some questions. We kept strong eye contact, which she remarked on later. I told her my story, in complete honesty. The lunch was good and included and bit of beer. She loves food, Middle Eastern food; she has an appetite! Me too.

She is so French and she does not like England or the English. Part of her reason for contacting me was because I am not English. She had noticed the paper I wrote to her on and the fact that I had used a fountain pen.

We drove back to Cambridge and walked around the colleges. There was a faint touch of spring in the air. We walked along the river, over bridges and into a gallery. At one point I said I had fantasies of staying the night. She said, "Oh! Did you now." Maybe it will happen. We walked around for a while and then went to a cafe for tea, chatting all the time. I could not keep my eyes off her. She just smiled at me. It's her elegance I like, her youth and vibrancy.

She took me back to the station. First I kissed her on her cheeks and then on the lips. On the way I asked her what she felt.

She said she does not need to say anything, it's understood. But she did say she wanted to see me again and she gave me her address in France, on holiday. Ever so gentle; ever so lovely; fragrant and sensual. I got on the train and thought of her the whole way back to Kings Cross, feeling at ease with the world.

At home I was content to do nothing. I lay on my bed thinking about her. I think Paula went out for while. I wasn't bothered. Progress. The kids came up and we listened to music. Value yourself, Leo. You are a fantastic fox.

12 Mar 1993

My anger has abated, probably due to the fact that Paula is away in Barcelona. She left me a note before she left to say she is sorry we had not talked. She also said she had spoken to Max and he thinks we should go there together again.

To revue my session with Max.
We spoke about Nadine. I told him I am interested, that she is attractive and interesting. It's what I need, confirmation of me as a person, more particularly, as a sexual person. After all, Paula has dealt my confidence a heavy blow. Be adult about it; pursue it and keep in touch. There is no need for me to define what I want or what I am "capable" of. Go with it and see what happens. If she is interested that is good enough. Maybe I expect too much from people, like these women I am meeting.

At the end he asked how Paula could simply impose her affair on me. "You don't just have an affair as she did, not after twenty years of marriage and three kids." Right on.

The question is, Leo: Do you want to get together with Paula? It's now on the cards that she will approach you. No. I want the new, the different.

13 Mar 1993
Hill Garden.
It's a beautiful, spring-like day. I am missing Nadine and I want her to phone. I have not felt this way about anybody else. I realize it is over with Paula, who phoned from Barcelona and spoke in a cheerful voice. I was short and polite. How can I still want her?

11: An Unexpected Turn of Events

16 Mar 1993

Well, well. It has all turned round again. What an unexpected turn of events. I had friends around last Sunday when a person called Sheila called for Paula, who was still in Barcelona. I asked if I could take a message. She told me that L.Z., Paula's therapist, had died suddenly.

Rachel and I went for a walk at about six. It was a lovely evening and we saw Venus shining brightly. I made dinner for us and we watched a bit of TV. Paula came back at about nine thirty, looking full in her long, red coat. I let her settle down and speak to the kids but I did not want to leave it too late till I told her the news.

She was in the kitchen making hot chocolate for the kids when I said, "You need to steady yourself." She replied aggressively, "What for?" I said, "I am going to give you some sad news—L.Z. died last night." She was shocked. I went up to her to say I am sorry. She blurted out, "Get away from me. Don't touch me." I could see she was devastated and I went to sit in the lounge. A short time later she came in and apologized and broke down briefly on my shoulder.

Yesterday morning she looked terrible and I asked her if there was anything I could do for her. She said, "No," gruffly. At dinner we had a small tiff but she offered me food in a way that she had not done for ages. It felt normal, almost friendly. I even detected a change in her voice.

This morning she said something about going to Max together. I said I was not keen. She said, "Then can we talk now." I agreed, seeing that she was distressed. She is falling apart, she said, and feeling suicidal, etc. I tried to calm her. She also said she "can't live like this." I have heard that one before. I said, "It's your choice; you want to." She answered, "I don't know what I want."

Her whole world has collapsed. She is astounded at the intensity of her feelings. I said it is probably similar to what I felt when she first told me about her relationship with Shawn. At one point I said, "You have driven a coach and horses through our relationship and marriage for two years and now you want to speak! Now you realize there is a cost involved in splitting up." Later, in the kitchen, our eyes met and we held briefly.

 Be careful, Leo. This is the same pattern, only more intense. Another crisis and she reverts to family; she looks for cover. Don't get sucked in again. The family is lost anyway and you have got better things on the agenda.

17 Mar 1993
She is talking like a human being and asking where I'm going! However, it may be easier to walk away. Slowly, slowly I part. Leo, don't pick up that stone again. Who do I want in the shower with me? Nadine.

 Splitting is like trying to break free from a plaster cast. Every move is painful and requires effort and drive.

18 Mar 1993
There is a whiff in the air of getting together. She even suggested that we take the kids to Wagamama's for lunch on Saturday and we spoke a bit about *Pesach*. I am apathetic.

I went to see Max yesterday.
After briefing him on what has happened recently he declared that Paula is in crisis and I am the one constant in her life. Consequently, I have to be caring and loving. I have been. He thinks that even before the crisis she had not made a final decision yet. He felt that I had now more or less decided it was off for me, that I didn't want to continue. I said I am moving that way but am not fully there yet and I am scared I will get sucked in again. I succumb to her pressure because I am not sufficiently sure of myself, I'm ambivalent.

 We spoke about the notion of comfort versus reality. What is "comfortable" is the status quo, the devil I know. But what do I really want? I replied that I will be fine either way, staying with Paula or going out on my own. Actually I am not sure I can be fine with her. She weighs too heavily on me and cramps my style.

 Max thinks there is a possibility the crisis will bring us back together. But I have to know what I want. That is crucial.

Every six months she has turned around and said, "I don't know what I want; I can't go on like this." Is it different this time? I am not convinced it is, so I am not even seriously considering it. And I am fantasizing about Nadine, who is in France. I tried phoning her but she was not in and she called back when I was out.

21 Mar 1993
This morning I took Paula tea in bed.
Since our walk yesterday, my thoughts have turned to lying with her again. Take extreme care, Leo. She suggested going for a walk and at about two o'clock we went up to the Heath. She was very glum, "sad," she said. "What have I got?" Is she saying she has nothing with Shawn? "Isn't separation our only option?" I asked. She replied, "Maybe not." I was saying we need to separate but she said we cannot make any decisions. Obviously she does not want to separate.
Should I take the initiative and say I cannot go on or should I wait and see? What is in my heart? The soft option: mending. Yes, but this time I am skeptical. Anyhow, the sum of it all is that I am a bit drawn to her and she is behaving decently and wants to talk more, perhaps with a therapist.

22 Mar 1993
You know what, Paula and I cannot make up. I cannot trust her. She has fucked me over twice and she will do it again. Walk away. For god's sake, walk away. I am not going to pursue her. If she wants me, let her say so. I have shown her I am open. Time is getting short.
For where I am now and what I want, separation is much better.

25 Mar 1993
I feel sick, and why shouldn't I? It's Rachel's birthday and there is a void. Paula says she is mourning; I should wait for her! I speak of divorce and phoning the lawyer. Divorce is the only choice. All that is stopping me is the tarot lady. I have decided: Tomorrow I'll phone the lawyer. Sad, but this is it. I have been doing somersaults for two years. Enough. There is nothing on the table. In the absence of anything substantial from her, I say divorce.

26 Mar 1993

The word "divorce" is ringing in my ears. I am uncertain, sad and angry but the time has come. I still cannot firmly answer the question: Do you want a relationship with this woman? However, I have been wavering for months, nay years, and we need to put an end to it. This "marriage" cannot continue.

Yesterday, however, was strange because we did "get on" in making the party for Rachel. She was almost normal and we smiled at one another. Leo, so you want this woman as she is now? NO. That is all you have to go on. The rest is fantasy. Why not just separate? Because we need the bureaucratic procedures; her conduct within the marriage is unacceptable.

At 1:05 p.m. today I made an appointment to see the divorce lawyer, for next Tuesday at 4:00 p.m.

27 Mar 1993

I phoned Harry in Israel last night. We had a wonderful conversation, talking with ease and joking about love, cricket, height and sandwiches. He is getting married on May 28 and they want me to come to the wedding. I want to go. I will, so help me. I played a few notes to him on my recently-made lyre. Maybe I'll play some to Nadine, too. I was so excited, so full of warmth and love, a rare feeling.

Yesterday I had a little scene with Paula about whether to turn right or left when starting our walk. I did not struggle with her; I don't have to struggle with her. I left her and went on a bike ride instead. If we can't go for a walk together that says something. Let it die, or, rather, recognize it is dead. Anyway, something else comes to mind. As we were leaving the house to go on the ill-fated walk I looked at her and said to myself, "I don't really want this woman."

28 Mar 1993

We did manage to go for a walk today. We talked a bit about mutual friends. Then there was silence. We were on Sandy Path. I told her I had made an appointment to see the lawyer. She asked what I was going to discuss. I told her I was going to file for divorce. She asked, "On what grounds?" I said that was what I was going to discuss. She responded, "Do you think it will go uncontested?" And she went home. I walked on to the Hill Garden. Since then she has avoided me. I don't feel easy but I feel better for it. I am acting, not being acted upon. Need I remind myself that she told me in June '91 that she wanted a divorce?

It's like walking out of concrete.

30 Mar 1993
There is anxiety and there is also relief at a sign of movement, like a trickle of water as a sign that the dam is about to burst. With the sadness and doubt also comes a feeling of having taken action and initiative. I feel slightly empowered. In the meantime I have all these women interested in me. What do I do?

Letter to P, which I left on her bed:

Dear P,
As we have not spoken...

In September 1972 we got married because we wanted to live together and intended raising a family. Now, in March 1993, in recognition of the fact that the marriage has ended and your continuing relationship with Shawn, I feel we need to get divorced in order to dissolve the marriage formally. I have contacted my lawyer and she will be writing to you shortly.

I have taken this step after serious deliberation and in the clear absence of any indication from you that you feel differently. I have given all I can in an attempt to heal things between us and until we met at Max's on February 8 I though it possible. I realized then there was absolutely no interest on your part either to mend our relationship or to restore the marriage, and so I was left with no choice. Furthermore, nothing has happened since then to alter my opinion.

I appreciate it is a difficult time for you but I want to start the process so that this state of limbo we are all in does not drag on unnecessarily.

I await your response.
Yours,
Leo

BREAKUP

Affair is her prerogative; divorce is mine. I feel a bit empowered. Take comfort, it was better with Charli last night than it ever was with Paula. Simple truth.

31 Mar 1993
Paula has received a letter from my lawyer. She said to me, "You can't file for divorce on grounds of adultery. You have committed adultery, too." She said she did not want to have her name blackened. She wants to separate. "Divorce is final," she says and claims I presented her with a *fait accompli* by saying I had arranged to see the lawyer. This time round I am more solid and she is much less sure of herself. I have to make her realize that it does not have to upset anything. It should all go quite smoothly if she wants it to.

01 Apr 1993
After yesterday's session with Max.
1. I am in a position of power; I am going for what I want; I can afford to be generous emotionally.
2. Deflect the onslaught, tai chi-style. Don't confront and never get into violence.
3. Don't take to heart what she says; let it wash over me.
4. I can approach her and say: "I did not want this."

And I think…be nice, caring and generous, but what about my anger, rage and disappointment? Where does all that go? I have been badly hurt, so I cannot simply let go of all that and say, "Let's make the most of things." Will we step back from the brink? I don't think so.

Nadine phoned last night, unexpectedly. Just to hear her voice. Man. We will meet on Wednesday. The world feels different again. I dread the thought of Paula coming to me and saying she can't go through with it. She looks terrible, on the verge of tears.

04 Apr 1993
I like being "single." I want my freedom.

The one clear fact is that Paula has initiated two walks/talks in as many days, something she has never done before. Suddenly she really wants to talk. I have entered a process of diminishing desire for her, not the opposite, though the erotic response is still there. I am prepared to go to therapy and say there what I have to say. As far as she is concerned the reasons for walking out of the marriage still remain, however, in reality she is now seeing it a bit differently. But that is her problem.

She is in a sorry state; she is running scared. At the moment she is "out," probably with Shawn, but I doubt if they are having a good time. The good times might be over for them. I feel fine, relaxed and confident. She realizes time is up; she is panicking and pleading, turning every which way. I feel sorry for her. I am also aware of what she tried to do to me for two years and that she would squeeze me tomorrow if she could. The balance has changed; I am holding the cards now.

I cannot recall all that has passed between us recently. The gist of it is that she wants to "talk," to go to therapy together "to explore." She also begged me to stop divorce proceedings "for Jessy's sake" and threatened to blackmail me if I didn't.

Yesterday, shortly after we set out on the walk she wanted to get straight to the point. She feels she still has a choice. Her expression was, "I don't know if I can go through with this." I asked her about her relationship with Shawn. She said it was okay but she was not sure if she could give up the family for it. She also feels she would have to give up her job if she ended her relationship with him.

For now I'll let the divorce procedure stand. It sort of balances things out—her relationship with Shawn is like a sword of Damocles hanging over our relationship; I have the lawyer's letter.

Maggie used the phrase "cosmic betrayal" to sum up Paula's feelings. Spot on. She has a fundamental sense of having been betrayed by the world, poor kid. So what does she do? She imposes a massive betrayal on me—getting her own back on her father (who died before she was born) by betraying her husband.

The bottom line is that I feel powerful because I don't need her anymore. Today she told me she was angry because I do my own thing. I replied that a comment like that is outside the brief of our present relationship. "It belongs to the relationship you walked out of," I said. She shut up. The boot is on the other foot now.

11:10 p.m.

Paula has just returned. I am off to see Charli.

07 Apr 1993
I had a session with Max today.
He asked me if there was anything Paula could do now to make me change my mind on the trust issue. I said: No. "No trust, no relationship," was his reply. And he added that I cannot fall in love now. It will take time.

16 Apr 1993
Having doubts is not sufficient reason for trying to get together. It needs to be more than that. Paula is up in arms about my going to Israel later this month. I don't like her whole tone and, in any case, I intend going.

20 Apr 1993
It's two years since she admitted being involved with Shawn. I think we are heading for divorce though I am not sure. My heart still says "mend"; my head says "no way."

On Sunday morning first thing she came into the kitchen and sat on my knee. I held her warmly and she responded. She says she needs time to "find herself." I don't believe it. I told her plainly she cannot both hold on to her anger and want to talk. At one point, on a walk, she blamed me for her life being a mess. She claims that had I taken on more of the domestic burden we could have had a good life, or something to that effect. Bullshit.

25 Apr 1993
Shawn phoned for her this morning as I was about to leave the house. I was mad. I don't want her affair flaunted under my nose. Why should I tolerate it? I shouldn't. Get out. I don't like it; I won't have it. End of story. I don't need this turmoil. She talks of going to see another therapist couple but we don't need therapy now. We need separation counselling.

28 Apr 1993
Nadine has suggested I spend the night. I feel better already. Jesus, a woman open to me, who turns me on. A certain sense of wellbeing has returned.

29 Apr 1993
Session.
All that happened in the session with Max yesterday is that he tried to pressurize me into making a decision, for my own sake, self-esteem and well-being. The decision has to be an expression of me, what I want. It has nothing to do with what Paula seems like or what I anticipate her response will be.

In fact, I have three alternatives:
a. Decide I want to keep the marriage and commit myself to that end.
b. Decide I recognize the end of the marriage and work towards separation.
c. Go on as we are.

At the moment I am tormented by having to decide. That cannot continue. I said to him that my heart is in "a." He says I have to go for that.

Last night Paula and I went to see *The Last Yankee* by Arthur Miller. The evening was a little tense, though pleasant overall. I liked the play more than she did. The bits in the dialogue that drew my attention were to do with the "failed" carpenter and his crazy wife. She asks him why he has stuck by her. He replies, "God knows. At best there is no one to touch you." I feel a little like that.

02 May 1993
The saga goes on. We "talk" on walks and what it boils down to is her venting her anger and me trying to restrain myself. It's like we are on different tracks yet we keep "talking." At least some feelings are coming out. There is a purging, a catharsis. And right now I feel rugged. I do not have to prove to her that I am "good enough." On the contrary, she has to prove to me that she is "good enough." Let her sweat. *First you end your relationship with Shawn and then we'll see where we stand.*

04 May 1993
I realize that something totally irrational is standing between me and separation, that I am clinging to some highly improbable dream. Why? The witches. And then later Paula came up to my room while Jake and Rachel were with me. That is a departure!

BREAKUP

06 May 1993
Looking back at my session with Max yesterday...
We covered my shortcomings in my relationship with Paula. In what way did I contribute to the breakdown? If I can take things on it will help with the healing.
1. I could have done more in the way of household chores.
2. R&L Designs: I was not sensitive enough to the effect of "failure" on Paula. The failure itself is not the problem; anyone can fail.
3. Sex did not work—a mutual problem.
4. I was difficult to live with. I exuded blackness and she let me down in my hour of need.

Perhaps I need to say something like: I can see where I was at fault and I am prepared to look at this and then negotiate the basis of a new relationship.

07 May 1993
Paula and I had an adequate relationship that needed a lot of work, which we did not invest, so we drifted apart. It was empty at the core. That void has now been revealed and is plain for everybody to see. The relationship ran down and she chose the "walking away" option. That is where we are today. I am looking ahead to the joint therapy session later today. However, I'm more excited about going to Nadine tonight.

10 May 1993
The story continues when we went to the joint therapy session last Friday. Paula and I met outside the venue and went for a coffee. I felt relaxed; she said she was tense and looked it. The session started with trying to sort out the seating arrangement. From the start and throughout the session Paula came across as confused, unhappy and singularly inarticulate. The details of the discussion are not important although a few interesting points emerged:
1. Paula views her relationship with Shawn as an alternative arrangement, not a passing affair.
2. L (the female therapist) said to Paula that she cannot expect to explore her relationship with me while holding on to her relationship with Shawn.

3. I said I was only prepared to be in this joint therapy if it is an "open book." Paula said it is.
4. L pointed out that we were trying to grind each other down and convince the other person of our point of view. That is not possible.
5. L very quickly saw a pattern in our relationship: Paula is more grounded than I am.
6. L asked why I am still keen to pursue this. I said: I love her. She asked what that means. I said I am attracted to her physically, I like her countenance and her energy. I like doing things with her. She asked Paula if she felt she was attractive to me and she said she felt she was.
7. G (the male therapist) asked Paula if there was a lot of feeling for me on her part. She replied, "Not really." I say to myself, "The rest is commentary."

We covered various other topics and got onto the early pattern of our relationship. I mentioned that when I got to England expecting to continue the relationship I started with Paula in Israel I found that she was involved in another relationship, which was dishonest. She admitted she could have been more honest. She went on to say that in Israel, "Leo was somebody; in England he was like a fish out of water." G said that Paula felt emotionally secure with my Israeli image, which was lost when I came to England. Maybe, but she got involved in another relationship before I got to England, while pretending to be faithful to me.

We agreed to meet again next week.

Overall, I think we gave the impression of not having had much together and failed to convey the level of warmth, love and affection we did have. I tried to say something with regard to our kids and how they reflect the solidity of our relationship. At least in the session we felt sufficiently secure to talk openly and freely, which we had not been able to do on our own, so at times it became heated. At one point the subject of our meeting with Max came up and Paula tried to fuzz the issue. I corrected her by saying exactly what she had said at that meeting and then went on to say I had subsequently decided on divorce. G said he understood that I had lost my patience. He validated my feeling/me.

I dropped Paula at Warren Street station, where she could not manage a "goodbye." I suspect because she knew I was going off to Cambridge, where I had a very good time. Nadine met me at the station and we went back to her place—on the couch with music, champagne and photos. Later we went out for a Chinese meal and then back to her apartment. We slept in separate rooms and in the morning she got into my bed. We spent a few hours together, relaxed but very, very nice. We went to have lunch at Madingly, which is beautiful, and then she took me back to the station. I was home by about five.

Back home and on the way to a party with Paula she got into a fit of jealousy, saying, "You probably slept with some woman in Cambridge. I don't want to talk to you again." Wild anger. In the end I dropped her off at the party and went home.

I was awake at about five o'clock in the morning when I heard someone at my door. It was Paula. She was in her gown but looked wide awake. She said she was sorry, indicated she wanted me to get back into bed and she would sit on the bed next to me. We chatted for a minute and then she got in next to me. We talked a little and then fell asleep with me locked in behind her. At about seven thirty she got up and left, after some gentle fondling. I told her I love lying with her.

Yesterday, Sunday, we had a good time together. We took the kids to Watford Springs and then we all went out to T.G.I.F. for lunch. After lunch we dropped Paula at home and I took the kids up to Hampstead. And a good time was had by all.

Why are we hassling each other? Because we cannot face the pain of separation.
Give it a chance, man. First there was a kiss, then another. Then she got into my bed. What next?

15 May 1993

At the joint therapy session today Paula started the ball rolling by raising the Jessy issue. She went on to say a few things, mostly in her bumbling, inarticulate way, adamant as all hell. L picked this up straight away and let her have it, by saying she was "making too much of it."

I felt I needed to tell our "story" and they gave me the floor, which peeved Paula. Afterwards she said that she had not acted "in her own interest" and that her first consideration was the kids! Total crap. She also said I did virtually nothing around the house. Absolute lie. L pointed out that whichever way she looked at it, Paula could not get away from the fact that she left the family home.

G made the point that I seem to have difficulty engaging with women, difficulty being intimate. I thought that was a good observation but qualified it, saying that when the circumstances are right I do open up and have had good relationships and good sex.

In the course of my talking about the family I said we are "gifted parents." L added that it does not have to stop in the case of separation.

In the car I could see that Paula was knocked flat. I asked her if she was okay. She replied, "Don't talk to me. Leave me alone." And we traveled the rest of the way in silence.

17 May 1993
Nadine phoned to say there is not enough between us. I agree. Some relief but I also feel rejected, again.

20 May 1993
Session.
Following my session with Max yesterday there has been some clarification. The kids, Jessy, etc., is a red herring. The only question is: Is there the sort of love, care and affection and trust between us to allow us to build up a relationship? Is there any real intention on her part to pursue a relationship with me, and if so, is she now prepared to give Shawn up completely?

I have not got answers to any of these questions. Surely the time has come.

Sex is not the main issue. It never is. It is always problematic and each can masturbate if necessary. She is rejecting me; plain and simple. Read the writing.

According to Max her choice is clear: 1) she comes with me; 2) she goes with S; 3) she goes on her own. It is not a mother/lover continuum; it is a practical choice.

In the meantime she is lapsing into further involvement with him and greater aggression towards me. Stop her fast.

BREAKUP

21 May 1993
It's a Friday afternoon and I am off to Israel on Sunday. Australia have just beaten England in the second one-day test. This afternoon we had the third joint session. It was fiery. I said my bit, saying I need clarity, and Paula has two weeks to decide. The long and the short of it is that she does not feel much for me but leaving the marriage is difficult. That says it all.

L is still going along with me in thinking that she cannot continue to see Shawn and expect to explore our relationship. We are grinding ourselves down. L also pointed out that I may now have become the sort of person Paula wanted to be married to. Paula said it was difficult living with me because I could not relate to the present. I did not argue as there is something in that. After the session she turned right to walk to the station without saying anything to me. I thought of approaching her but decided not to. Fuck her. I am fed up.

Last night I lay awake for some time. I thought to myself that there is no love between us. No flow. It is time to act. *I have had enough of your fury. That's it.*

22 May 1993
This morning when I returned with the food shopping she helped to get the things from the car and said, "We can't go on like this, Jessy is upset." Later she tried to hold me and put her arms around me. I remained limp.

She started saying things like, "Yesterday (at the joint session) I saw things differently; I want it to work." I said, "You are not capable of it, I have heard it before." She insisted that she is. I was very fierce. I said she must go and do her homework, go away and bury her anger and fury and only then send me a clear signal. "Till then go and get fucked," I said. And I meant it.

02 Jun 1993
Jake was happy to see me when I returned from Israel, as I was to see him. He told me that Paula and Rachel are away.

Once I realized she was away I felt much better. Life is better without her. I can almost see another life, almost. I see that wanting her is sick. Something turned in me yesterday: I became aware of thinking that ending with Paula is the equivalent of death. It is not. I also thought about how I cling to my destroyer, partly because it is all I know. We hold on to what eats us—Faulkner.

03 Jun 1993
I went downstairs with some trepidation this morning, knowing that Paula was there. She came up to me and we hugged. She looks terrible. She asked about my trip but could not listen to what I had to say. I told her I had confirmed the appointment for the joint session tomorrow. She asked if we would be able to talk beforehand. I said, "Talk anytime, but no fights."

When I got up to leave the room she came up to hug me. I held her and she cried a little on my shoulder. I don't know what it means. I am certainly not dying for her to say, "It's on."

08 Jun 1993
I feel different today because I decided last night, after much deliberation, to tell Paula I am sticking to my ultimatum of wanting a decision soon, and I handed her the briefest, pencil-written note.

At the joint session last Friday I was calm until the end, when Paula launched into a diatribe about the way I put the kids to bed. I really blasted her and she was astounded. L wanted to know what my response was to Paula saying neither yes nor no to my ultimatum. I said I was uncertain. We discussed a few things, including our sex life, and she was generally less angry.

Going home was tense but she weathered the storm. I went to her on Saturday morning as she lay in bed with only panties on. She did not want me to stay so I left. Later she came to lie in my bed for a while, but pre-empted it with, "No touching."

09 Jun 1993
Session.
At the session with Max today I did not want to spend the whole time dealing with my "marriage." In the end I did. I said I am ambivalent about Paula and Max remarked that was the first time I had expressed ambivalence, which surprised me because I thought that is precisely what I feel. He says I will be ambivalent when we split up, too, which is normal. I said to Max that I had tried to heal and failed. He says I should not regard it as a failure. I did my level best at great personal risk. It didn't happen.

While I was trying to get to sleep Paula came into my room. I was lying on top of the blankets. She indicated that she wanted to get into the bed with me and then realized I had nothing on. She said, "Put something on." At first, I thought she meant a condom. Then I realized she wanted me to cover up a bit. I did. "I am sad," she said, which, if I remember correctly, was a prelude to her leaving before.

12: END THIS LIMBO

12 Jun 1993
On a church bench in Hampshire.
The world feels extraordinary: bike at my side, beautiful flowers on a grave, late spring. I have got the bit between my teeth. Nothing can stop me now. I am strong; Paula is weak and distraught. When she came to my bed last night I wanted to explode inside her but restrained myself. Where will it all lead? God knows. I am still smitten. I don't think it will happen and it will need a lot to make me give up my freedom. She said she does not want to end the marriage. Do I give her more time?

18 Jun 1993
I want to end this limbo as I have all but lost hope of mending. I need some positive indication from her now, or else. It seems she is happy to go on like this while I need decisions, clarity; I need to get my life moving. I have just retuned from a short "circuit" walk and I feel fantastic. I am free. Paula is off my back. Now, listening to Beverly Craven sing *Promise Me,* I feel energized and empowered.

This afternoon we had the last joint session. I told Paula I wanted to know what she really felt. At first she could only say that she was in no state to decide. Eventually she said she thought our relationship was a fantasy for both of us. She also said she wants my "behaviour" to change before we can get together. I let it go. Finally I said, "We have to separate." L spoke about the symbiotic aspect of our relationship and suggested that Paula left in order to gain a separate identity. Good point.
 I wanted clarity and I got it.
 Paula and I got into the car. There was silence. After a minute or two she put her hand on mine, looked at me with tears in her eyes and said, "It's very sad." I said, "Sad, but true." Then she said she wants us to be "friends." She went on to tell me that she had contacted an astrologer. I told her that I had consulted two, and told her briefly what they had said—that we would get back together.

BREAKUP

29 Jun 1993
During break at school this morning I popped over to the graveyard to relax and saw the following inscription on one of the gravestones: "Perfect husband and devoted father." Somehow this steeled my nerve and I decide to phone the divorce lawyer. I walked stridently across the grass to the public phone outside Graham's butcher. I told her to proceed with the divorce. She will write to Paula to ask if she will admit to adultery, as this would make the procedure easier.
Later I told Paula I had contacted the lawyer and that she can expect a letter. I said I had reached the end of my tether. She was upset but seems resigned to us splitting. She "wants to do it decently." She kissed me goodbye.

01 Jul 1993
People, including Max, have suggested opting for separation rather than divorce. I want divorce. Among other things, I want it because I do not accept my wife having an affair with another man. I have put up with it thus far. No more.
Today I went for a walk with Sue, a colleague and friend, in Fryent Park. She boosted me by saying I am easy to talk to, that I am interested and that I listen. She was amazed when she heard how I had handled things when Paula left. She made me value myself and feel attractive. These are not major things and yet they made me feel I have not been appreciated, quite the opposite.

06 Jul 1993
I gave Paula the letter from the lawyer.
She appeared in my doorway at about two o'clock in the morning, hesitated at the door till I told her to come in. She got into my bed and we hugged a bit. She said, "I don't think I can go through with this," i.e., the divorce, and went on to say again, "I think I am prepared to end my relationship with Shawn." I remained calm and relaxed. She said, "I don't love anyone at the moment except the kids." We lay together for some time before she went back to her bed at around four or five. I realized she is in dire straits.

08 Jul 1993
Session.
Since the session with Max today I have come out with something new: no more Greek tragedy. Let's have fun; it's time for me to lift off the lid; get some fire in my belly; express my feelings. GO FOR BROKE WITH PAULA. Take the initiative and don't take no for an answer.

Last night she did not feel like talking. Early this morning I felt a strong urge to be with her. After restraining myself briefly I let go, went to her and got into her bed. We lay together for a while. I told her I was not going to let her go, that I loved her and desired her. Tears came to her eyes as she said, "My life is in a shambles." When I asked her to tell me what she is going through, she wouldn't. In the end she got up and told me to go away. I went upstairs.

09 Jul 1993
Funny times because I am still trying to pursue her and she is trying to keep away from me. She is hostile and remote and I just come right back in. Last night I told her to cut the hostility. After dinner, when we were about to go to a movie with her sister, who is visiting, I handed Paula a note that said, "Listen, you horror, how about coming to sleep with me tonight." She read it, smiled, tore it up and tried to put it back into my pocket. Methinks she protesteth too much.

16 Jul 1993
A full three days have passed since my session with Max. It was the Waiting for Godot session—I am waiting for something that is not going to come. It's in me and not out there. We spoke about this seesaw pattern and I told him I could not do any more. He suggested that I could still approach her seriously, say I don't want a divorce and set a time-limit for trying to rebuild, at the end of which we separate if we decide not to stay together.

21 Jul 1993
Session.
There is a simple message from the session with Max today: I am depressed. I need to pull out of the trap and do what I need to do for myself. The rest will follow. He pointed out that I am flat and

monotonous because all my energy is directed towards something I have no control over: my relationship with Paula. Leave it and start thinking about my options. I have been like a puppet, with her pulling the strings. The question is: What do I want?

We are stuck and I have to come unstuck. Without having a clear idea of what I want, I must start the process and that way I will find the direction in which I want to move. He says I am an interesting, talented person who is not expressing it. I need to stop thinking about the world and engage it.

22 Jul 1993
This morning, early, following a strong urge, I went down to Paula. She was not interested in engaging in what I wanted to engage in, so we talked. She wants to talk about the present; I want to know where we are going. She says she needs "weeks." I say, "In matters like this there can be no certainty. Make a decision and stand by it."

28 Jul 1993
At about seven this morning I put on my gown, took the earrings I recently bought for Paula and went down to her. She was reading in bed. As I walked in she said she was about to get up. I gave her the present and she seemed to like them. All in all she left me cold. I went upstairs and had a shower, saying to myself, "It's over."

She suggested going for a walk and we chatted in a reasonable fashion. Later I contacted the lawyer and told her to hold fire, thinking that Paula needs time.

29 Jul 1993
Session.
I started the session with Max yesterday by talking about "not letting go of my mother," as per Clive. He said this is trite, adding, "We never fully let go of mother, from whence we came." Because of my childhood I do not value myself and do not recognize my talents. I must blow my own trumpet. Max says Paula needs to hear who I am—talk straight for ten minutes.

Paula says she does not want me to come to her room or touch her. So be it. In the meantime I see that she is due to visit another astrologer and I wonder what that means.

31 Jul 1993
I am in my beloved Hill Garden. It is almost seven o'clock on a lovely Saturday evening. The garden is all shades of green and rabbits are nibbling at the grass. I hear the din of distant traffic on the slight breeze.

As Max says, "Time, longer than rope." So this morning I asked Paula if we are agreed on splitting. She said: yes. She told me she has seen an astrologer, who had told her to make a change; that it won't work between her and me. She reiterated that she was in a terrible state and is under pressure at work. I said I wanted to use the summer to move.

05 Aug 1993
We said we were separating and then we retracted. We had long, intense talks; the upshot is that she does not know what she wants and I don't know whether to give her more time or not.

Session.
Nevertheless, I went to the session with Max determined to decide. He explained that I have to be myself in everything I do, respond to x, y or z according to who I am. For instance, if somebody comes up to me and accuses me of stealing a thousand pounds, how do I react? I have choices. How do I react when my wife tells me she is still emotionally involved with Shawn? I have to maintain my identity whatever and the moment that starts being eroded I have to call a halt to it. That central person, ego, self, has to remain whole. Me.

08 Aug 1993
Lynbridge, Devon.
What can I say? I am sitting on a bench above the valley, facing the sea. It's beautiful and I feel fantastic, at ease. The air is fresh and I'm out walking. It's the ultimate moment, again. I don't want to be anywhere else in the world, or anybody else. I am 100 percent. It's all in me.

Woody Bay.
I am resting now after about a two-hour walk along the coastal path west from Lynton. I feel great, seeing the birds below, sea,

sky, cliffs; the edge. It's the best day of my life. I feel like the ice that can crack the rock. I know what I want. Stand still and things will come to me. I am confident.

09 Aug 1993

I have just got back to the cottage after an hour in the rain and I am soaking wet. I had a shower and got into bed to read *Prince of Tides* (having seen the film a while ago). I have not read a novel in ages. I really enjoyed the first chapter. Again I saw parallels with my life: he, a teacher in crisis; she, a doctor, wage-earner. She has an affair, etc.

I slept for a while, lovely and relaxed; no worries or stresses, only the bubbling of the river outside. I woke feeling I want Paula and must do something about it. I have a burgeoning feeling that I need to speak to Shawn to tell him what I feel: Leave her alone and give us a chance. It has taken a long time to get here, two years. I feel really good now. Sigh.

I am sitting in the middle of the East Lyn, Devon.

All is peaceful, beautiful, exquisite; such lovely energy. The water is flowing fast as I look up at the trees, the greenery and the sky.

There was a flood here in 1952, right where I am sitting now. The image of the tree in the flood comes to my mind. That's me. The tree will outlast the flood. I believe it. Stay steady. Do nothing and breathe. Leo, does she mean so much to you? Apparently.

11 Aug 1993
Rockford Inn on East Lyn.

I have just walked down from Doone Farm and have stopped at the inn for a drink of scrumpy. I decided to go out on the bus to Malmsmead and walk back. As it was raining I decided to keep to the road. I felt good walking, though I also felt very sad at the impending separation. I have to accept that she is dead to me. I could give her time but I sense that we will split. Anyway, I came to this absolutely beautiful mill. I stood there and nearly cried. The loss, the sadness. "Mill, give me strength." Leo, give it to yourself. Right now I feel I could slay a dragon.

Riversmeet.
I have plucked two stones from the river. One says: All roads are good; the other says: It's time you got what you want. Now they are both in my pocket and I'm thinking I feel deeply for Paula. I want her in every sense. At the same time, I realize she may not want me. *Ah-so!*

Along the final stretch, the Cleaves, I heard clearly what Max said, "You have to know what you want. It has nothing to do with Paula or anybody else."

13 Aug 1993
Lynbridge, Devon.
Last night I nearly went crazy. I have never felt so bizarre. I started seeing things and hearing noises; my mind was tied in knots with Welsh names and I felt trapped. I saw weird images and shapes and I felt terrible. I must have been disturbed about thoughts of returning to London after being in Devon. I felt I was going back into a trap, a horrible situation that I/we cannot get out of—a sort of pressure cooker. I had a bath and was feeling fantastically angry: angry with the world, with my mother and with Paula for abandoning me. I wanted to shout and scream. Instead I went to bed to the gentle light of the oil lamp and calmed down.

I then started thinking that I want Paula back. She is still away in the country with the kids and I began toying with the idea of phoning her and suggesting that she should move in with me, man and wife again. I was prepared to take a chance and ask for what I want.

I phoned. She was cheerful enough and I told her I wanted her to move in with me. She said she could not and that she had made her own decision: to be with Shawn. We had a long, calm discussion, during which I reminded her that only the other day... But she seemed pretty certain of herself. I did not relent and told her I was determined to continue. She said she had planned to see Shawn on Sunday and "spend time with him."

15 Aug 1993
London.
Yesterday was one of the most amazing days of my life. I slept reasonably well the night before and woke thinking: this is it; the

marriage is over. Let's celebrate—I'll hold her in peace, real reconciliation; forget acrimony, conflict and strife.

So I went down to her and got into her bed. I told her why I had come and that I accept her decision. I want her but let's live in peace and with care. I just opened my heart to her. We did kiss a bit and she admitted that I am a "good kisser" but she could not handle it. I told her my sexual fantasies and felt better for it. She hardly reacted. She did, however, like the idea of living in peace.

At about eight thirty she wanted to shower and we got up. I felt fine. As I was walking out of the room I looked back to see her. There I saw this heavy, dour figure. She looked about one hundred years old.

I went up to my room and got into bed feeling fantastic, thinking about Roni, whom I met the other day and who really turns me on. She is exciting. The release and ease were phenomenal. I felt a million dollars. I have never felt like that before. Sheer joy and bliss. Yesterday my hand was in the pocket of powerlessness but today it is in the pocket of omnipotence. I am king. I can be here and do virtually as I want. I felt good for the rest of the day.

16 Aug 1993

Something Cecil said to me clinched it for me. In answer to his question: Why have you continued to have hope in what appears a no-hope situation? I replied, "The tarot ladies." He said the witches were just reflecting my wish. The penny dropped. There is no hope for Paula and me. I have woken up.

17 Aug 1993

We had a reasonable talk this morning. From 08.05 a.m. we are going to be "friends." She is saying she does not want us to be man and wife. I KNOW IT IS OVER. Recognize that it is dead. Look forward and plan. Sell the house. Divorce. There is no point discussing anything except practical issues. We are adversaries.

Paula and I have been discussing the kids and whether to sell the house or not. She said the kids need a mother and a father and they don't have to be together. I said, "That is the watershed between us—they do need their mother and father together." Her response was, "Not if they are fighting." I left it at that.

We have a mountain to climb: separation, divorce, house and kids. Once it is broken down it does not feel so daunting. Small steps. In the meantime I had a lovely time with Roni last night. We lay in the grass in Hyde Park marveling at the gas lamps. Her body is beautiful. We just slipped into each other's arms. So, so easy. Incredible.

20 Aug 1993
I have written to the lawyer:
Dear Mrs. H,
I definitely want to proceed with the divorce. Please file straight away.
I have enclosed the marriage certificate.
Yours sincerely,
L.A.

I went on my bike to deliver it to her. When I got there I took the letter out of my rucksack, looked up at the blue sky, thought for a moment and put the letter through her letter box.

I told Paula I had delivered the letter. She was upset and cried. I asked her what the tears were for. After all, it is what she wants and we have, in effect, been divorced for the last two years. She said, "Yes, but it means the loss of the other." All I said was, "That's the price."

Up till now I have mistaken those tears for a change of heart. They are not. They are sorrow for what she is losing. Crucial point. I, too, feel the dull thud of pain. But I know it will pass. I have finally realized that all along she has wanted to separate but has been unable to. It is now blatantly obvious. Why did it take me so long?

And Leeds University has offered Jessy a place at medical school—the final piece of the jigsaw. She deserves it.

22 Aug 1993
Divorce until proven otherwise, although Paula is saying she is still confused. She says she wishes none of this would ever have

happened! I told her I had been prepared to give her time until she told me of her decision last Friday, when she clearly said she did not want to be man and wife with me. She replied, "That is when you should have given me time."

We went to the Roth's party this evening. After getting home and seeing to the kids I was walking upstairs when Paula indicated she wanted to say something. "I don't want to get divorced," she said. "What does that mean?" I replied and continued upstairs.

I used to think it means precisely that. I now think it means something like: I would rather just separate now, or I want to stay married and carry on my affair.

I used to think I had my share of bad luck with my mother's death, so Paula would not leave me in the end. Today, after chatting to my Aunt Anne in Bournemouth, I realize there is no limit to "bad luck." My dad's father died on him when he was six and his wife died on him when he was forty.

24 Aug 1993

It's a nice day, though autumn is in the air.

Paula still says she does not want a divorce and the fact that we are talking indicated it is not over. I disagreed.

It's ridiculous: we can't separate and we can't get together.

04 Sep 1993

Paula told me that she and Shawn have ended their relationship. He called it off because he is finding it too difficult, her not able to leave the family. I was shocked. We'll see. She wants to play it cool. And I was just thinking that I don't want her. After spending a little time by myself I decided I had to call an end to our relationship and I told her. She begged me to change my mind, saying I was making a "terrible mistake." I relented, again.

Shortly after that she came up to my room and got into bed with me. We lay and hugged for a while. Then we kissed, properly. I sensed she wanted it. There was an ease and sensuality about it all that I do not associate with our love-making. In our moment of intimacy she said she does care for me, and then went on, "…it's just…" and wouldn't say what. Of the time around getting Jessy's results she said, "There is nothing like family."

07 Sep 1993
It is staring at me; the writing is on the wall. For my sake I have to make a decision. I feel bad, hurt, out-manoeuvred and manipulated. I have laid myself open and she has spat on me again. I feel humiliated and ashamed. How can I allow her to do this to me?

Now she speaks of confusion and uncertainty, so I was wrong to relent. I should have pursued the divorce at the time. Clive was right—she will continue to come back. "Don't touch her with a barge pole," he said. "Tell her where to go." Each time I have tried to end this set-up she has baulked. What I want most of all is an end.

A kiss does not mean anything.

08 Sep 1993
I had a session with Max yesterday, the first after the summer break.
Max changed my thinking yesterday; he shattered my illusions. I thought we were still talking, whereas she is prevaricating while carrying on with Shawn. He spoke yesterday about the difference between dependency and inter-dependence. In inter-dependence the two people consult, confer, talk openly and honestly. In dependency the one person is dependent on the other for things, e.g., a decision. I am becoming dependent on Paula for a decision. That is not good. My only way of changing that is by making a negative decision. A positive decision of mine would not carry.

My simple answer to her is this: You want to end the marriage, leave. That feels good.

Now, at about six o'clock in the evening, I am feeling decidedly better. I have written a bit, prepared some clay and bashed away at a piece of sycamore that is beginning to look like a woman. I can see a new life taking shape for me just as the sculpture is emerging from the wood.

09 Sep 1993
This morning I was reading an article on the new Pinter play, *Moonlight*. The writer says that "love and friendship are subject to betrayal", which is what I have come to realize. It is a time of compromise and reconciliation in the Middle East (the Oslo Ac-

cords are due to be signed soon) and here it feels like the parting of the ways.

Paula returned from somewhere, all very calm and decent. We had a nice family scene for a while, chatting about all that had gone on here and her telling us about her latest trip. We soon descended into a sort of dull heaviness. There is an air of mourning about her and I ask myself: Who is it for, for Shawn or for me? I think it is for me but nothing has been said. We are all trying to be awfully nice.

We are the only ones who know what goes on between us. To everybody else it looks crazy. Maybe it is.

12 Sep 1993
I have just had an interesting talk with Elaine after going on a walk to the Heath. She thinks Paula is not in a state to decide anything now; she needs a lot of time. She is obviously not clear what she wants and the sexual pull to Shawn is not what it was. In other words, give it unpressured time and there is a possibility we can rebuild, but it might fail. Elaine also said that for Paula this is a crisis, not just an affair.

15 Sep 1993
Session.
My session with Max yesterday made it clear: I expect that one day she might make up her mind in my favour, which presupposes two unlikely events: 1) that she will decide; 2) that it will be for me.

Yesterday, while walking across Twickenham Bridge, I realized it is over with Paula, and my heart ached.

18 Sep 1993
Oh Hill Garden,
Dissipate my sadness,
Suck up my tears.
And I ask a simple question: Why is it so difficult for me to recognize that this relationship has ended?

21 Sep 1993
On Saturday night I waited for Paula to come home, supposedly from a dinner party. She arrived at about one o'clock in the

morning. I gave her a few minutes and then went down to her. I said, "I am waiting for you to ask me into bed." She did. I confronted her with, "Where are we?" She said she cannot decide to end her relationship with Shawn now so we have to separate. We stayed together till about three, partly in embrace. We chatted. I said I accept her choice. I went to my bed and slept from about three till five or six and then went down to her again, feeling it was our last chance to be together. Then I went to sleep again, relieved I suppose.

On Sunday I went to bed feeling more relaxed than I have in a long time. I slept like a baby. In the middle of the night she came up and got into my bed. She was affectionate and put her head on my shoulder. We slept together till it was time to get up. I said she must come up again. She said she would.

Max had said at the last session that she does not want to lose me. It's not something I would have considered but it rings true.

The session with Max.
I told him the whole saga. The question is: Is it the epilogue of the third act or the start of something new? He thinks it is the former and I agree. At the end of the session he jested about the different expectations men and women have of each other. At the time of the wedding the bride is thinking: I hope he has managed to separate from his mother. The groom is thinking: I hope she is like my mother.

When I am in a session with him, as with Clive, it all seems so clear and when I leave the ambivalence sets in. Essentially he is saying that giving it more time will get me nowhere; there is no basis for a relationship and I cannot allow her to control me like this. I, on the other hand, feel that time might allow a healing but I am less and less convinced. Put the house on the market and divorce now. Jessy leaves for Leeds on the weekend. We are planning to take her up and stay over.

06 Oct 1993
On Saturday we set out *en famille* to take Jessy up to Leeds, where she is about to begin her medical training. There was some tension over finding a place to stay and when we eventually set-

tled for the first place we saw, Paula made it clear she wasn't intending to share a room with me. "I'll share with Rachel," she declared. I felt we should have discussed it.

By this time we were all tired and hungry so we went in search of a place to eat. We ended up at a Chinese restaurant and I went for a short walk as there was a half-hour wait. When I got back they were looking at the menu. Anxious about the cost, I said, "I want to economize." Paula got really angry. "You order then," she screamed. Very soon it descended into a fight and we walked out. Everybody was upset; all the kids were crying. Terrible.

I slept really badly, thinking only of ending. At about eight I got dressed and was already downstairs and about to go for a walk when I noticed Paula looking out of her window. She indicated she wanted to join me. We walked down the road and through a park. I told her how angry I was and that separation looked like the only option for us. I said, "If you can't be reasonable with me then get away from me." She admitted to being unreasonable and said she would try to change. She returned to the hotel while I walked on a bit, flooded with emotion. In the car on the way back to London we talked and I expressed my feelings of ambivalence.

15 Oct 1993

When I went downstairs she was in the kitchen. I made her sit on my knee and caressed her. She did not protest. When she got up she threw an overripe lemon in my direction. A gesture? During the brief conversation we had before she left for Madrid she said she would like to find a "creative" way of living here together, perhaps dividing the house up. When I asked what is happening with Shawn, she indicated it was so-so. He is not going with her to Madrid.

Maybe I should pursue this against all odds. How can I seduce her? Get her drunk.

Either shack up with me or get out. I am staying put. That's being assertive. She tells me she wants to speak to me about Allan Bullock (British WWII historian); I want to tickle her parts. Talk about conflicting needs.

19 Oct 1993
Session.
I saw Max today and a few points emerge clearly:
1. Paula and I are both acting within a hypothetical relationship and defining ourselves within it. I/we need to get out of it. I need to define myself outside the relationship.
2. It is not that we are scared to face the void, we are in it and unable to get out. We are stumbling around, trapped. The golden path is out there. Take it.
3. Face the fact that there is no relationship, and there has not been one for more than two years.
4. I have to act to change the situation otherwise it could drag on and on.
5. Freedom might not be far away. Just start the process.
6. I have defined what I want in a relationship and I am not going to get it here, so look somewhere else.
7. Where is my anger? I try to give the impression of calmness but actually I am seething. What is the process that still permits me to chase after her?
8. This is not healing anything; it is allowing the wound to fester. Perhaps if we make a clean break it will allow us to find each other. Perhaps not.

The long and the short of it all is that the time has come to recognize and accept that the only way out of this trap is to separate. I feel sad and heavy but I know this is true. On the way home I couldn't even think of trying to drag it any further. There is nothing left.

I had a nice evening with the kids.

21 Oct 1993
We have spoken. We will put the house on the market. Now I have to hold my nerve. I will file for divorce tomorrow.

22 Oct 1993
I have shilly-shallied for too long and I have to extricate myself from this mess. I had a brief talk with Jake. He said he would be happier if we split because things are so bad between us. Jessy has left home. It's time to separate. I have exhausted all ways of staying together. I cannot climb this mountain.

Questions of where I want to live and how come to mind.

BREAKUP

23 Oct 1993
Today I almost felt like a *mensch*. I spent time in Hampstead with Rachel and had a nice dinner with her and Jake. The time has come to start drawing my bits together and creating a life out of who I am: father, lover, craftsman, teacher, writer, friend, lover of the outdoors and aesthete. Man of love, laughter, beauty and perfection. Something is burgeoning; it may flower once I leave this relationship.

The thing is I still feel the pull of her sex. I still see her as the incarnation of c--t. There are others but it is hers I feel drawn to most powerfully. The strange thing is that I feel this way despite the fact that sex was not good between us.

24 Oct 1993
In June 1991, at Clive's weekend workshop, I said I would rather be in hell with my mother than out of it without her. I now feel differently. I am leaving hell, the void, limbo.

25 Oct 1993
Paula returned a little earlier than expected from Madrid. Straight away she intimated that, "We are not doing things correctly." She wanted to talk, which we did later when I came back from seeing *Three Colours: Blue*. We had a rather tense talk. She seemed to be saying that we have not really tried properly to get together and she may now want to! She spoke of moving into my room with me and began to lay down conditions.

I asked her if she has ended her relationship with Shawn. She said she had not but would if she moved in with me. I said it has to be the other way round. I asked her what had changed since last week. She said she cannot let the family end and that she does not know what she really wants. It's the same old story and I don't feel like battling with it. I said I would think about it.

26 Oct 1993
I asked a realtor to come over yesterday evening. Later, when Paula came home she asked me about the realtor in a very agitated way and then started talking to me angrily. I told her that sort of talk is not in our game plan. She went on. I got really an-

gry. "I'll kick your teeth in," I shouted. Then we tried to patch it up. But it makes me sick to the core. We seem to be reaching a situation where I want to sell and she doesn't.

28 Oct 1993
I am tired because Paula came to my bed at about three this morning and I could not get back to sleep afterwards. She came as a result of yet another bad scene. I had told her I wanted her agreement about putting the house on the market. She was adamant that she would not give it. Says she wants it all to mend but I don't think it can. She says we need to court. She wants to be courted!

When she got into bed she said she does not want to fight. She feels too confused to have sex. We lay together. I said, "No penetration?" She replied, "No movement." I laughed.

When I suggested that because she is uncertain she should follow my lead, she took objection to it, saying she is an independent woman. I answered by saying I am also independent and can decide to end it. She really objected to that. No win.

31 Oct 1993
I go down to her, she comes up to me. We lie quietly for a while. I want more and she says she is not ready for it yet. When the paper came I went to fetch it and then made tea for her. We read the paper together.

02 Nov 1993
We had a short chat this morning. An hour later she phoned to say, "I am prepared to go the whole way with you." I said not until she can meet my conditions: a) she must give up her relationship with Shawn; b) she must want a relationship with me; c) be prepared to work on it. When she knows, she can approach me.

Yesterday I was in turmoil too but I decided to contact Greene & Co. (realtors) to put the house on the market.

I was resting when she got back and she came straight upstairs. She said straight away that she wants to mend. I told her about the house being on the market. She was not too upset and asked me to phone the realtor and cancel, which I did. When I asked her why she wanted to get together she said, "Because there were some good things in our relationship." For her the only certainty is that she wants the family. I said, "That means a relationship with me." She said she knows. She has not ended her relationship with Shawn yet and her pain is about ending it. She doesn't know if she can give up her fantasy of freedom and fears being trapped again.

06 Nov 1993
On the path in the graveyard I suddenly had this thought: if I had a magic wand, what state would I grant myself, would it be bliss with Paula or with another? I'll go for the other. I was able to grant myself an alternative; that's a revelation.

08 Nov 1993
We have had a torrid time. Since the letter arrived from the lawyer on Saturday morning Paula has been in a frightful state. What is more, I suspect she is still seeing Shawn and I wanted to confront her about it. She lied to me about him not being at the party the previous night. I asked her how she can say, "I'll go all the way with you" on Tuesday and then change her tune on Wednesday.

This morning I needed to talk to her. I sat on her bed and spoke. I just spoke and she listened like she has never listened before. I made it clear that I want a divorce now because there is no other option for me.

09 *Nov 1993*
We are not talking.
I have to express anger. *I am wild with you. You bastard. You go off and have an affair and carry on with it while pretending to get together with me. GET OUT.*

Admit, Leo, admit that you are hurt to the quick by her affair. Tell the world that you have been fucked over, cuckolded. Don't stand for it any more.

This morning, early, I vaguely thought of going to her. Then I said to myself, "That is the last thing to do." Slowly it came to me: this is the time to end things. No more waiting for Godot.

11 Nov 1993
Paula has spoken to a lawyer and she is at the stage of saying, "I feel terrible about this." I told her on the phone that it is clear cut: we have to divorce and sell the house unless she comes out with an unambiguous statement and action to make me think otherwise.

12 Nov 1993
We have agreed to put the house on the market. I have a new stone. It says: I am definitely better off without her. And I feel good.

16 Nov 1993
Session.
After a very difficult session with Max and a lot of soul-searching there is no question in my mind that I do not want what is on offer at the moment. If I see there is something new available I will go for it. I am in a reasonable place to face all possibilities, even separation and rejection.

When I told him the details of recent events he said it sounded like a nightmare, even allowing for exaggeration. He said she is emasculating me and I am agreeing to it. There is no dignity left; I have surrendered everything. In an attempt to keep the family together we are destroying it. When the kids see their parents at a loss it must be frightening for them. I, too, am responsible because my vacillation has permitted this state of affairs. In fact, there is no relationship and no family.

The kids, the poor damn kids!

17 Nov 1993
I was out at the theatre when Paula received a call from a Mr. Jennings, who wanted to come around to see the house, and she had arranged for him to come at ten in the morning. She came to my bed very upset. What really upset her was that she learned from Mr. Jennings that I have already begun looking at apartments. She asked me to cancel everything. She is running scared and wants to try to make a go of it with me from today. Shawn is away in Australia.

When I left the house on Sunday morning I noticed that Greene & Co. had put up a For Sale sign outside. It hit me that things were moving. On my return in the afternoon, Paula went hysterical. She screamed at me, knocked down chairs and broke a chopping board. She was foaming at the mouth. She took out a pen and tried to write in large letters: NO SIGN. She called it a "cross of blood." I have never seen her in such a state. I remained calm. We took the sign down.

She had invited some friends to come to tea in the afternoon and asked me to join them. I refused and went upstairs. She begged me, saying she would move in that night! She went on to say she missed me that morning, unheard-of things. In the end she did not come up, saying she was tired.

18 Nov 1993
Yesterday, while working in the Hendon Library, I came across the myth of the Gordian Knot, cut eventually by Alexander the Great—a decisive, bold act. That is precisely it, as Clive said all that time ago: cut, man.

GET AWAY FROM IT, MAN.

The usual doubts return but I see it is just fear of separation that has kept me from reading the writing on the wall. She has nothing to offer me except her sex and that is hardly on offer. Let's face the truth, she is not interested either. It has taken me a long time to get here.

22 Nov 1993
This morning I decided to end it; it is all too much. It would be healthier if I did the cutting. On the weekend she did say she does not want to end it but my estimation is that she will not be able to make a decision she can stick to, although she says she is "trying."

27 Nov 1993
I have put the For Sale sign up again. I sort of want her to say stop. Let's see what she does.

I came back from seeing a few lousy apartments on Friday afternoon and after a long bath I felt determined to have a final answer from her by the end of the day. She came back late from work and after some indecision we decided to go out to eat. We went to The Little Bell on Belsize Road and had a nice meal of tomato-onion soup and lamb casserole. £5 each. Half-way through the meal I said, "I want to keep this marriage." She said she couldn't. She had tried and it didn't work. I accepted there and then. We talked about how we would end it and went home. When I got home I wrote a letter to the lawyer requesting her to definitely go ahead with the divorce.

13: I AM STILL STANDING

28 Nov 1993
This morning we chatted gingerly, saying we would try to make it smooth and that we would buy houses close to one another to make it easier for the kids to move between the two of us. All lovey-dovey. The day passed reasonably.

However, I am in a cauldron of emotions, of grief, sadness, anger, shame and relief. This morning, for one brief second, I realized (again) that I did not really want her. In the graveyard tears came to my eyes because nobody has stood by me. I have stood alone and not because I wanted to. AND I AM STILL STANDING.

Yesterday morning after she got up and went into the bathroom I offered to wash her back. When she refused I said, "But we love each other." She said: "Not in that way." At the time I felt it an achievement for her to admit that she loves me.

29 Nov 1993
I am at school on Monday morning, with a feeling of slight emptiness and a sense of optimism. There is a new little stone in front of me. It says: STEP AWAY AND MAKE A LIFE. It is reasonable to get divorced and it is also an expression of anger, as is putting up the For Sale sign.

So, the tarot ladies were wrong. They raised my hopes and made me hold on beyond reason; they also gave me hope in my hour of darkness. Somehow, with the pressure off, things are healthier between Paula and me. She is being very calm and decent.

An edge of what I am feeling has to do with the fact that she said "no." It leaves her with the guilt and me with the feeling of rejection because I went for what I wanted right till the end.

The wild man has appeared on the scene; I am having a lot of angry thoughts at the moment. All the hate and fury and sense of rejection and betrayal are coming up. The pain will pass and who knows, maybe I'll start tasting some joy. The load has got off. Thank the Lord. Walk away from the wreckage. I desire her and want to explode inside her but deep down I don't care. My task is to walk away; clear out and build my own life.

I went down, called her into the kitchen and said, "I want to make peace with you." She was clearly relieved, held out her hand and said, "You are a *mensch*." That meant something to me. Then she came up to me and kissed me. She apologized for hurting me. I could feel Max's influence on me, for had it not been for him I would have resorted to hostility.

Maybe we will be better off as co-parents rather than as husband and wife. No more Greek tragedy.

30 Nov 1993
We have crossed the Rubicon. We have gone too far to turn back. I want to get rid of my ring.

When I went downstairs this morning I noticed her door was open. She had already gone to the airport to fetch Shawn. At first I was shocked, then I felt nothing, not deserted or betrayed. Just relief. It was as if she had left forever. What a blessing. I have been living two parallel lives: the real one and the dream one. Accept what you see in the wreckage, man.

For me, the idea of breaking out of the prison was crucial. I allowed myself to think of being in a relationship with another person, not Paula. I remember the tale of the prisoner vainly attempting to escape through the ceiling light instead of venturing into the darkness/light. Like Robinson, he expected darkness and he found light.

It is now just a matter of hanging on till we separate.

The session with Max.
He recognizes it is finished and says it should have happened after our joint meeting with him. He says I should not get rid of my ring yet; I must hold on to what was good. The questions arise: Why have I acted as I have? What can I learn from this? I need to be kind to myself and be patient with relationships. It will take time.

01 Dec 1993
At Brondesbury Station.
She is off somewhere. This is an extremely difficult time. We kissed goodbye in a caring and gentle way. She said, "I'll be think-

ing about you." I know we have to go through with this but it is so painful.

I still lapse into thinking this is just a charade and we will make up in a year's time. That is my problem. I need the divorce proceedings to keep me on track. I didn't believe this could happen to me/us. Stop! It's good news, a blessing in disguise. Why do I not feel it so? Because I still have to come to terms with it.

02 Dec 1993
I still wait for her to come begging, but I find myself letting go a little. The marriage has finally ended. Amen. Go out and live. My life is in tatters. Thank the Lord. I am hungry for life: a place to live; more money; a woman.

She fell in love with Shawn and ended our relationship. Then she destroyed the family and now she says there is nothing there. She's right. It's an explosion, a volcano. The landscape has changed forever. It changed nearly three years ago. The pain now is living with shame, rejection and betrayal.

06 Dec 1993
For some reason that is not clear to me she just descended into her old hostility from the moment she arrived home. At every point she breathed fire at me. Twice I told her calmly to cut the anger but she didn't. She hurt me and diminished me. I spoke to her firmly without blowing up. Her behaviour was intolerable.

We have to separate ASAP, though in reality we will be in the house together till the summer as we have to sell and buy new places. In the meantime I have to keep away from her; just the bare minimum. Don't expect anything from her, not even to be reasonable or decent. Never mind attention or appreciation.

07 Dec 1993
On Saturday night I saw *Medea*, a real Greek tragedy, with the Lewis's. The message I got is that it's a cruel world. Perhaps this is the turning point.

My lawyer wrote to ask me to phone. She said Paula indicated through her lawyer that she would prefer to separate, sell the house and divorce in two year's time. Should I agree? I think

not. Is there any reason not to divorce now? I have to divorce now.
    I phoned to confirm.

08 Dec 1993
The session with Max.
He says I must not hold on to my anger, it will eat away at me. Our relationship ended years ago. However, I was not prepared to hear it at the time of our joint meeting. For me it was a no-win situation. I gave everything, maybe too much, but it had no effect on her. I told him of my plan to join a therapy group and he welcomed it. His parting words to me were, "Keep your anger away from each other. It is a time of mourning and grief. The children need you. Put yourself centre-stage."
    After the session I went for a walk up Parliament Hill. There I shouted and raged against the wind. "I am here and I am strong."
    I have a new stone. It is bright and powerful. It says: I am the wild horse. There is excitement running through my veins even though it is a time of mourning.

09 Dec 1993
At six this morning I wanted to go down to her. I didn't. I can feel the anger decreasing. Now I have to find a way of relating while staying apart emotionally. I came home this afternoon to find a note from her to say she is sleeping out. I thought of lashing out, locking her out. No. Leave her, man. She is bad news. I can do a thousand times better.

12 Dec 1993
Take care. This morning I found myself lapsing back into feeling for her and thinking she will come back. She won't. The reality is harsh.
    I want to cut her down. I hope she suffers and sweats blood. Let go of that, too. Drop the Paula issue. She is nothing to me. I feel my experience is like a death. There is no compensation, no blessing. It is pure loss and pain.

13 Dec 1993
I feel okay, though still shocked and depressed. It's time to recover and regain my strength. I have been thinking about my

idealized view of the world, which I "inherited" from my mother; my need to see the world in idealized terms in order to keep her alive. With Paula I have clung to an idealized view, i.e., that we would re-build. I was unable to accept reality, the grim reality. It's over. Grieve, cry, shout, kick, go crazy but recognize it. Not only is divorce reasonable, it is essential.

14 Dec 1993
I am beginning to see my story as a Stones story. Just think about the stones at the side of my bed.
1. The crucial stones from last summer: Most roads are good; go for what I want.
2. The stone that said, "I don't want her as she is."
3. The little stone: I am infinitely better off without her.
4. The beautiful white one: Keep my eyes on my own ship. I have a lot going for me.
5. The one that said, "Leave the Paula issue. Step away and make a life."
6. The flat, brown one: Cut the Gordian knot.
7. The power stone that allows me to take power to myself, to kick the tarot ladies and allows me to walk into the dark/light.
8. The magnificent stone in my pocket that announces, "I am the wild horse. It's all in me."

All along there were two sides of the story, fantasy and reality, represented by two schools of thought. On the one hand there were Clive and Max, representing masculine realism—it's finished; get on with your life. On the other, the tarot ladies and Elaine, to some extent representing feminine romanticism, who counseled giving it time to heal—okay, she is in love with him; let is pass and she will want to come back. And it will be good.

I was caught in the middle, wavering between the two poles, hoping and wishing the ladies would have it while thinking that the men were right. My heart was feminine, my head masculine. I acted with my heart, owning my feelings till the end, when I finally saw there was no hope. It all seems so simple now. To think, how I agonized. But I am still standing.

She fooled me. All the tears and the joint therapy! What irresponsible, ridiculous behaviour—all the fights, because of her. She has been leading this double life all along.

First you killed our relationship. Then you destroyed the family. Then you left, saying there is nothing to stay for.
The pain, of course, is of rejection and betrayal. Face it squarely, man. It could be a blessing in disguise. I feel eighteen. I have never been eighteen! It's all ahead of me. The joke is on her; I am free as a bird.

21 Dec 1993
This morning Paula said we have to greet each other. She slept out again last night but still pretends to be living here with us. She said I am destroying the family!

30 Dec 1993
What will 1994 bring? Something in me says I have reached the sea, the light. The tree has withstood the flood. New life beckons. Yes. I think I have reached a turning point. I really feel I am better off without her, and I grant myself power to move on to better things. I am bubbling.

14: THERE IS NO CIVILIZED DIVORCE

03 Jan 1994
I feel tense, anxious and despondent, aware of an emptiness that I fear cannot be filled. On Saturday I felt a million dollars; now I am low. It has partly to do with Paula, whose presence and seeming confidence alerts me to my own situation. Her life is so set up while I have nothing. Stop. Look at my own ship—I have a lot going for me.

In *The War of the Roses*, which I saw last night, Gavin D'Amato (Danny DeVito) says there is no civilized divorce. Spot on.

I am sleeping much better. It has never been so calm in our house. What harmony. It's wonderful having nothing to do with her. She left me a note re finances, and saying she won't be back tonight.

09 Jan 1994
I have a new orientation: I bought a copy of *Elle Decoration*, though I don't yet know what house I am going to be redecorating. Last night in the bath I realized what "living in the moment" means. I suddenly stopped anticipating, thinking about the future and hoping things will get better. I removed the future dimension and have not been harking back to the past. I remained in the present, able to extend the moment. Just the moment. It was a great, new feeling.

While working this morning I realized that small increments create things, not giant leaps. It is a matter of: one brick on top of the other; one foot in front of the other; one word after the other. What a revelation. Life is good to me.

10 Jan 1994
It's one of those hard spots, brought about, I suppose, by the sense of finality, rejection and betrayal, sadness and my own feeling of emptiness. I just let things go through me. This morning Paula tried to engage me in conversation and I avoided her. Actually, I wanted to lash out, hurt her, damage her car, who knows what. Leave her completely alone. She is bad news, man. She has had it all her own way. No more. I want nothing to do with her.

23 Jan 1994
Jessy's birthday. I prepared a card for her and doing so brought tears to my eyes. I am now feeling the anger I should have felt towards my mother and I feel the overlap of mother/Paula. It suddenly struck me: Paula had it in her head all along to split and just used me for her own ends. How did I fail to see it? I believed what I wanted to believe. I could not see what was in the wreckage. Now I am furious. I was taken for a ride.

We have *never* had such peace.

02 Feb 1994
I was standing at the sink and Paula came up to me, trying to force me to talk. She put her hand on me in an aggressive way. I said, "Don't get physical with me." It descended into a shouting match; real anger both ways. I want her out of the house, out of my sight. I am adamant. I gave her every possible chance so now I can grant myself permission to be angry, cold and remote. I still have not "gone for the jugular." In time, perhaps. She looks terrible and she hates me. What's new?

I know I am a thousand times better off without her but it still hurts. I feel rejected and sexually diminished and I feel the sadness of the breakup of the family. Accept. *Ah-so!* New doors will open and more importantly, now is okay.

07 Feb 1994
Gail says I have done my job as a father so I can feel sure of myself. It has taken me three years to get to the point where I can say: FUCK YOU.

Paula is in a rage. She hit me this afternoon. I just took it calmly. I don't want to get into a physical fight with her, or any other kind. She does not scare me and she didn't hurt me. Poor woman. She tells me I have been behaving badly! Get away from her, Leo.

11.40 p.m.
After my bath I agonized about whether I should go down and smash her face in or not. Stay away, man. Leave her. I am experiencing continuous déjà vu and think it is a prelude to "reconciliation." It's madness, the child. Stop it.

BREAKUP

23 Feb 1994
Being Jake's birthday, I wonder what we have done to the kids. In fact, they seem fine. Jake is handling it well. He wanted me to come down while he opened his presents. I did not want to join in, with Paula there, but I did go down to the kitchen. I can't tell what is happening with her. She looks grim but manages to laugh a bit.

I went down to Barn Breaks in Somerset for the weekend and met some good people, who I would like to keep in touch with. Last week I was out almost every night.

For a long time my friend Gail, herself a therapist, had been suggesting I join a therapy group. She felt I could really benefit from the experience. I made approaches to a number of group leaders and was finally accepted into Manny's group, which met on Tuesdays.

I have joined a therapy group. We are struggling to find a new format, as Derek and Ann are leaving and new people will be coming in. We need more fire, from within. Give ourselves life; give myself life. It does not come from outside.

I have been reading Robert Bly's *Iron John*. I need to get in touch with the wild man inside me. He is there. I think I am fiercer than I was, not always looking to please. On the contrary, I am sticking my neck out. When Paula and I got into a little fight the other day I told her I didn't want to hear her voice. That shut her up. I don't want to see her. "You dismissed me so I will dismiss you a hundredfold."

05 Mar 1994
We had a little fight this morning. I didn't let her get away with hitting and pushing me. God, I was naive. Get away from her. I have nothing but contempt for her. This is what was needed ages ago—have nothing to do with her.

Don't wait for love to fill your life. Live now. Let it fill now.

14 Mar 1994
I had a devastating dream. There was a fire in a hotel we were at but our family was okay on the first floor. We got out by the time

the building collapsed. It is not hard to see the symbolism. We were all right as parents; no longer.

We have absolutely nothing to do with each other. She looks terrible but tries to act okay. Rejoice: I am away from her anger. Perhaps go for the jugular now, or just be shot of her ASAP.

I am feeling young again. I have escaped from the wreckage. Amen.

28 Mar 1994
Last night, after coming home from seeing *Short Cuts*, I flared up in response to a despicable act—an example of Paula at her worst. Word reached my ear that she had secretly arranged and had a birthday/bat mitzvah party for Rachel at her uncle's, in the afternoon. I felt hurt, mad at her for manipulating the kids into not revealing the plan to me, and betrayed by my friends, who had not said anything to me about the planned party. Paula was out and I locked the front door and left the key in the lock on the inside. Jake and Jessy got upset and left the house. Paula tried to get in and eventually went away.

I have been too soft and accommodating. Now I am looking for the wild/angry/masculine side. I have not got it right yet but I am on the way. Cut her out, Leo. Don't give her the time of day. I am entitled to be angry.

29 Mar 1994
Group session.
I was given time and attention so I brought up what happened on Sunday—lock out. People asked: Why have I tolerated it; what has it done to me; why is Paula so angry with me? I have been infantilized. Manny suggested it was a corpse of a marriage, like my dead mother again. I am living with a corpse.

10 Apr 1994
This afternoon I went down to Zimbabwe House to see an exhibition of stone sculptures. I met Nellie at the exhibition, where she bought a piece. Well, well. Thinking: Nellie, Nellie, Nellie.

12 Apr 1994
I met Nellie in Hampstead to celebrate her birthday and we went for a walk on the Heath. I got her a pair of earrings. She is lovely

but I don't think she will want to get involved. Ooh! A night with her. We had a meal at the Shahbag. Little kisses on her cheek, no more. I just ooze love for her. I am crazy about her.

The good news is that I am not interested in Paula, not one little bit.

18 Apr 1994

The unthinkable has happened: I am getting divorced. Three years on, and I feel pretty good. I am the child and the father; the priest and the sacrament; taker and giver. It's all in me. But the pain, sadness and loss are there too.

20 Apr 1994

In the mornings I feel the hurt; in the afternoons I thank heavens for where I am.

A few things have been going through my mind. One negative one is the recurring theme that I am the kind of man that women leave, like a few men I know—gentler men. Yet I can hear Clive waxing lyrical about my strengths. "You have a lot going for you; your best years are ahead of you," and so forth. I am more open, more aware and more assertive.

I have virtually nothing to do with Paula; I hardly see her. She barely talked to me for years and she had a special voice for talking to me when she did. No more.

On Sunday night I went to the West End with Sarah to see *Stalingrad*, the movie. She drove. At one point a car pulled out and she wanted to park in the place it had vacated. To me the line marking was unclear. There was one clear yellow line and one not as clear, so I half thought it would be okay to park there. She got out to have a look and in a split second saw that it was a double yellow. Influenced by what I wanted to see, I was unable to see the reality—a salient lesson. I have been unable to see the writing on the wall, the death in the wreckage.

21 Apr 1994

Gail's divorce joke. An ex-couple meet after twenty years apart. They exchange niceties. How are the kids? What? I thought you had them!

27 Apr 1994
It is the day of the first democratic election in South Africa. I am moved by what I see and read, as I still have strong emotional ties. What will be? I'll speak to my dad on the weekend.

In the meantime we have had a good offer on the house. They want the fridge-freezer and kitchen island included. I said I would have to ask my wife! After some opposition, she agreed and then went on to say, "You are liable for the realtor's fees—3 percent." I just walked away. Later she came to her senses and wanted to talk. I didn't want to know her troubles and felt like suing her, or tearing her apart.

I am reminded: freedom is just around the corner, in the dark.

The other day I went for treatment to an osteopath, a gifted man by the name of Lennox, who, besides manipulating my weary body, made some interesting remarks. I have to bounce back, claw my way back, he says. The world does not like losers. I have to side-step trouble (P) and "hate binds." Let go, which is what I could not do in relation to my mother. When he heard my deep laugh he felt it indicated I was a "good man." Nice.

26 Apr 1994
Group session.
We spoke a little about grievances. Who am I without my grievances? And about honesty vs. playing games. Do I say what I think? What is politic? When I told of the incident with Paula regarding the realtor's fees, they made me aware I am in the middle of an acrimonious divorce, whereas I thought we would be able to do things in a reasonable way. I am too nice to be in this! Somebody said she wants to shake me because I appear to be this caring father and yet I have not got things organized for them. I also realized that letting Paula back in in April 1992 was a mistake.

We are all scared to try freedom. We all have prisons. The discussion led Manny to suggest that we are all exploring what is possible with the other sex; what can or cannot be done.

Nellie and I have been to Kew Gardens, spent time in the country and been to see *A Month in the Country* in the West End. She is so sorted out, perhaps too sorted out. However, she has suggested we go away for the weekend. Sounds good.

BREAKUP

08 May 1994
Our garden.
It's the last few months in this garden. Sad. Stay calm, sell up and get my own place. Paula is away, which is why I feel so relaxed. Forgive myself *everything*. I had to let her back. Oh, to separate physically! Three months.

11 May 1994
Group session.
A short message from a powerful group session yesterday: When we are alive, we also feel pain and sorrow. For me it is a time of sorrow and grief.

What I feel is not fear or anger, just profound sadness. Loss, ending.

I feel good that I am doing what I have to do: sell up, get my own place, side-step trouble. Sam Keen: don't settle for a false peace. Move into the deep, uncharted waters. That is the male voice.

12 May 1994
This is a profoundly sad time but I feel okay.

Two days ago I got a letter from my lawyer to say that the Decree Nisi will come through on 27 May and the Decree Absolute on 11 July. I felt sad though I did not hesitate to phone her to let her know that I want to proceed...to the end.

Paula and I have had to sign various papers related to the sale of the house and our joint endowment policies. There has been a little conflict, where I have remained calm and firm, knowing that this has to be tied up. At one point, when I handed her some documents, she said, "Give me five," as a gesture of friendship. I declined. Obviously she is trying to be friendly. I just take no notice. Strictly business. Is this not anger? It is. Be the brute; set limits and set them short.

15 May 1994
I had a fight with Paula this morning—same old anger. I just cut her short. I have been through the mill: abandoned, defeated, emasculated. But I feel good now.

I might go to Cape Town next week!

25 May 1994
I can see a beautiful sunrise over Africa from 30,000 feet.
Table Mountain comes into view. Absolutely amazing. I feel good. My whole life passes by me: my father, my childhood. What will it be like, how will I be regarded now that I am on my own? Don't forget: L—P = 1½L.
I am almost fifty. My dad was this age when I left South Africa. I can picture him. There are similarities but crucial differences. I long for the open spaces, sea and fresh air. It's time I got what I want.

Later.
I went for a lovely walk but I was warned that I should not go alone! That is the political reality.
I have been looking at the photo album my mother compiled and I can see I had a proper infancy: beautiful boy, juicy mother, real father. What went wrong? My mother died on me. Yesterday I went to my old homes in Cape Town. I have roots. Cape Town is beautiful.

03 Jun 1994
Sea Point.
Earlier I went to Pinelands Cemetery. I was sad at my mother's grave; happy at my granny's. I left a stone on each and took a stone from each. What a child I was. What a mother. I would like to come here again. This is far, far away from London.
The message from my mother: *I have spunk.*

04 Jun 1994
The Gardens, Cape Town.
Table Mountain is in front of me and the sky is almost clear. I have been walking around town and am on my way to the Waterfront. I need to get into making, where my happiness lies. Earth, Fire, Water—Pots and Tables.

05 Jun 1994
35,000 feet above central Africa.
London lies ahead. What does it hold for me? Selling our house and buying my own one, I hope. My kids, Sue, Nellie, Sarah, work. Look after yourself, man. *Alles sal rektum.*

BREAKUP

I sat at Skeleton Gorge this morning and picked up three stones. My real roots are here. Europe is alien to me. I see it now. I said goodbye to my dad. Will I ever see him again?

07 Jun 1994
London
I am going to see a house in Child's Hill, NW2, this afternoon. I like the location.
All I have to do now is sell up and get a place of my own.

12 Jun 1994
Nellie and I arranged to meet at the Royal Academy's Summer Exhibition. As we walked in I saw Paula with a friend. We looked at each other for a second and then she turned away. It felt like a bit of one-upmanship: the heavy, plodding Paula in sharp contrast with the elegant, beautiful Nellie. How did I stick with her for so long? I want to have nothing to do with her. Nothing. All I have to do is get out and into my own place. Then I can start life again.

20 Jun 1994
Generally, it has been a time of reflection and sadness, partly brought about by my visit to South Africa, seeing my dad and going to the cemetery.
It is painful being left; it robs me of my manhood. And, to rub salt in the wound, while on the Heath yesterday, throwing Frisbee with Jake and Rachel, I was telling them about the remains of a stone-age man that had been found nearby and that women were clamouring for his (frozen) sperm. Rachel said, "You should get some." Why? "Because your balls are too small," was her answer. "Where do you think you come from?" I replied. Was she thinking that Paula left me because I am "not man enough" and is she angry with me for that? I left it but would like to talk to her about it. She is hostile. Ultimately, I have to face the fact I am not Vlad the Impaler.
Leo, you have spunk, man.

21 Jun 1994
There is a slight chance I will be able to buy the house on which I have made an offer. I am not excited about it and neither are Jake

and Rachel. Nevertheless, I like the area and, with money and work, it could be turned into a nice place.

Group session.
It was a session about tempering one's temper, of finding the right measure, of not going over the top and not crumbling. Fine-tuning. It rings bells of making something of what is available. Life is not about creating out of nothing; rather it is a matter of lifting things slightly, of transforming the ordinary into the extraordinary.

I realized I have come a good way on these matters, and that I do not explode as easily as I used to. The problem is the difficulty to feel, to feel pain, but not too much. I was able to speak without filtering. At the end of the session I felt drained but good.

24 Jun 1994
Paula is poison. Keep away. It's absolutely simple.

I realize that what is different about this situation is that I am not the good guy. I am the same as everyone. I have a dark side. She had to end with me; now I have to end with her. Okay, she started. Anyone is free to choose but there is a price. I am so hurt, so ashamed. How do I heal it? Can it ever heal? Will the pain ever go? The voice of father: the pain will pass. You will thank your lucky stars she ended it. It's a blessing, believe me.

26 Jun 1994
I am angry, furious, enraged. I feel like ripping her open with a knife. Let it come out, Leo. Feel free to express your murderous rage; you could not express it against your mother (and father).

I have been happy to spend time on my own. I went to the British Museum this afternoon to see an exhibition of Indian drawings. Peace. I am itching to move. Oh for the new.

28 Jun 1994
I woke up at a reasonable time and just lay in bed. Dead, empty, enraged. I want to throw a grenade into their bedroom. Perhaps I should go down to her tonight and taunt her and then rape her. She put a knife into me and I still wanted her. Admit the dark, dark feelings; admit even that she arouses them. I am just as base as anybody else.

BREAKUP

30 Jun 1994
We have agreed on the sale of 25 Solent Road at twenty-five thousand pounds less than we should have got. That's it. Ending. And what have you learnt from your divorce, Leo?

04 Jul 1994
I went up to Leeds on Friday to fetch Jessy. She is in good shape and has got through First Year well. Good for her. At home, all was tense, as usual. I watched the Wimbledon final—Sampras in straight sets vs. Ivanesevic. Then I cut the hedge, probably for the last time, and went out at night with a few people.

I have been reading *The Dark Side of Love: the Positive role of Negative Feelings* by Jane Goldberg. It makes me think we could have repaired if we had tackled it earlier. Instead, we played out our anger in a destructive way, particularly Paula. Now, I wouldn't go back.

05 Jul 1994
All I need is ten grand. There is less than a month still together. That is a cause for celebration. I am thinking of having a party at no. 26 Nant Road in September.

07 Jul 1994
Gail phoned me to suggest running pottery classes on Saturday mornings as a way of making extra money. Good idea.

11 Jul 1994
Decree Absolute.
   I believe that from today I am divorced. Hooray. Inwardly I feel strong, good, relieved. There is an element of sorrow. I am shot of her and now I can get on with my life.
   It has always been a futile endeavour, a bottomless pit. She was never right for me, I remember saying so years ago. It was dry. There was no receptacle for my love. She did not love me. Period. Now I am free. Rejoice. We had a nice weekend while Paula was away. The weather was good and we watched the World Cup, which was disappointing: Brazil finally beat Italy on penalties.

17 Jul 1994
It's a lovely Sunday morning and I feel good: fit, lean and confident. My new motto is "Don't tread on me." As Sam Keen says in *Fire in the Belly*, you have to "defend the sanctuary of the self" and "once the stream runs clear express your outrage against those who violated your being."

22 Jul 1994
The certificate dissolving the marriage arrived today. I feel a bit nervous but fine. It's all happening. I'M FREE.
    I got my new phone number from a phone box in Barnet.
    They can all handle me not being Mr. Nice Guy. Here it is: absolutely ruthless; no truck; no half-measures; total cut-off. Firm, hard, cold anger. It is not malicious. It simply says: that's the limit. I'm saying: don't mess with me. I take guard, like a warrior. And will I find new love? I think I will. I have a lot going for me.

24 Jul 1994
A moment of bliss with Danna in Holland Park. It's there, man.
    The final separation is pending; a division of the spoils. It's hard.

15: Clear the Decks!

27 Jul 1994
Clear the decks, man. I got a phone call from Fiona, the lawyer, to say the deal on my house is going through. I have given Paula a list of things I want from the house. It's the beginning of the end.

04 Aug 1994
I feel numbed, waiting for my new life. I bought the new kitchen yesterday. Take chances, I'll manage.

06 Aug 1994
Thank God I am shot of her. This morning she hit me.

08 Aug 1994
I have slept my last night at 25 Solent Road. I could not fall asleep till three o'clock in the morning and then slept till seven o'clock. I am excited and anxious. I am on my own. Smile. What I need most are a crowbar and a ladder to begin working on 26 Nant Road.

09 Aug 1994
Jake, Rachel and I slept in my room in our new house last night.

06 Sep 1994
I am now sitting in the sun on my patio in my new house. I am home and dry. Keep your eye on your own ship. It's right but it hurts. There is still a residue but I want to be where I am and nowhere else.

17 Sep 1994
I don't know what it is but I feel good. I have been thinking about Paula and loss but most of the time I feel at ease, strong and content. I want to share but also want this utter freedom and joy of being here alone. I have been looking at old pictures—my beautiful kids. It brings tears to my eyes.

People say my eyes are sparkling. A long time ago Clive said to me that I have to make the south of France in Golders Green. I am close. I can breathe here.

05 Oct 1994

It is the third night in a row that I am home alone. I like it, but I miss the warmth of other people, the kids, a woman. I want my freedom and I also want a body next to me in bed. All in good time.

I feel my power much more than I did. My task is to build a new life, this time on firm foundations. I am rearing to go. I have started an interesting work-related course, The Atypical Child, at the Anna Freud Centre.

09 Oct 1994

At home in jeans and a T-shirt. My new house is good, very good. I am at ease here, relaxed and strong.

As a result of a small incident involving Rachel's keys, I started thinking about what I am suppressing. What do I feel about Shawn? What do my kids think about my having been replaced as their mother's man? I have been shunted aside, overlooked, abandoned—a victim. Yes, but stop. It is the best thing that could have happened to me. Drop shame and embarrassment. I am deeply wounded and it takes time to recover and, who knows, maybe the pain doesn't ever go away.

I keep thinking about a report meeting at Jake's school, when I might have to see Paula. I have not seen her since early August.

18 Oct 1994

I bought a wisteria, my favourite creeper, and planted it near the fence. May it grow. The weekend was spent working on the kitchen.

Here and there I catch sight of Paula bringing or fetching the kids. I feel vulnerable, a bit battered. The kitchen is nearly done. I feel so fucking good.

01 Nov 1994
Group session.

James Watt: a boiling kettle turned into useful energy—steam power. How do we transform anger/steam into something useful that we can use? I guess I am puzzled by the step required to move from steam to steam power, from anger to real work. At some level I think anger is "wrong"; there shouldn't be anger; we should all be friends all the time. For me, anger = death. I might not survive it, and it is therefore to be avoided. There is nothing in between calm and rage. Can you be angry with somebody and love him/her at the same time?

Perfection is the enemy of the good. Someone told the story of an old man who walks through the forest rejecting walking sticks because he expects to find a better one further on. Eventually the forest ends and he is left without a stick.

At the session I came to the realization that Paula is a thing of the past. I don't have to dwell on my difficulty with her.

I have been looking at slides with Jake and Rachel. They are amazing pictures, beautiful places we went to as a family: the tree house in Kent, Bardou and Nizas in France, Yorkshire. We were a couple. What happened? We drifted apart but obviously we had something.

08 Nov 1994
Group session.
The group session was about Letting Go, what I started on with Clive. Disengage from battle. Focus on relationship with kids and leave Paula alone completely. No communication is better than acrimony. Manny: only mother's love was complete. Nothing can match it, yet we yearn.

I spent the weekend at home doing the kitchen. It's all I want.

02 Dec 1994
Hill Garden.
There is only one pressure: to be myself.

I feel fantastic. The world is beautiful. All I need is five thousand pounds.

13 Dec 1994
I realize that it is hard for me to admit to weaknesses because it has the implication of shared responsibility for the breakdown of

the marriage, when I need to lay the blame on Paula. In truth, there is shared responsibility for the breakdown; regarding what happened after that, she wrought destruction in every form.
    Irishman A: How do I get to Dublin?
    Irishman B: If I were you I wouldn't start from here.

14 Dec 1994
Paula has written me a moderately decent letter re finances and communication—joke. I will not give one inch. What is more, she rejected me, I will reject her tenfold. Let her struggle and suffer. I am dating a few women but I am fed up with it all. Stop looking.

20 Dec 1994
Hill Garden.
I have found the south of France here today. The smell, the feel of my body—loose. Sun and ease. This is it; there is nothing more.

31 Dec 1994
Home alone and fine. Serve your own inner king, Leo.
    I still think a lot about the state of things with Paula. My heart says "embrace" her as well as throttle her. But I have to protect myself. She is inimical to me. She represents the death and destruction of my ego.
    Will there ever be anyone special in my life?

24 Jan 1995
I feel like the poor relative; my family goes on without me. I want people to ostracize Paula. It's not fair. She abused me. What was my part in it? All my aggro came out—she is a bastard and people should see her like that. Now I have said it and it's out in the open.
    What J.C. Fields wants on his tombstone: I would rather be in Philadelphia.

16 Feb 1995
Hill Garden.
In the sunshine with my bike, thinking about last night with Kate. It was one of the better bits of love-making in my life. She is eas-

ily aroused and satisfied. I like that. And I want her again tomorrow.

23 Feb 1995
I feel amazingly good having worked in the garden. Sing for joy, Leo. You are shot of Paula. It was all worth it just to be done with her. I can breathe and smile. Thank the lord she is off my back.
    Something is stirring in me. I feel good because I am in charge of my life. I am building a life: house, pottery, work, kids.

07 Mar 1995
Some lessons from the group:
I say I have no sense of a future and the reply comes: that is rooted in having a tenuous hold on the past. We are all looking for where we are rooted and can grow. We all have a story. We either tell it or we don't and each time we tell it it is different; it becomes lighter and feels easier.

20 Mar 1995
I have not written for ages. It's a sign of the times.
    In the bath yesterday I started thinking I would like to have Paula with me…to torture her. I found myself saying, "I'll take you to within an inch of your life." And I realized that is exactly what my father used to say to me, and do. I was taking out my anger against my father on her. And she has been doing the same to me. I also have played out the feelings of betrayal and abandonment I have towards my mother. What agony to go through it again, as I did. Now I find myself making sure it will not happen yet again. In other words, don't get myself into a situation where I can be abandoned again. Does that mean not getting into a relationship? Perhaps. I will abandon them, rather, and get my own back. I am an abandoned kid. I was, and the scars still show.

28 Mar 1995
It's a time of re-adjusting to a new life, of realizing that this is it. I am not going to slip into a new romance or just feel at ease, or get together with Paula again. I am fixing up the house, getting the pottery functional and seeing to the kids.
    Regretfully, this is not a work of fiction. It is a true story.

10 Apr 1995
Stocklinch Ottery Church, Somerset.
This is a time of special peace. I am staying with Adam after a Barn Break weekend, feeling at one with the world—driving, walking around the villages and churches in the area, just going where my nose leads me, and talking to a few people.

Barrington Court Garden.
It is a moment of definition, of being here and darting back to the past, to loss and pain. As well as an awareness of loss I have a wonderful sense of being here, as I am, taking in the exceptional beauty of the place. In front of me is a pond with small fountains and I am surrounded by flowers, smells, butterflies, birds twittering. It's a beautiful sunny day. I have taken my socks off.

11 Apr 1995
Bagsborough, Quantocks.
A beautiful evening, still sunny. I am sitting on a bench after a long walk. Feeling weary, so I can hardly write. Peace and tranquility, sunshine, fresh air; what more can I want? Nothing. There are cows in the field below me. It's England at its best.

12 Apr 1995
Parnham.
I am sitting on a wooden bench at the top of a stone stairway, with water gushing from the fountain at the bottom. The sun comes out. There are conical conifers to the left, in rows. The house, in its splendour, is to my right. The whole thing is inspirational.

14 Apr 1995
Bridport, Dorset, coastal path.
I can see in front of me…forever. I wanted to be by the sea today. No pressure from anybody. Rejoice. I just popped into a village church. Outside the door was a poster that read: Each day is gift from God. Use it.

BREAKUP

13 Apr 1995
Hill Garden, London.
I have to start pulling it all together. I am a good teacher, good potter and good maker. My mind is poetic; my gift is material.

19 Apr 1995
Flowers from the garden are all around me. Beautiful and enervating. Reading Campell: life is not about finding meaning but about experiencing living.

2:30 p.m.
My kiln is connected up. Amen. The pottery is taking shape. I have worked in bursts most of the day on fixing the workbenches.

01 May 1995
Nice weekend. Jessy was down. The four of us sat around on Saturday having dinner with a good feeling. I am still preparing the pottery and have a second definite student for pottery classes.

08 May 1995
A fresh start. I am going to begin making pots this afternoon.
 Leo, she never cared for you. Leave it all. You are a thousandfold better off. Guilt-free freedom. Thank the lord. When I took Jake and Rachel to Paula I saw Shawn arrive, I think. First it touched me a bit then I thought: he can have her.

18 May 1995
6:45 p.m.
I am under the beautiful old wisteria in Golders Hill Park again. No more West Hampstead cemetery. This is my pitch now. The change symbolizes my shift from ending to a new beginning. Renaissance, rebirth. I am making a life, some of the pieces are already in place. I am overawed by the beauty of this place.
 Saul Bellow: I spent many years with a woman who did not care for me very much.
 I share the sentiment but it took me till December '93 to realize it.

06 Jun 1995
Letter to friends in Cape Town, written after South Africa won the Rugby World Cup:

Dear Syd and Roslyn,
It's not because of an event that took place at Newlands the other afternoon that I'm writing, but I was so emotional I imagine you must have been ecstatic. Were you there? Rainbow people. Let's hope so.

How are things with you? I have been meaning to write for ages but have not got round to it, for very good reasons, of course. Now, in a more relaxed frame of mind, I can get swanky on my computer.

I suppose I am more relaxed because I feel my life has some shape to it. Work, which still primarily means trying to help children with learning difficulties, is okay, and is well balanced by everything else that is going on, viz. being a father, getting my house fixed, starting up a pottery and a bit of socializing.

I love being in this house and I really enjoy spending time here. I feel free and at ease with the world. I don't feel I need to rush out or entertain lots of people. Apart from work on the house itself, the garden and the pottery, I have started running two pottery classes a week. Somehow, I feel more complete now, and I think it has got to do with making pots again. It has added a fresh dimension to my life.

The arrangement with Jake and Rachel, whereby they spend half the week with me, is working out well. It's nice when they are here and it's fine when they are away. They have both grown and matured; Jake is a lot taller and is strongly built. It is weird when your kids are bigger, stronger and cleverer than you. But what can one do? Accept. (You must know the feeling.) Jessy is coming to the end of her second year at medical school and starts her clinical in September.

*Over the Easter/*Pesach *holidays I went down to Somerset for a week. The weather was exceptionally good, and I spent some time with friends and some time on my own. I went walking in*

BREAKUP

the hills, visited quaint churches, public gardens, stately homes, potteries and the most amazing furniture-making enterprise— John Makepeace. All in all, England at its best.
  Back in London, I am opting for the quiet life. I meet women; nobody too exciting. I go to movies, exhibitions, dinner with friends. Pretty low-key, and just how I want it. Correction. I do want more companionship, intimacy and money than I have. But I feel really good (most of the time).
  A year ago, while still living in the old house, I used to go on a daily pilgrimage to a cemetery nearby to find peace and quiet. I really loved the place, its connection with the past, the colours of the lichens on the gravestones, the changes of the seasons. I thought I would never be able to leave it for long.
  However, since moving to this house, I have not been back there. I now go for walks in a park—a place of growth and renewal. It has ponds and trees and lawns and beautiful flowers and plants. I treasure it. And I think it epitomizes the change in my life, the change from ending to starting afresh; from a sort of death to re-birth. But, it has been a long road.
  I wonder how you are faring. How are things generally, and are you still feeling as optimistic as you were a year ago? Any travel plans?
  I hope you are well, and I'd like to see you but unless you get to these parts we aren't going to meet up for a while. Sad.
  Take care. Much love,
  L

18 Jun 1995
Today I was with Katie at the Royal Academy Summer exhibition. We kissed and held momentarily afterwards. I kept my hand on her back. Paula and Elaine were there. And me with this lovely, young woman. Paula could not restrain her surprise and disappointment. Perhaps she recalled seeing me there with Nellie last year.

02 Jul 1995
Alone and feeling it but ultimately feeling I am at my best. The world is good, nay great. I am full. I am thinking of getting in-

volved in some kind of arts & crafts centre/sanctuary, possibly providing facilities for people. I remember Clive saying: be authentic, do your thing and people will beat a path to your door. It's happening in a small way.

11 Jul 1995
The first anniversary of my divorce. Hurray. Last night—Katie. What it is to kiss a lovely woman. She was warm and loving. Hang in there. Not sure whether I want a relationship or not.

Group session.
At the group we discussed controlling the pain because relationships never end. Someone asked whether I hate Paula. What do I feel about her? Mixed. I had better get used to the idea that she is thriving and will continue to do so.

05 Aug 1995
Saturday morning. I am working in the pottery on my own and I feel good. I am meeting new people, different people

25 Aug 1995
My house is taking shape and it's lovely to be here. What I have learned this holiday is that I can have a good time without my ex-family and friends and that they can have a good time without me. I understand that Paula has her life together and that she is with Shawn. No surprise.

11 Sep 1995
I have been talking to Bahti, a friend and neighbor, over the weekend. She says for adults there is no such thing as abandonment. It takes two. I wonder. We all have it in us to be very destructive. Some control it, some don't. We can only make contact to the extent we can let go of ourselves and only change if we let go of our old self.

30 Oct 1995
On Saturday night I went to see *Il Postino* with Bahti. Then dinner, which she made, chatting all the while. We spoke about past

loves and I realized I have had quite a few. She thinks Paula wanted a non-Jewish, English man and that I am attracted to women who reject me. I want women to be in love with me. She also thinks I am a puritanical moralist on a tirade to purify myself and the world.
On Sunday I fired the kiln for the first time in years. Amen.

07 Nov 1995
The group session.
It gave me a sense of my power, which is difficult for me to see. I have an image of myself as small and ineffective (a legacy of my childhood). Not true, I have power. I must use it.

14 Nov 1995
Last night I bathed in my new bath. It was lovely and satisfying after all the hard work to install it. A fire is burning in the grate and I am eating lovely baked vegetables on my own.

23 Dec 1995
At home. Rachel is here too. I realize I have had almost nothing to do with Paula for two years. I regard that as a triumph. I don't remember ever having a period of such calm. My corner table is so beautiful. I sit at it in the bright winter sunshine.

01 Jan 1996
I had a nice, relaxed walk in Hertfordshire with Don and Isaac and I got thinking about women. I don't think I'll find anybody here.

16 Mar 1996
Last Thursday I met two people at Sainsburys in Golders Green: 1) Inga, who may give me some private work, 2) Yael, an old friend, who suggested that I contact Iris, an Israeli neighbour of hers. I phoned Iris an hour ago. She sounds lovely. We are due to meet on Thursday. Stand still, man.

18 Mar 1996
I am continually thinking about Iris. What does she look like? Does she smoke? Chances are I won't find her attractive.

20 Mar 1996
Yesterday (Tuesday) was an extraordinary day. Unable to wait till Thursday, Iris phoned me at eight o'clock in the evening, just as I was about to start teaching a pottery class. I said I would phone back after the class. I phoned soon after ten o'clock. After talking for a few minutes I said, "I want to come over. Where are you?" I went over to her in Golders Green and within the hour our relationship was consummated.

EPILOGUE

September 2009
It has not been easy revisiting the sorrows of the past, though there is an element of satisfaction in having been through the mill and surviving to tell the tale.

When I look back on the turbulent period laced with sadness and anguish described in *Breakup,* I console myself with the thought that it was only after passing through the mythical nine layers of divorce hell that I reached the point where I could initiate and carry off my landmark visit to Iris on March 19, 1996. From the moment I met her, I knew that this was not going to be just one more in the string of brief flings I had been having. With her eager cooperation, I seized the moment and we have been together ever since—thirteen years. Iris is the love of my life.

I am also convinced that, were it not for the personal transformation I underwent during the course of the breakup of my first marriage, I would not have been able to sustain the relationship I have with Iris. She is very different from Paula, and our relationship is built on an intimacy and openness that were lacking, and of which maybe I was incapable of, in my previous marriage. We have had our difficulties, but we were able to overcome them because, among other things, we both believe the other person to be the most suitable partner we could have.

Concluding this project on a positive note is a testament to the unpredictability of events. While in the throes of divorce, I was sure my days of despair would never end. I certainly did not think my best years were ahead of me. They were and, who knows, they might still be.

www.ingramcontent.com/pod-product-compliance
Lightning Source LLC
Chambersburg PA
CBHW051421290426
44109CB00016B/1382